SOUTHERN COMFORT

REVISED AND UPDATED EDITION

Southern Comfort

The Garden District of New Orleans

S. FREDERICK STARR

Photographs by Robert S. Brantley and Jan White Brantley

PRINCETON ARCHITECTURAL PRESS, NEW YORK
THE FLORA LEVY HUMANITIES SERIES

PUBLISHED BY
Princeton Architectural Press
37 East 7th Street
New York, New York 10003

Visit our web site at www.papress.com.

EDITOR: Jan Cigliano Hartman
BOOK DESIGNER: Sara E. Stemen
PROJECT EDITOR, PAPERBACK EDITION: Dorothy Ball
COVER DESIGNERS: Deb Wood and Elana Schlenker

SPECIAL THANKS TO: Nettie Aljian, Nicola Bednarek,
Janet Behning, Penny (Yuen Pik) Chu, Russell Fernandez, Jan Haux,
Clare Jacobson, Mark Lamster, Nancy Eklund Later, Linda Lee,
Katharine Myers, Lauren Nelson, Jane Sheinman, Scott Tennent,
Jennifer Thompson, Paul G. Wagner, and Joseph Weston
of Princeton Architectural Press —Kevin C. Lippert, publisher

LIBRARY OF CONGRESS CATALOGING-IN-PUBLICATION DATA
Starr, S. Frederick.
  Southern comfort : the Garden District of New Orleans / S. Frederick Starr ;
photographs by Robert S. Brantley and Jan White Brantley.
    p. cm. — (The Flora Levy humanities series)
  Reprint. Originally published: Cambridge, Mass. : MIT Press, c1989.
  Includes bibliographical references and index.
  ISBN 1-56898-546-0 (alk. paper)
  1. Dwellings—Louisiana—New Orleans. 2. Architecture, Domestic—Louisiana—New
Orleans. 3. Garden District (New Orleans, La.)—History. 4. New Orleans (La.)—History.
5. Garden District (New Orleans, La.)—Buildings, structures, etc. 6. New Orleans (La.)—
Buildings, structures, etc. 7. Garden District (New Orleans, La.)—Biography. 8. New
Orleans (La.)—Biography. I. Title. II. Series.
  F379.N56G377 2005
  976.3'35—dc22
                              2005007739

*The Kemper and Leila Williams Foundation of New Orleans, Louisiana, is proud to have
supported research of this book. The Foundation, established 1967, is dedicated to the collection and state-of-the-art preservation of manuscripts, paintings, and artifacts pertaining to
Louisiana. The foundation operates under the trade name The Historic New Orleans
Collection and is housed in six historic structures in New Orleans' Vieux Carré district.
Many of the documents and historic photographs on which this book is based are to be found
in The Historic New Orleans Collection, which is open to researchers and the general public.*

*The Flora Levy Humanities Series was endowed by the late Flora Levy to promote the
creative work of artists, poets, novelists, and historians. Entrusted to the University of
Southwestern Louisiana Foundation, the Levy Humanities Series publishes the quarterly
journal* Explorations *and monographs on Southern history, culture, politics, and literature,
and also sponsors the widely regarded Annual Lecture in the Humanities.*

CONTENTS

To the heroic men and women of New Orleans
who have braved hostility and, worse, human
and natural disasters. This revised and updated
paperback edition of Southern Comfort
first reached bookstores in 2005, just days before
Hurricane Katrina struck. Thankfully, the
Garden District's higher elevation was nature's
barrier to protect and preserve the neighborhood
from the flood waters that devastated many
of the city's historic buildings.

ACKNOWLEDGMENTS

BUILDINGS DON'T JUST happen. Every architect gratefully acknowledges indebtedness to those other designers from whose work he derives inspiration and also to those craftsmen and specialists who provide components and raw material for him. The architect alone bears responsibility, but the credit extends far beyond him.

An author of a book about architecture is in the same position. Although the Garden District in New Orleans is geographically small, it has attracted the attention of many devoted students, whose work both inspired and enriched the present study. Among these, none stands out more than the late Samuel Wilson, Jr., of New Orleans. In his pioneering work on the Vieux Carré, Mr. Wilson demonstrated the exceptional documentary riches of the Crescent City's architectural archives. He generously shared with us insights and files on every aspect of New Orleans architecture. Victor McGee graciously put at our disposal his vast knowledge of the life and works of Henry Howard, one of the Garden District's and the South's greatest architects. Dr. Joan G. Caldwell meticulously documented the luxuriant growth of Italianate architecture in New Orleans in her doctoral dissertation. Had it not been for this pioneering study, that movement would have figured far less prominently in this book. The same must be said for Arthur Scully, Jr., whose fine book on James Dakin demonstrated the urgent need to view the work of New Orleans architects in the context of their careers nationally. A deep bow, too, to Ray and Martha Ann Samuels, for their published compendium on many Garden District houses and for their willingness to share with the author the materials assembled during the course of their research. It is sad to note that Mrs. Samuels, too, passed away since this work first appeared.

Among American cities, New Orleans is particularly rich in citizens who, working largely on their own, have developed great expertise on local social and architectural history. The late F. Monroe Lobouisse, A.I.A., was notable among such people and spent many hours sharing that expertise with the author. Henry Krotzer, A.I.A., of the architectural firm of Koch and Wilson, spent many years pondering details of New Orleans architecture and made many pointed observations from which this study has benefited. The late William Cullison, curator of the Southeastern Architectural Archives at Tulane University's Howard-Tilton Memorial Library, amassed formidable knowledge of the work of architect James Gallier, Sr., which he kindly made available to us. John Ferguson assembled a similar wealth of data on New Orleans architect Thomas Sully. Like Cullison, he generously opened it to our use, even prior to the completion of his own work. Ann Masson of Gallier House, New Orleans, shared her great knowledge of New Orleans ironmongers, while Jessie Wing Sinott provided an invaluable listing of buildings by her grandfather, architect Frederick Wing. Thomas Bernard kindly made available a rare manuscript on the early history of his home at 1328 Harmony Street. And Roulhac Toledano, one of the most productive specialists on New Orleans architecture, offered excellent suggestions on the manuscript.

In addition to these various local perspectives, many people elsewhere in the country provided both general inspirations and specific suggestions. Roger G. Kennedy, former Director of the National Park Service, U.S. Department of the Interior, led the authors on many architectural prowls in diverse locales that helped shape this book both directly and indirectly. Geoffrey T. Blodgett of Oberlin College drew on his subtle knowledge of social history and architecture to provide many useful suggestions for revision of the text.

Photographs for this volume are principally the work of the illustrations editor and photographer. The text is also graced by the timeless photographs of the late Richard Koch, A.I.A., made available to the author by his devoted partner, Samuel Wilson, Jr. The comprehensive photographic guide to the Garden District prepared by Tina Freeman of New Orleans also proved a useful reference, which we gratefully acknowledge.

The fine maps, plans, and elevations are the work of Luis Vildostegui and Alan McGillivray, both formerly of the New Orleans architectural firm of Eskew, Vogt, Salvato & Filson Architects. Their work in turn was facilitated by David Lee Jahncke, A.I.A., who photographed many now lost buildings and began the difficult task of preparing plans and drawings. Help in preparing the many drafts of the text was provided uncomplainingly by Connie Cooksey Gardner, now of Stowe, Vermont, with the assistance of Patricia Peacock, of Oberlin, Ohio. Even with word processors their task turned out to be formidable.

A word of gratitude is due to Colin Hamer of the New Public Library, to the archival staff of the Howard-Tilton Memorial Library at Tulane University, and to specialists at the Historic American Building Survey in Washington, D.C., all of whom extended themselves on behalf of this project far beyond what reasonably could have been expected. Warm thanks, above all, to many hospitable and intellectually curious Garden District residents, among them Mr. and Mrs. Prescott N. Dunbar, Mr. and Mrs. W. Boatner Reily, Mr. and Mrs. Thomas Favrot, the late Ms. Murial Bultmann Francis, Mr. Thomas Bernard, and Mr. and Mrs. William von Puhl Trufant, to mention only a few. These kind friends not only opened their doors but often their attics as well.

The Kemper and Leila Williams Foundation of New Orleans provided major support for the research leading to this volume. It is a pleasure for the author and photographer to acknowledge this, and also the assistance provided by many members of the staff of The Historic New Orleans Collection, the splendid archive maintained by the Foundation. A deep bow in this connection to Ms. Lyn Adams of New Orleans, whose superior work as research assistant was also supported by the Williams Foundation. That the Foundation and Collection should be so thoroughly engaged with architectural history is no surprise since the chair of its board, Mary Louise Christovich, is herself a major authority on New Orleans architecture and one of the city's most effective preservationists. It is hard to imagine the completion of this study without her friendship and encouragement.

Finally, we acknowledge with gratitude and affection Professor Maurice du Quesnay of the University of Southwest Louisiana and Jan Cigliano of the Princeton Architectural Press. It was Professor du Quesnay who conceived the idea of a new edition of this work and who brought to bear the resources of the Flora Levy Humanities Series in support of the project. Ms. Cigliano brought the original book to the attention of Princeton Architectural Press and saw this revised edition through to publication with patience, humor, and good will. To these good friends is due the publication of *Southern Comfort*, but none of its faults.

S. Frederick Starr
Washington, D.C., and New Orleans

Robert S. Brantley
New Orleans

SOUTHERN COMFORT

I N THE HISTORY of modern cities, nineteenth-century America achieved distinction in two areas. First, its restless people established settlements with a rapidity that surpassed even that of the burgeoning empires of the sixteenth and seventeenth centuries. In scarcely two generations, cities like Chicago, Cleveland, and St. Louis arose from the wilderness to become major centers of commerce and culture. Second, with a haste that is no less startling, those Americans who could afford to do so fled these same cities, establishing instead suburbs of an entirely new type.

Such suburbs, which eventually ringed the cities of the entire country, embodied the most diverse and contradictory impulses: extreme individualism coexisted with an ideal of village-like collectivity: rustic simplicity was enriched by all the comforts modern technology could afford; and the romantic call of a lost bucolic world was audible within minutes of some of the world's most bustling commercial centers.

Every major American city founded in the nineteenth century is a monument to this process of simultaneous urbanization and disurbanization. The metropolis fostered trade and manufacturing. Commerce generated new opportunities for personal enrichment, which drew waves of poor immigrants to the city. The arrival of these new Americans in turn caused the exodus of the more

[FACING PAGE] *"No houses could well be in better harmony with their surroundings, or more pleasing to the eye." Mark Twain on the Garden District*

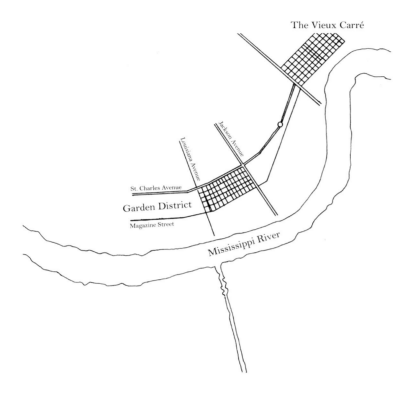

The Garden District in the Crescent City (ALAN MCGILLIVRAY AND LUIS VILDOSTEGUI)

prosperous classes to suburban enclaves. These distinctive suburban neighborhoods created by the upper classes came to symbolize achievement in the United States. Both as symbol and as physical reality, the new suburbs were potentially accessible to all. Anyone could aspire to the worldly success that the suburbs represented. By investing a penny in a horsecar ride, even the lowliest immigrant could see firsthand what the future might hold for him.

This is a book about one such suburb, the Garden District in New Orleans. It is situated two miles upriver ("uptown" in New Orleans parlance) from the historic Vieux Carré and a half mile north of the Mississippi River, which at this point in its course flows east before dipping south and southeast toward the Gulf of Mexico. In modern times the Garden District has generally been taken to include the sixty-six blocks bounded by St. Charles Avenue, Magazine Street, Jackson Avenue, and Louisiana Avenue. In its nineteenth-century heyday, however, the Garden District was assumed to comprise a larger if somewhat less defined area, beginning approximately at Felicity Street and extending uptown at least to Louisiana Avenue, and reaching several blocks north from St. Charles Avenue and south from Magazine Street. Initially part of the City of Lafayette and, after 1852, incorporated into New Orleans, the Garden District was never a distinct political entity. It was, rather, a metaphor that embraced notions of high economic status, political and social identity, a gracious style of life, and architectural opulence.

This historic district of New Orleans warrants national attention on several counts. First, in the nineteenth century it was a truly suburban neighborhood, not a zone of country villas like Philadelphia's Chestnut Hill or Cincinnati's Walnut Hills, or an only slightly less dense bedroom extension of the city, like Brooklyn Heights. Initially incorporated as part of a separate municipality, the Garden District prefigured the process of urban expansion and absorption that has occurred throughout the United States in the twentieth century.

Situated along one of the first street railway lines in the country, it reveals the impact of modern technology on transportation in America and hence on various aspects of daily life. By its very existence as an enclave, the Garden District helped over time to create the standard two-part American city, what Sam Bass Warner, Jr., has called "a city of slums and a city of suburbs, a city of hope and failure and a city of achievement and comfort."[1] However strange to American sensibilities, this situation reversed the conditions that long prevailed in the ancient cities of Europe. There, as Chaucer observed in the fourteenth century, wealth was concentrated at the center of cities and suburbs were places of "fereful residence."[2] Only with the rise of commuter suburbs in the nineteenth century did there emerge what Kenneth T. Jackson termed this "new pattern of peripheral affluence and central despair."[3] The Garden District is a monument to this great reversal.

Second, through its organic tie with New Orleans, the Garden District reflects economic and cultural developments in one of the largest and most prosperous cities of North America in the first half of the nineteenth century. A minor town of only 10,000 inhabitants at the time of the Louisiana Purchase in 1803, New Orleans had grown to 100,000 by 1840, making it the fourth largest city in the country.[4] With a population that included virtually every ethnic group represented on the continent and having direct communication with both the Mississippi Basin and the Northeast, New Orleans was truly a national city, and its evolution a central element in the story of America's urban growth.

Third, the Garden District remains an enduring achievement of architecture and of residential planning. This fact is all too easily ignored or taken for granted. In recent years America's suburbs have been the favorite target of attack by urbanists and others who regret the decline of the old central cities. Only now are we coming to recognize, as one specialist has observed, that the Anglo-American suburb is "a remarkable achievement, not the degraded form of city planning that so many have called it."[5]

To contemporaries, the nineteenth-century Garden District was an object of awe. Mark Twain, a frequent visitor there, wrote that "[its] mansions stand in the center of large grounds, and rise, garlanded with roses, out of the midst of swelling masses of shining green foliage and many colored blossoms. No houses could well be in better harmony with their surroundings, or more pleasing to the eye, or more homelike and comfortable looking."[6] Of the plantings, Thomas K. Wharton, an English-born architect and diarist, observed that "The [Garden District] is richer in flowers and tastefully adorned residences than any other suburb I know except Brookline near Boston."[7]

The beauty of the Garden District naturally gave rise to some highly romantic notions concerning the suburb. Who has not heard that the great houses there have been passed down through the generations by ancient patriarchal families? What tourist in New Orleans has not conjured up the image of well-to-do antebellum planters holding gala receptions at their city residences in the Garden District? A whole school of writers has labored mightily to promote such *Gone with the Wind* imagery. To take one example, John P. Coleman, an enthusiastic New Orleans journalist of the 1920s, described antebellum life in the Henry S. Buckner residence at 1410 Jackson Avenue as "all gay and exciting, and every pulse throbbed with exhilarating emotions." Coleman went on to gush over the "wealthy aristocracy" that once inhabited the mansion.[8]

Most such accounts are grotesquely inaccurate. Pulses may have throbbed, but the exhilaration arose more from the prospect of financial gain than from any more tender emotions. Mr. Buckner was indeed wealthy, but he was a hustling self-made man, an entrepreneur rather than an aristocrat. There may have been graciousness in the Garden District, but few families succeeded in maintaining their property from one generation to the next. As to the planters, most of those who came to the pre-Civil War Garden District did so as guests, not as homeowners.

Surrounded by absurdly sentimentalized myths, the Garden District has come to be seen as a noble relic quite out of the path of American urban development as a whole. No wonder that the major specialists on nineteenth-century architecture and social history pass it over (and the entire city of New Orleans, for that matter) with scarcely a word.[9] Even the Historic American Buildings Survey of the U.S. Department of the Interior has recorded only two houses in the Garden District, although it documents dozens in other suburbs of major cities of the Northeast.

In the absence of adequate coverage of the Garden District in the broader architectural literature, it is a relief to turn to a purely

A postwar taste for the eclectic drove Willis H. Hogan to combine Greek Revival motifs on the first floor, Italianate on the second, and New Orleans' cast-iron grillwork on the side porch, 1138 Third Street, 1869–70

local tradition of study within New Orleans. The Friends of the Cabildo, a volunteer support group for the Louisiana State Museum, has made heroic efforts to document New Orleans architecture on a neighborhood-by-neighborhood basis; the work of its members has revealed the sheer volume of documentary materials available.[10] For soundly practical reasons, however, the various authors contributing to these volumes have concentrated on those areas of the city most threatened by destruction. Hence they began with the imperiled Lower Garden District, a neologism they coined, but did not deal with the Garden District proper. Several garden clubs have compiled brief guides to the major homes in the Garden District, perpetuating many old myths in the process. Far more useful is the booklet, *The Great Days of the Garden District*, published in 1961 by Martha Ann Brett Samuel and Ray Samuel; here at least is the tentative beginning of a genuine history of the suburb.[11]

If there has been no comprehensive study of New Orleans' great suburb, several architects practicing in the city today have amassed immensely valuable information in the course of their work on specific restorations. Henry W. Krotzer, Davis Lee Jahncke, Jr., George Denegre Hopkins, Jr., and the late F. Monroe Labouisse and Richard Koch all gained useful insights about specific aspects of the architecture. Among the leaders of these skilled restorationists was Samuel Wilson, Jr., who combined scholarly research with his practical experience in such a way as to establish himself as the leading authority on New Orleans' architectural history as a whole.

Several researchers have studied specific architects or eras in the Garden District's history. Victor McGee and Robert S. Brantley's studies on Henry Howard; John Ferguson's research on Thomas Sully; William Cullison's documentation on James Gallier, Sr.; Arthur Scully, Jr.'s book on James Dakin; and Joan G. Caldwell's exhaustive study of the Italianate style all contributed to the realization that the Garden District presents an unparalleled museum for the study of nineteenth-century architecture and society. In the course of their work, these scholars have posed many of the fundamental questions addressed in this book.[12]

How should we look at the architecture of the Garden District? The simplest answer is the one assumed by writers of popular guidebooks. They explain a building by giving the date of its construction, the name of its architect, and perhaps a word on

Diversity: Tuscan and Greek revival elements on the gallery of the William H. McLellan house, 1006 Washington Avenue, 1868–69

A doorway to the out-of-doors. Public and private space at the Joseph Fernandez house, 1302–04 Jackson Avenue. Fernandez paid for his lots in piasters, Spanish currency, then built his residence, 1850–51

the significance of the building in the context of the architect's work as a whole. The closest such guidebooks come to accounting for the building's character is to comment on the supposed aesthetic influences of its design.

If the goal is truly to understand a building, however, this approach does not suffice. For architecture, by its nature, is the most social of arts. Provided they have paint, brush, and canvas, painters can bring their ideas to fruition, without compromise. But architects need patrons who prescribe the nature of the building and sometimes even its form. Architects and patrons alike are enmeshed in the daily economy, which not only generates the money that pays for buildings but, through its technology, determines the materials and techniques available for the work of construction. Houses, unlike paintings or works of sculpture, are lived in. However lofty the architect's aspirations, he or she must satisfy the practical needs of actual households. What role is played in such households by women, men, children, and servants? What kind of public social life does the family maintain? To what extent do such diverse factors as health, sanitation, transportation, and the need for security shape the design of houses and even of whole neighborhoods?

The answers to such questions, no less than the architect's talent and training, determine the final outcome. One can imagine some dictator or grand planner commanding that an entire district and every building within it have a certain character. This actually occurred in many closely controlled sections of Europe, but the laissez-faire and individualistic world of nineteenth-century America entrusted such authority to no one. Not only did each patron exercise an often decisive influence on the design of buildings but so did the various builders, artisans, and even the suppliers of building materials.

The architect, then, was but one element in a series of independent forces acting on the design and execution of the building. In the actual process of designing and building a Garden District home, each factor— patron, architect, builder, artisan, and supplier—interacted with the others and assumed virtually equal importance. Each could exercise the power of veto over the final product. Unless each was willing to acknowledge the other's requirements, their individual efforts would all be in vain. Nineteenth-century Garden District architecture was thus a

surprisingly democratic endeavor. It was also, in this sense, a collective enterprise.

The architecture of the Garden District is best understood as the crystallization of a range of cultural forces at work in the suburb and in nineteenth-century New Orleans generally. To make contact with these forces, one must have access to a wide and diverse body of information from the past. For most American cities the paucity of surviving building documentation would make this all but impossible, but New Orleans is a happy exception. One reason is the existence of remarkably detailed records left by past notaries public. Under Anglo-Saxon law the notary public is little more than a commissioner of oaths, who certifies that oaths are properly sworn and that signatures are authentic. In the French, then Spanish, and then again French legal codes that prevailed in New Orleans to 1803 and in the Napoleonic civil code largely perpetuated thereafter, the notary public fulfilled this function but was, in addition, the state's monitor of every legal transaction and even a kind of savings and loan agency. The notary public worked closely with investors and property owners to arrange mortgages and loans. As the manager of loans, he kept a percentage himself, which caused notaries to be branded "paper shavers." Every transaction was duly recorded and the copies preserved in archives that constituted the communal memory. Such notarial archives, unique in the United States to those regions once ruled by France or Spain, offer an unparalleled resource to the historian of architecture and society.

No less important is the testimony of the buildings themselves. Provided the observer is prepared to examine even familiar building types with fresh eyes, the old houses can reveal the most elusive dimensions of their inhabitants' lives. Why, for example, does one occasionally encounter formal doorways on the facades of otherwise plain dwellings in the Garden District, doorways that lead not to the interior but merely to open side galleries?[13] The use of such doorways, unusual for New Orleans, can probably be traced to prototypes in the Carolinas. There, as in New Orleans, they served as a useful means of delineating the public and private zones, mediating between the desire to present an orderly facade to the street and the practical need to move about relaxedly in a semitropical climate.

Many details of the surviving buildings reveal aspects of the original occupants' lives. Unfortunately, however, a number of the

The local fire truck: Jefferson Fire Co. No. 22 tomb, Lafayette Cemetery, Prytania and Fourth Streets

Fire tower at Magazine and Washington Avenue, 1850s (THE HISTORIC NEW ORLEANS COLLECTION)

finest Garden District residences have been lost. The urgent tolling of fire bells formed an incessant refrain in nineteenth-century New Orleans. In 1850, for example, the local *Deutsche Zeitung* reported on a fire that destroyed the German theater in Lafayette and forty other buildings.[14] In spite of several fire towers in the Garden District, few conflagrations were successfully quelled there.

In addition to losses caused by fire, numerous houses have perished by their owners' choices. Many of the splendid late-nineteenth- century mansions on St. Charles Avenue were pulled down in the twentieth century simply because architectural fashions had changed. Faced with the choice between adapting them to new uses and starting over, many property owners chose the latter course. There have also been numerous instances of wanton destruction. As recently as 1970 a mansion on Magazine Street was destroyed when its owner decreed in her will that it be demolished "as quickly as practicable after my death."[15] Yet more recently, the Uptown Development Corporation, the owner of two handsome galleried houses on Josephine Street, had them demolished at the very hour the New Orleans City Council was debating the desirability of introducing an Urban Conservation Zoning Plan for the city.[16] Such brutally primitive methods have elicited so much criticism that they are generally avoided today, demolition by neglect (or sometimes by arson) being far more common. This has been the recent fate of a venerable home at 1129 Jackson Avenue, replaced now by a modest row of condominiums, and also of a rare Second Empire house at 3005 St. Charles Avenue.[17]

Happily, enough of the historic buildings within the Garden District have survived to enable us to form a picture of nineteenth-century life there. They reveal the story of a notable American suburb whose patrons were conscious of its uniqueness from an early day. With careful research and a dose of historical imagination, one can conjure up the world in which the men of New Orleans made great fortunes overnight and lost them as quickly and in which they endeavored during that fleeting moment between success and failure to give permanence to their dreams by building worldly mansions.

The British historian Peter Laslett portrayed the vanished life of agrarian England in a book provocatively titled *The World We Have Lost*. The rhythm and impulse of nineteenth-century America have slipped away no less completely. We are fortunate to have in the Garden District of New Orleans an enduring reminder of that life as it was lived by some of the most ambitious people of an expansive age. The purpose of this book is to use the surviving buildings—both the opulent and the humble—as a window through which the evanescent society of Victorian America can be perceived. Let the readers peer into that window and, having done so, take the actions that are urgently needed to assure that this gracious and distinctive monument to the suburbanization of America might be preserved in its entirety for the future.

[FACING PAGE] *Neglect ravages the house of A. W. Bosworth, the ice dealer from Skowhegan, Maine, 1126 Washington Avenue. Thomas K. Wharton, architect, 1859*

CHAPTER ONE

Uptown and the Americanization of New Orleans

THE GARDEN DISTRICT was laid out in the 1830s and settled in the 1840s, approximately 120 years after New Orleans was founded but only three decades after Louisiana came under American rule. American society was thus a late transplant to Bienville's city of La Nouvelle Orleans. Yet the new Anglo-Saxon colony had already passed through three distinct but overlapping phases of development by the time the Garden District was established.

The first phase of Americanization in New Orleans began at the dawn of the nineteenth century and extended through the 1830s. In this period immigrants from elsewhere in the United States moved into the Faubourg Ste. Marie, the commercial and residential city immediately upriver from the French Quarter that extends to present-day Howard Avenue. The second phase began in 1806 and accelerated into the 1830s and 1840s. In these years an attempt at grand planning was made still further upriver, in the newly subdivided land between the modern Howard Avenue and Felicity Street. A low-density elite suburb came into being, but this area—known today as the Lower Garden District—represented only a partial break with the earlier pattern of settlement. The third phase began in the 1820s and intensified into the early 1850s. During this period lower-class immigrants and artisans settled along the riverfront further upriver from the Lower Garden District. The city of Lafayette

[FACING PAGE] *Stylish, but heat absorbent and prone to flooding: downtown Julia Row, by New York architect Alexander Thompson Wood with James Dakin, 1833. A restored survivor of the nascent Garden District in the Faubourg Ste. Marie*

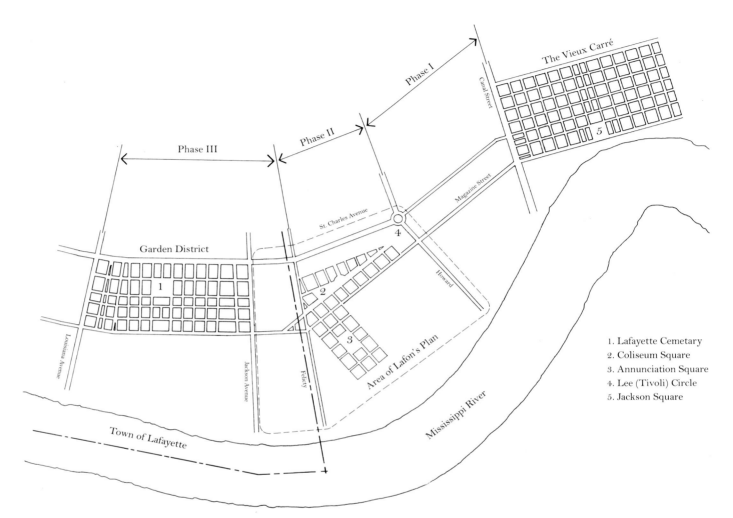

Phase III

Phase II

Phase I

The Vieux Carré

Canal Street

Magazine Street

St. Charles Avenue

Garden District

4

Howard

1

2

3

Louisiana Avenue

Jackson Avenue

Felicty

Area of Lafon's Plan

Mississippi River

Town of Lafayette

1. Lafayette Cemetary
2. Coliseum Square
3. Annunciation Square
4. Lee (Tivoli) Circle
5. Jackson Square

Three stages of uptown development: moving west-
ward, Canal Street to Howard Avenue, to Jackson
and Louisiana Avenues (MCGILLIVRAY AND
VILDOSTEGUI)

comprised both the brash port city thus formed and also the area
later known as the Garden District. The raucous riverside zone that
stretched upriver from Faubourg Ste. Marie threatened not only to
erode the existing uptown suburbs but to preempt with inexpensive
development the very territory on which the Garden District would
eventually be built.

These three overlapping phases of development encompass the
process of Americanization in New Orleans and set the stage for the
creation of a special garden suburb by and for the city's new Anglo-
Saxon elite. Because the Garden District was created to some
extent in reaction against the older American sections of New
Orleans, an examination of the earlier phases of Anglo-Saxon settlement will be instructive.

❧ THE FIRST PHASE: FAUBOURG STE. MARIE

For seventy years after its foundation in 1718, La Nouvelle Orleans was limited to the Vieux Carré, the seventy-one squares known today as the French Quarter. Following the disastrous fire of 1788, however, Bertrand Gravier petitioned the Spanish Royal Surveyor, Carlos Trudeau, to divide into city blocks his plantation adjoining the Quarter. Gravier named the development Ville Gravier and subsequently called it Faubourg Ste. Marie, after his deceased wife.[1] It extended along the Mississippi River from Iberville Street to the present Howard Avenue. Shortly afterward, in 1795, the Spanish rulers gave American vessels free use of the New Orleans port. American traders and manufacturers had already been visiting the city for many years, and had settled both in the French Quarter and Faubourg Tremé. After 1803 they came in great numbers, eventually moving into the part of town that Bertrand Gravier had recently opened to settlement.

As in colonial situations around the world, the Anglo-Saxon newcomers to New Orleans encountered coolness and hostility. As late as 1845 they still found the Creoles to be "remarkably exclusive in their intercourse with others."[2] Few of these American residents understood French, as evidenced by the fact that the word *faubourg* regularly appears in early English-language New Orleans publications as fauxbourg.[3] Epithets like "Cray-owls" abounded, and the Creoles reciprocated by marking such important events in France as the death of Napoleon with ostentatious pomp.[4] Besieged, the downtown Americans still referred to themselves as a "colony" as late as the 1840s.[5]

Nevertheless, Americanization rapidly transformed the city. Comprising only about one-tenth of the population in 1806,[6] Anglo-Saxons by the early 1850s had become a majority of the voting population. Architect Benjamin Henry Latrobe in 1819 concluded that "in a few years this will be an American town."[7] Yet the Anglo-Saxons' earlier experience of being treated as outsiders left an important mark on their life in the city. Huddled together in their quarter of town like the French in Algiers or the Portuguese in Macao, they staunchly resisted Creole influences, even in areas where they would have been of potential benefit. The Yankee newcomers "showed the flag" by clinging doggedly to the way of life they had known in the Northeast. They arrogantly refused to observe the Creoles' long midday break and insisted instead on working through the heat of the day so as to be able to take dinner early.

For their houses, most spurned the plastered, pastel-painted exteriors favored by the Creoles and imposed the more familiar dark red brick, which Latrobe sagely ridiculed as "red staring brick-work, imbibing heat thro' the whole unshaded substance of the wall."[8] Instead of interior service courtyards and portes cochères they favored narrow, airless alleys. Spurning the Spaniards' sensible rooftop gardens, they built steep-pitched roofs, as if anticipating snowfalls. Most foolish of all, Yankee newcomers often followed the Philadelphia practice of building the main family rooms only a few steps above street level, thus exposing the living quarters to floods that rarely reached the Creoles' second-floor salons.

Only in the face of absolute necessity did the Anglo-Saxons adopt local practices. Kitchens, which in the Greek Revival houses of lower Manhattan were in the basement, were shifted to the wing extending to the rear. Servants' rooms, which throughout the Northeast were under the rooftop eaves, were also moved to the rear extension.[9] By rejecting most indigenous architectural practices, the Anglo-Saxons transformed Carlos Trudeau's Ville Gravier into a fairly precise replica of Philadelphia, Baltimore, or New York. Even row houses in the Georgian style imported to Philadelphia from England in the eighteenth century became popular, especially when it was discovered in the 1830s that they could be lucratively built on speculation.[10] The recently restored Julia Row, designed by New Yorker Alexander Thompson Wood together with James Dakin in 1833, is the best surviving example of some two dozen such groups of houses.

The few remaining early buildings in the Faubourg Ste. Marie are rightly treasured for their Greek Revival design. More than one contemporary observer found them ridiculous, however, and ill-suited to the Caribbean environment. Latrobe complained that "the suburb St. Mary [sic.], the American suburb, already exhibits the flat, dull, dingy character of Market Street in Philadelphia, or Baltimore Street...."[11]

Part of the problem was that many of the newcomers did not see themselves as residents for life. They wanted only to live efficiently while they made money. Their first dwellings met this objective, as did the granite-piered business blocks that were transplanted from Boston via New York. As their resources increased, and as they considered the possibility of settling permanently in New Orleans, these Anglo-Americans began thinking about more commodious and airy living quarters. As this occurred, they began eyeing the used plantation land immediately upriver as a new zone for development.

THE SECOND PHASE: BARTHELEMY LAFON'S GRAND DESIGN

The second phase of uptown growth began in 1806, when Madame Marguerite Delord-Sarpy decided to subdivide her plantation into a new faubourg, or suburb. Although at no point more than a few hundred yards in width, this long narrow wedge of land running on both sides of the modern Howard Avenue through Lee Circle to the river was of central importance to the planning of uptown New Orleans. It was there that the system of blocks that had earlier been extended upriver from the French Quarter finally had to be realigned to accommodate the Mississippi River's bend. To plot this pivotal acreage, Madame Delord-Sarpy turned to Barthelemy Lafon, deputy surveyor of Orleans Parish. Only a few months earlier this same Lafon had successfully subdivided Bernard Marigny's sprawling plantation below the city. For the Faubourg Marigny, Lafon had specified a simple grid system. He now proposed the same plan for Madame Delord-Sarpy's plantation.

Scarcely had Lafon set to work on his task than Madame Delord-Sarpy sold her upriver holdings to Armand Duplantier, a Creole who had served as aide-de-camp to General Lafayette during the American Revolution and was now intent upon entering the real estate business.[12] Compared with Marigny or Delord-Sarpy, Duplantier was a visionary with ambitious ideas about the future of New Orleans, far more expensive than could be achieved through Lafon's simple grid. He therefore requested Lafon to submit a second plan that would be worthy of his, Duplantier's, private vision.

Lafon responded with by far the grandest urban scheme yet devised in New Orleans or, indeed, in the entire Mississippi Valley.

Lafon proposed to establish a new Faubourg Annonciation extending from the modern Howard Avenue to Felicity Street. The scheme centered about a grand canal, named the Cours des Tritons (now Howard Avenue); a circular park (now Lee Circle), which Lafon named the Place du Tivoli after the town near Rome; a long park dominated by a huge collisée or coliseum (present Coliseum Square); various intersecting canals; a prytanée or classical school; and a large Place de l'Annonciation on which a cathedral was to stand.[13] Here, finally, was the recipe for a true metropolis, as opposed to the blandly bourgeois commercial settlement left by the earlier French, Spanish, and American residents of Bienville's city.

It is not clear where Lafon got his idea. American planners at the time were absorbed in what has been called their "Roman period."[14] Pierre L'Enfant had already laid out Washington, D.C., in the grand manner, and between 1797 and 1805 radial avenues were proposed for Cleveland, Buffalo, Detroit, and West Philadelphia. There is no clear link between any of these projects and Lafon's proposal for Armand Duplantier, although it is quite possible that Lafon had examined them. Lafon may also have had in mind the elaborate town plans of eighteenth-century France, even though he had not actually studied architecture in his native France before coming to New Orleans in 1790. That Lafon was keenly intelligent is certain, for he possessed an extensive library and spoke four languages.[15] Benjamin Latrobe described him as being "no fool." Whether Lafon derived his planning ideas from other American or European urban schemes or borrowed them directly from the grandiose Romanisms of Napoleon, he was clearly intent on setting New Orleans on a new course.

For all the brilliance of his proposal, Lafon failed. Neither the coliseum nor the prytaneum was ever built. Only one of the many canals got beyond the drawing board, and both Coliseum Square and Annunciation Square remained dusty parade grounds until the 1850s.[16] The only element of Lafon's scheme to be fully implemented was the least interesting, namely the system of grid blocks that was extended all the way to the parish line at Felicity Street in what is now called the Lower Garden District. Thus, in the same year in which a legislative commission in New York decided to cover all of Manhattan Island with checkerboard squares, American New Orleans backed away from its one opportunity to follow a different type of development and opted for the same rectilinear plan.

Lafon did not succeed in introducing a grander and more spacious way of life to New Orleans. Nor did anyone else attempt to realize his grand proposal, or seek to apply the lessons of bucolic urbanism that John Nash successfully elaborated in his plan for Regent's Park in London only a half decade after Lafon's proposal was drafted. Eventually Lafon abandoned architecture, and in later years he drifted into other activities, including piracy and the study of Egyptian hieroglyphics. Even in his failure, Lafon helped pave the way for the future Garden District. The Faubourg Ste. Marie had been sliced up into narrow lots similar to those in Philadelphia and Manhattan. In Lafon's new neighborhood, lot sizes were far larger. This fact, combined with the mounting prosperity, cracked the hegemony of standardized row houses in Anglo-Saxon New Orleans. Thanks to Lafon, more individuated residences in a wide variety of styles could be accommodated within a single neighborhood.

The diversity of architectural styles that blossomed in the Lower Garden District is bewildering. William Carr Withers built a serenely handsome Georgian villa on New Levee Street in the 1820s. With its galleried portico and elevated basement, the Withers house borrowed directly from Charleston, South Carolina.[17] Some blocks away, on Annunciation Street below Race, the New York architect James Dakin built the imposingly porticoed Robert Slark house, an adaptation of the Greek Revival style as it had flourished in upstate New York. On Carondelet Street near Melpomene, Dakin built a mansion for Peter Conrey that is strikingly similar to the residence of Reverend Edward Everett Hale in Roxbury, Massachusetts. On property at Constance and Euterpe Streets the architects Antonio Mondelli and John Reynolds created a series of four exotic garden dwellings reminiscent of an Ottoman serai. One house from this group still stands at 928 Euterpe Street in mutilated form, and the garden has been overbuilt with a twentieth-century structure.[18]

Wags were quick to poke fun at this hodgepodge of borrowings. One visitor ridiculed the Yankee architects' attempt to create "here a little of Boston, there a trifle of New York, and some of Philadelphia...."[19] The more perceptive critics understood that the variations were not merely aesthetic but reflected deeper differences in the backgrounds and tastes of the various owners. On the one hand, the new suburb permitted a degree of freedom and individual expression that had not existed earlier in the American quarter of New Orleans. One need only compare the once fashionable thirteen downtown row houses on Julia Street with Mondelli and Reynolds's Euterpe Street house in the Lower Garden District to see the difference. The former dwellings are not only absolutely identical to one another but, on the exterior at least, they are nearly indistinguishable from the barracks-like housing built for mill workers in Lowell, Massachusetts, at the same time. The latter is a delightfully informal conceit that proclaims the individual uniqueness of the people who inhabited it. By comparison with the Lower Garden District, even the contemporary suburb of New Brighton of Staten Island in New York appears uniform and monotonous.[20]

On the other hand, the new suburb had little social cohesion and showed it. As in so many areas of nineteenth-century American cities settled by the wealthy, people built their individual houses and assumed that the welfare of the neighborhood as a whole would arise naturally from the aggregate. Beyond the well-kept yards, conditions were primitive. Knee-high grass sprang up in the unpaved streets each summer, rubble and debris clogged the so-called parks, and mosquitoes infested the ponds of water that appeared everywhere after each rain.

In spite of these shortcomings, Lafon's Faubourg Annonciation (or Lower Garden District) was a genuine suburb and one of the first in North America. Without making the slightest architectural concession to the several Creole plantation houses nearby, it introduced a welcome bucolic note into the densely urban world of mercantile New Orleans. By so doing, the new Faubourg marked a dramatic change in upper-class life; as in all eighteenth-century American cities, the line between a man's work and his family life was thin, while women carried out their family responsibilities in close contact with their husbands' professional world. In the Faubourg Ste. Marie, for example, it was a simple matter for men to go home each day to have lunch with their families. Faubourg Annonciation, by contrast, one-and-a-half miles from the commercial district, was so much more than an easy walk to make this practice impossible. Business and home life were sharply segregated, the latter becoming more exclusively the domain of women. This was considered at least as much a virtue as a necessity, as attested by the writings of such feminists as Catherine Beecher, sister of Harriet Beecher Stowe, who found the protected home environment more conducive to the spiritual and moral uplift of the nuclear family.[21] The men, meanwhile, smoking cigars and perusing the *Louisiana Courier* at some downtown cafe, could do no more than romanticize and sentimentalize the home life in which they played so small a part. This change, essential to the mentality that created the Garden District, made its New Orleans debut among residents of the Faubourg Annonciation in the 1830s.

❧ THE THIRD PHASE: THE UPTOWN BOOM AND MR. PETER'S SUBDIVISION

For a few years the old parish boundary running along the present line of Felicity Street marked the limit of uptown development in New Orleans. The Reverend Theodore Clapp, arriving in the Crescent City from the North in 1822, found the area beyond Lafon's planned zone to be "unenclosed fields, which a few years before had belonged to a large sugar plantation. They were adorned with a carpet of green grass, where herds and flocks grazed in common. Here and there we passed a farm house in the midst of gardens, luxuriant shrubbery, and orange groves...."[22]

These fields, too, quickly succumbed to the surveyor's rule and compass. Much of this land had been owned by the Ursuline nuns, who used it for truck gardening. In an effort to consolidate the convent's holdings downriver from the city, Sister Ste. Marie Olivier arranged to sell off the entire uptown tract to developers. Again, Barthelemy Lafon was called in to do the surveying. His simple grid opened the area from Felicity Street up to St. Andrew for settlement. However, St. Andrew Street, originally named Chemin de St. André after the trustee of the convent, was fated only briefly to mark the uptown border of settlement.[23] Eventually, the entire area was incorporated into the City of Lafayette.

Immediately upriver from the narrow Faubourg Nuns (or the Faubourg Religieuses, as it was variously called) was the plantation of Jacinto Panis. A captain in the Spanish garrison in New Orleans, Panis had died a decade before the end of local Spanish rule. His German wife had watched the land boom on the outskirts of town and resolved to take advantage of it. In 1813 she subdivided the acres closest to the river, and in 1829 she had the rest of her plantation plotted into squares. Extending the line of the oak alley that formerly ran from the Panis plantation house to the river was the broad Cours Panis, later renamed Jackson Avenue in honor of the hero of the Battle of New Orleans. The establishment of Jackson Avenue was to be the last attempt to lay out a grand thoroughfare in uptown New Orleans for some years.

The speed with which both the Ursulines' tract and the Panis plantation found buyers caused developers to shift their attention still further upriver. Here they encountered the large plantation of Jacques François Esnould Dugué de Livaudais, which dominated the entire block now bordered by Sixth, St. Thomas, Washington, and Tchoupitoulas Streets. To all appearances, the Livaudais plantation seemed the very embodiment of the gracious Creole way of life. By the 1820s, however, the Livaudais family was experiencing a series of economic and personal misfortunes. Beginning in 1825 one branch of the family sold off large plantations in Lafourche Parish.[24] Jacques Livaudais meanwhile had separated from his wife. A judgment of divorce in 1826 required him to deed the entire New Orleans plantation to his former spouse, who promptly left for Paris, where she established a new life as the "Marquise de Livaudais." Before leaving, she turned over her affairs to her solicitors, who in 1832 sold the entire plantation to a partnership of Anglo-Saxon newcomers for $490,000.[25]

Together, the former Ursuline, Panis, and Livaudais plantations constituted the land on which the city of Lafayette eventually rose. Stretching upriver from Felicity Street to Harmony Street and from the riverbank to the marshes at the present Claiborne Avenue, this tract also comprised the territory on which the future Garden District would be built. In each case the sale, surveying, and resale occurred with blinding speed—never stretching over more than a few months. Here was a land boom of staggering proportions, com-

Rivals: Developers Samuel Jarvis Peters [ABOVE]
and Bernard Marigny [LEFT] (NEW ORLEANS
PUBLIC LIBRARY)

Nicolas Destrehan's ill-fated Cosmopolite City, across the Mississippi from New Orleans (THE HISTORIC NEW ORLEANS COLLECTION)

parable to John Jacob Astor's real estate bonanza in New York and the Chicago land rush of exactly the same years.

One man dominated the entire uptown land boom: Samuel Jarvis Peters (1801–55).[26] Sprung from an old family of Boston Puritans, his grandfather had fled to England after the American Revolution and his father settled in Toronto, where Peters was born. After studying French briefly in New York City, young Peters arrived in New Orleans in 1821. He opened a wholesale grocery firm and soon entered the field of politics, siding with those sympathetic to national commerce who later came together to form the Whig Party in 1834. By 1829 Peters represented part of the old French Quarter on the City Council and seemed destined for further political triumphs. In 1822, Democrat Bernard Marigny (1785–1868) upset his race for the state legislature. One of the richest Creoles in the state, a former member of the Louisiana Constitutional Convention, and a fop, Marigny was almost Peters's undoing.

This was not the first tangle between Peters and Marigny. Some years earlier Peters had approached the Creole with a proposal to develop a large tract on the downriver edge of New

Orleans that Marigny owned. Marigny, who had introduced the game of craps into America, was not about to gamble on an unknown Yankee immigrant. It is not that Marigny was hostile to Anglo-Americans. He had married Mary Ann Jones, the daughter of a Philadelphia merchant; he strongly supported the American cause against the British; and he idolized Andrew Jackson.[27] Marigny's admiration for Yankee initiative began to wane only when Anglo-Saxon settlers in New Orleans began to pose a threat to the Creole hegemony. While he may never have become a notorious Yankee-hater, as one historian claimed, Marigny reacted vehemently to the intensifying competition.[28] No wonder, then, that when he was approached by Peters—Anglo Saxon, aggressive, and a political opponent to boot—Marigny turned him down. Worse, he delayed his refusal: he led Peters along to the point of signing and then saw to it that Madame Marigny, whose signature was also needed, did not appear at the crucial meeting. Peters, enraged, is said to have declared, "I shall live, by God, to see the day when rank grass shall choke up the streets of your old *faubourg*."[29]

Later, as he watched the Livaudais fortunes decline, Peters saw the chance to take revenge on Marigny and make a financial killing in the process. As it happened, Madame Livaudais was a Marigny, the sister of Peters's rival. By taking over her plantation and transferring it into a suburb of his own, Peters settled his score with the renowned Creole.

Peters had as partners in the half-million dollar purchase three fellow New Englanders: William Chase, Matthew Morgan, and Levi Peirce.[30] Peters and his partners had to move fast. The short terms for mortgages (usually five years) forced entrepreneurs to turn over their property quickly. After completing the arrangements with Madame Livaudais's lawyers in March 1832, Peters managed to subdivide and auction the entire tract by the end of April. His surveyor was the New Orleans-born Creole, Benjamin Buisson. There was no time to lay out anything so ambitious as the Faubourg Annonciation, let alone the elegant but financially disastrous Cosmopolite City, which the Creole magnate Nicolas Noel Destrehan had planned in the late 1830s for a plot of land across the Mississippi in what is now Harvey, Louisiana.[31] It had been Destrehan's hope to found a city of broad boulevards punctuated by public squares designated for churches, schools, and hospitals.

When lots failed to find buyers, he abandoned the project. Buisson, probably conscious of all the risks involved in more ambitious undertakings, settled for a simple grid.

It is evident that Peters and his fellow speculators counted on the Anglo-Saxon market. In all likelihood they knew that suburban enclaves for the affluent were being planned at the same time in Philadelphia, New York, and Boston and assumed that an analogous quarter in New Orleans would be attractive to immigrants from such cities. They followed the model of Philadelphia in numbering the north-south streets and using names such as Chestnut for those east-west roads not otherwise named by Lafon when he established the adjoining Faubourg Annonciation. By these means, Anglo-Saxon newcomers were encouraged to feel more at home in their new surroundings, the impact of exotic flora and the alien environment having been softened by safely familiar place names. The Peters group achieved its objective.

Most purchases were made by hastily organized partnerships, such as the one formed by John Egerton, a banker, and Edward Ogden, an insurance agent. More than one irregular deal was struck in the process. Yet no one seemed to mind, nor did eyebrows rise when non-Anglo-Saxons invested there. A Spaniard named Francisco Canellas bought into the district and settled there with his children, all quadroons.[32] Lucile Vivant, a free woman of color, purchased an entire square bounded by Sixth, Coliseum, Washington, and Chestnut. She in turn sold one of the lots to another free black, Jean Baptiste Clauveau, who then profited from a subsequent sale to still another free Negro, Barthelemy Rey. It was Barthelemy Rey who, in the late 1830s, erected a house that still stands at 2830 Coliseum Street.[33] The bonanza was open to all, cash on delivery.

Speculators preferred to take their profits immediately. Most of those who waited were ruined by the Panic of 1837, which subdued the real estate market for some years thereafter. The bubble had burst. The astronomical prices that had prevailed during the boom sale of 1832 encouraged a few of the surviving speculators to wait until well-heeled buyers came into view. By 1838, though, it was far from certain that such people would ever appear, and when lower-class immigrants unexpectedly began pouring into the edge of the tract nearest to the Mississippi, the uncertainty deepened.

Homes, hovels, and tannery on Laurel Street in Lafayette City, 1866
(NEW ORLEANS NOTARIAL ARCHIVES)

THE BRAWLING RIVERFRONT

Those Yankees who moved out of the original American quarter in the Faubourg Ste. Marie to settle uptown practiced urban flight as surely as any ex-urbanite a century and a half later. They fled congestion, noise, crime, and the poor. Imagine their alarm, then, when a sprawling and brawling frontier neighborhood sprang up on the very border of their sanctuary. This was the riverfront district of the city of Lafayette, and it stretched from Felicity Street to Harmony Street.

Named for George Washington's renowned comrade in arms, Lafayette took its name as early as 1824, a year before the French marquis visited New Orleans to check on land given him by President Jefferson.[34] Lafayette City was incorporated in 1833 amidst extravagant hopes for the future. Barely two miles from the French Quarter, the new town of Lafayette made rapid inroads into the commercial monopoly of the old downtown. By 1840 it threatened to usurp New Orleans' place as the chief entrepôt of the lower Mississippi.[35] It failed in this great hope, but Lafayette briefly did become the teeming center of manufacturing and industry in Louisiana.

No business that turned a profit was too indelicate for that section of Lafayette that huddled along the river's edge. Slaughterhouses abounded at Bull's Head, near the mouth of St. Mary Street. Other slaughterhouses a few blocks upriver attracted so many scavengers that the local baseball team was later named the "Buzzards." The stench of tallow factories rose nearby and enormous steam-driven cotton presses pounded away, audible for

Commercial building on Soraparu Street at Rousseau, near Lafayette's riverfront

miles. A sugar refinery covered nearly a city block on Second Street near Annunciation. Cotton spinning gave Lafayette the promise of becoming a southern version of Lowell, Massachusetts. To meet the demand for manpower, a booming slave market imported laborers from Virginia.[36] All these enterprises, it should be noted, were only a ten-minute walk from the future heart of the Garden District.

The diversity of Lafayette's economy is astonishing. In the decade before the Civil War the local census recorded the presence of soap boilers, tailors, blacksmiths, coopers, bricklayers, engineers, tinsmiths, hatchmen, saddlers, brewers, confectioners, watchmakers, bakers, cigarmakers, draymen, stone masons, undertakers, river pilots, and tanners, not to mention circus actors and musicians.[37]

Most of this activity was linked to one innovation: the flatboat. By 1834 Lafayette was the greatest flatboat port on the Mississippi, surpassing New Orleans. The official port register lists up to ten arrivals a day, bearing cargoes of corn, cattle, brandy, bacon, wood, and other raw materials. Most flatboats floated down the Ohio and Mississippi rivers from Kentucky and Indiana—the crew of one of them included a rawboned Abraham Lincoln. Tennessee and Ohio were the other main points of origin.[38]

Since these powerless boats relied on the current to carry them downstream, they each made only one trip to the Crescent City, after which they were broken up for lumber. (A whole industry was devoted to dismantling flatboats.) Their beams were then used for everything from attics to privies. There was even a "Flatboat Church" on Felicity Street. Later, flatboat planks were often placed at the bottom of the foundation trenches of Garden District mansions. The homes of Luther Stewart, James Pagaud, and Robert Grinnan are but three of the big houses which, according to building contracts, rest on foundations footed on barge planks.[39]

Lafayette's prosperity was a magnet for the footloose and restless. Census figures for 1850 list merchants from nine countries.[40] Germans began settling in Lafayette in the 1840s, the same decade in which the Irish tide hit. By 1850, 11,000 Germans and 20,000 Irish resided in the burgeoning towns. Soon the entire neighborhood around Adele Street at Tchoupitoulas was Irish, giving the whole district the name "Irish Channel," which remains today.[41] In addition to these voluntary immigrants were blacks, most of them slaves, who constituted thirteen percent of the population.[42]

THE ARCHITECTURE OF LAFAYETTE'S RIVERFRONT

The plan of the city of Lafayette that lay along the Mississippi River was a low-density settlement of one- and two-story buildings, most of them wooden but some of brick. The sole element of planning consisted of the old French and Spanish practice of building shops on the street corners with residential housing between. Even this soon gave way to the more informal American custom, originally borrowed from England, of combining shops and homes in small compounds, as at the bakery that still stands in modified form at 719 Fourth Street at Chippewa.[43]

Many business buildings were indistinguishable from those in New Orleans proper. Two- and occasionally three-story brick structures were common near the levee. Their French doors, sidewalk overhangs supported by posts, hip roofs, and Greek-key doorways reflect a comfortable merging of national traditions. Other business blocks seem almost to have been transported whole from cities of the Middle Atlantic states or the Ohio Valley. Occasionally designed by architects, such characteristic commercial buildings as can be seen at Soraparu Street at Rousseau were commonly the work of craftsmen-builders.[44]

The diversity of styles made the town seem like an exhibition of regional and ethnic architecture. A splendid dwelling near the river at 436 Seventh Street, for example, hails directly from the Carolinas via the Feliciana Parishes of Louisiana.[45] No less distinctive are the many one-and-a-half-story houses based on prototypes from Connecticut, New York State, and especially the Western Reserve in Ohio. Remarkably ill suited to the hot climate, they were nonetheless built in some numbers before 1850. There were even attempts to enrich this style by the addition of pompous classical porticos.

Appropriate to both the climate and limitations on land were the countless one-story houses with three or more rooms stretching back through the narrow lots. Among the earliest such houses in the uptown area was one built for Miss Mary Neilson at St. Andrew Street in 1848.[46] Sprinkled throughout Lafayette by 1850, they are the direct forebears of the "shotgun" houses of post-Civil War New Orleans. In spite of their purported West Indian or even African origin, most were built by Germans or Yankees for

[ABOVE] *The rural Carolinas on urban Seventh Street in Lafayette*

[FACING PAGE] *A simple cottage in Lafayette, the early Garden District: square columns, after the Western Reserve tradition in Ohio* (NEW ORLEANS NOTARIAL ARCHIVES)

transplanted Anglo-Saxon immigrants. Multiple dwellings in this style also abounded and are still to be seen today.

New immigrants from France and local Creoles tended to stick with their traditional architecture. The ancient French half-timbered, brick-between-posts mode of construction was used for a number of dwellings in Lafayette, while cottages in the style of eighteenth-century Louisiana continued to be built into the 1840s. There were even narrow one-floored houses of a type that the earliest French settlers formerly built along the Gulf Coast, a surviving home at 2709 Camp Street being a particularly interesting example.[47] The vitality of these retrogressive local styles is measured by the fact that many immigrant Americans and Germans picked them up. Gerd Heinrich Wilhelm Lehde adopted a typical Creole floor plan when he built a group of houses at 730–736 Washington Avenue, while at John Friedenstein's brick home at 2308 Chippewa Street chimneyed gable ends add American flavor to a typical Creole double.[48] Such amalgamations reached a high point with the elegant Isaac Bogart house at 1020 Fourth Street. Designed by the Scottish-born architect George Purves in the 1840s, this exceptional residence weds Greek Revival, Creole, and South Carolina elements to achieve an exceptionally impressive dignity.[49]

As builders, the immigrant Germans were both active and adaptable. Scarcely had they arrived in New Orleans then they began constructing homes for themselves and others. For the most part, however, they assimilated whatever was best in the buildings around them rather than impose some Germanic prototype on the city. To be sure, various features of the simple buildings along the riverfront in Lafayette reveal German influences, notably the popularity of gable-end facades along the streets. However, it is in the quality of crafts-manship in both wood and brick in which the German's hand is most readily discerned, rather than in the type or design of the buildings.

Irish settlers along the Lafayette riverfront left fewer traces of their presence than the Germans. Poverty and their unfamiliarity with wooden construction forced these immigrants to rely on builders from other ethnic groups for their homes. Most became renters. Even the heart of the Irish Channel—the block bounded by Adele, St. Andrew, Rousseau, and Levee Streets—was owned not by Irishmen but by people with names like Conrad, Muller, DeBlieux, and Livaudais.

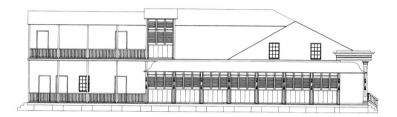

[ABOVE] *A cottage expanded to ten rooms on two floors: the Bogart house at 1020 Fourth Street, 1849–50* (RON FILSON)

[FACING PAGE] *Scottish architect George Purves's handsome adaptation of classicism in a small dwelling, for sugar broker Isaac Bogart's house, 1020 Fourth Street, 1849–50*

[ABOVE] *German tomb in Lafayette cemetery*

[RIGHT] *German Presbyterian tombs in
Lafayette cemetery*

View on *Coliseum* (late *Plaquemine*) *Street.*

Jean Dominique Esquèrre's bucolic island in the riverfront area, 3232 Laurel Street, 1856—58. Perfected with a charming garden (NEW ORLEANS NOTARIAL ARCHIVES)

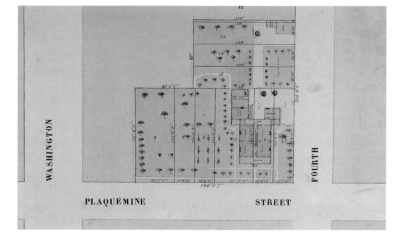

Certain aspects of the riverfront area were undeniably attractive. Back of town at 3232 Laurel Street, Jean Dominique Esquèrre created a charming formal garden beside his house.[50] The vine-covered trellis and gazebo formed a pastoral island, as did the tidy gardens that surrounded an otherwise ordinary cottage, now destroyed, on Fourth Street between Magazine and Camp.[51] Herringbone brick walks, bird houses, whitewashed walls, green shutters and red roofs imparted a picturesque quality to the neighborhood.

In the early years Lafayette as a whole was anything but picturesque. A rough boom town, it soon sank into a state of civic chaos. The one percent ad valorem tax on land, buildings, and slaves produced scarcely enough revenue for city improvements. Most of the money went into wharves, breastworks, and fire equipment rather than more visible amenities. A large combined courthouse and market building was constructed at the foot of Jackson Avenue in 1834, but it fell into decay within the decade and had to be demolished.[52] The only substantial civic building, significantly, was the jail, designed by the surveyor and engineer Benjamin Buisson in 1836.[53] Two four-room schools were also constructed, but virtually all other civic functions were left in abeyance. Even in 1850 there were only seventeen tax-exempt institutions in Lafayette, including orphanages, churches, and a synagogue.[54]

Paving was almost unknown in Lafayette except for plank roads, that primitive form of surfacing that had migrated to the United States from Russia via Canada. Even with the help of a steam-powered pump purchased by the municipality, streets and yards were deep in mud most of the year. There was no gas for lighting until the late 1840s, and, at nearly a dollar a gallon, sperm whale oil was too expensive for public use.

If the physical city was primitive, social conditions were still worse. Pickpockets, prostitutes, and drunks prowled the rat-ridden wharves. Six-foot-high picket fences surrounded most yards, reflecting not so much a desire for privacy as for protection against bandits and thugs. Nostalgic literati today tend to blur the realities of grim living conditions when they retrace the daily route of the young Walt Whitman, who lived for a few months on Washington Avenue. Contemporaries, even those who believed the situation was improv-

ing, acknowledged that the area as a whole was generally believed to be "synonymous with midnight robberies and assassinations."[55]

Much of the worst behavior was linked with the Irish poor. As renters, they lived six or eight to a boardinghouse room. A visitor to St. Thomas Street in the Irish Channel found the alley filled with "offal and refuse of every description."[56] It is hardly surprising that the gruesome yellow fever epidemic of 1853 began precisely in this area.[57] Considered lower on the social scale than free blacks, the Irish were the object of "vile and opprobrious epithets."[58] They danced at numerous social halls, drank at the Bull's Head and other taverns, and engaged in gang wars against each other and the surrounding neighborhoods.

Such were the conditions prevailing along the riverfront in the city of Lafayette. Barely twenty years old, it already suffered from what a nearby resident called "suburban poverty and neglect."[59] This urban blight cast a shadow over the development of uptown real estate generally. Even without the squalor, the rise of industry and a lower-class labor force in Lafayette imperiled the gentrification of adjoining neighborhoods. Had it continued to expand as it did between 1825 and 1845, the Lafayette riverfront would have preempted the establishment of a garden suburb in uptown New Orleans.

The rate of growth of this riverfront area, including the Irish Channel, eventually subsided. The city fathers boasted that their port would overtake New Orleans, but by the 1840s they could see that the basis of their wealth—the flatboat—was dying. As New Orleans rebounded with the new role of a steamboat port, Lafayette settled down to a more subdued existence, although not without one last political contest with New Orleans, waged over its incorporation into the larger city in the early 1850s. No longer did the spread of lower-class slums threaten to consume Samuel Peters's vast tract. Thanks to the decline of the flatboat, the future territory of the Garden District was spared funkier development of the type that had prompted American business leaders to flee from downtown in the first place.

As a result of a chain of actions then—some deliberate and others unplanned—there existed in uptown New Orleans a large, subdivided tract of land back of the river that was suitable for the establishment of a garden suburb. Down to the mid-1840s this tract

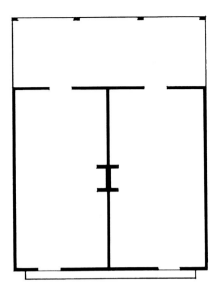

[LEFT] *A minimalist house: two-family dwelling with one room for each. Built in a few days with no facilities except a fireplace, these houses became instant slums* (NEW ORLEANS NOTARIAL ARCHIVES)

[ABOVE] (VILDOSTEGUI AND MCGILLIVRAY)

was nearly devoid of houses. Those speculators who had brought blocks and lots from Samuel Peters and his partners had found few buyers.

The question now was whether the renewal of commercial life in New Orleans during the 1840s would bring new purchasers to their doors. If so, what kind of people would they be, and what would they be seeking as they followed the now well-trodden path into the suburbs? Would they be seeking rural cottages, summer houses, or isolated villas where a businessman could play at being a country gentleman? Or would they wish to establish homes in a

stable suburban neighborhood where they could raise families, socialize with business colleagues, and enjoy physical comforts beyond what they could expect either in the teeming city or in the countryside?

A fresh wave of suburbanization began in the 1840s. A new and in many respects distinctive breed of businessmen evolved. As these people moved uptown, they placed their stamp permanently on the Garden District. To understand their suburban enclave, one must first comprehend them and their world.

BEHIND EVERY BUILDING stands a patron, the individual or organization that commissions the design. In their relations with the architect, patrons can be domineering or self-effacing, visionary or pragmatic, open-minded or downright mulish. New Orleans, like any city, offers a gallery of all types of patrons. At one extreme stands the board of La Banque de l'État de la Louisiane, which in 1818 charged the great Benjamin Henry Latrobe with nothing more specific than to design a porticoed office, "which in its construction shall unite both convenience and taste."[1] The former Surveyor of Public Buildings under Thomas Jefferson produced a tour de force. On the other extreme stands the Baroness Micaela Almonester de Pontalba, the red-haired whirlwind who in the 1840s and 1850s conceived, financed, and all but designed the impressive row houses facing Jackson Square.

Patrons in the Garden District shunned both extremes. They would hire an architect when one was at hand but would rarely invite him to indulge his fancy. When instead they worked with builders, patrons made it clear what they were after. The results were astonishingly pleasing and harmonious, more so, indeed, than the architecturally more lively but at the same time less integrated Lower Garden District. Three-quarters of a century before there was any zoning in New Orleans, Garden

[FACING PAGE] *Michel Musson's Creole outpost at 1331 Third Street. Musson, Edgar Degas' uncle, built his residence after 1850; the cast-iron gallery was added after 1884*

Before the Musson house was dressed up with a cast-iron gallery. (COLLECTION OF SAMUEL WILSON, JR., SOUTHEASTERN ARCHITECTURAL ARCHIVE, TULANE UNIVERSITY)

District patrons created for themselves an impressively unified neighborhood. This occurred through separate, individual decisions. Patrons could define or subdivide their lots at will, build up to the street or at the rear of their lots, and choose whatever style pleased them. That a coherent plan and impressive unity of architectural style could emerge from such unguided freedom attests to the fact that the various patrons had much in common. They constituted a distinct group.

To be sure, there were patrons who stood outside this group. Joseph Fernandez, the Spaniard who paid in piasters, or Spanish currency, for his lots at 1302–1304 Jackson Avenue, was an outsider.[2] So, too, were Winnefred Hubbard and Sarah Johnson, free women of color who owned properties at 3116 Prytania Street and 1229 Second Street, respectively.[3] Even Michel Musson, the wealthy Creole and uncle of painter Edgar Degas, stayed only a few years in his Italianate home at 1331 Third Street before moving back to the securely French world downtown.[4] Needless to say, the Creole sugar planters who had originally exploited the land on which the Garden District rose had long since abandoned the neighborhood to newcomers.

The Garden District was overwhelmingly Anglo-Saxon territory. Common background, professions, religion, politics, and economic interests linked the principal patrons as a group. Even without reading Englishman John Claudius Loudon's popular tract *The Suburban Gardener and Villa Companion*, published in London in 1838, New Orleanians seized on his main point, namely, the desirability of social homogeneity in one's neighborhood. During the late 1850s a number of their most prosperous members, including Henry S. Buckner and John Burnside, would gather in the late afternoons on the benches placed in front of Pope's Pharmacy at Jackson and Prytania. When local wits began referring to the group as "The Club," they inadvertently defined one of the principal keys to the architectural tone of the District as a whole.[5]

New men built the great houses of the Garden District with wallets swollen by one of the biggest booms in American history. They were clever, opportunistic, and energetic. The boom created them, however, not vice versa. To understand these men, it is helpful first to focus on the economic conditions of their era.

Until 1837, many of the largest New Orleans fortunes had been built on sugar. Several factors combined to trigger the advance of cotton after that date. The "Petit Gulf" strain of cotton, newly imported from Mexico, was more heat resistant and had a longer growing season than the older varieties and hence reduced the risk to planters. Improvements in ginning, packing, and shipping made it possible to process the local crop and move it to wherever it was needed, and the voracious cotton mills of northern England provided an endless demand. The only missing ingredient was capital. In their zeal to acquire it, the business leaders of New Orleans ended up in a major crisis, which in turn transformed the local leadership, opening the way for the new men of the Garden District.

The Mississippi Valley's thirst for capital was unquenchable, and in response to it the banking houses of the Northeast, first those in Philadelphia and later those in New York, issued paper in ever greater quantities. Even before the charter of the second Bank of the United States expired in 1836, the credit system was stretched dangerously. Only the slightest tremor of fear was needed to collapse the entire structure. When a few New York lenders demanded payment in specie in the spring of 1837, they unwittingly unleashed chaos. The ensuing panic eventually reached every corner of Europe and the Americas. Overextended New Orleans bankers were particularly vulnerable, since many could cover no more than a sixth of their liabilities with specie. The local economy remained in a shambles for half a decade. Only with the passage in 1842 of a state banking act that required Louisiana lending institutions to hold a dollar in specie for every three dollars they lent, did confidence rise.[6]

The economy of New Orleans in the 1840s was not so much revived as reconstructed. Many, though by no means all, of the old leaders had been wiped out. They were replaced by financial entrepreneurs whose wealth was based on new and burgeoning fields of enterprise. The lucrative activity of the 1840s and 1850s was concentrated in three areas in particular: cotton, wholesaling, and such allied fields as insurance and shipping. These were to be the three pillars upon which the wealth that built the Garden District was founded.

Pope's Pharmacy: where "The Club" of the Garden District gathered under the eaves in the 1850s, 1456 Jackson Avenue

[ABOVE LEFT] *Fast money. Cotton factor, banker, and speculator Jacob U. Payne built his residence at 1134 First Street, 1849.* (NEW ORLEANS PUBLIC LIBRARY)

[ABOVE RIGHT] *Kentuckian Jacob U. Payne's dignified dwelling at 1134 First Street, 1849* (RUDOLF HERTZBERG, PHOTOGRAPHER; SOUTHEASTERN ARCHITECTURAL ARCHIVE, TULANE UNIVERSITY)

[FACING PAGE] *The house of London-born Thomas Gilmour, 2520 Prytania Street, 1853. Conceived as a galleried residence, builder Isaac Thayer instead created this Italianate villa*

Residence of Virginia-born banker Walter Robinson, 1415 Third Street. Henry Howard, architect, 1859

THE COTTON BARONS

The cotton business in New Orleans was Janus-like, with one face peering upriver to the planters who grew the raw material and the other face gazing across the Atlantic to the Liverpool merchants who fed the spinning mills in Manchester. Two stalwarts of the Garden District, Jacob Upshur Payne and Thomas C. Gilmour, epitomized the two aspects of this new trade.

Jacob Payne was a cotton factor, and his handsome columned house at 1134 First Street bears witness to what an industrious cotton factor could achieve in the 1840s. Built in 1849, its dignified but unornamented exterior hides rooms decorated with a profusion of flamboyant classical moldings, cornices, and woodwork. It exudes old wealth, or so many people have thought. To be sure, when Payne died, the local press hailed him as "one of the grandest lord masters of the old regime."[7] Yet this lord master had made his entire fortune in less than a decade.

As a cotton factor, Payne earned his money by marketing cotton shipped to him by planters upriver. The standard fee for this service throughout the South was approximately 2 1/2 percent. The planters around Vicksburg all knew him, for he had spent many years there after he closed his small store in Fulton, Missouri. Like other factors, Payne did not simply sell the baled cotton consigned to him but also extended credit to his planter clients, usually at 8 to 12 percent interest. They borrowed against their future crops. Cotton factors thus became bankers and speculators, borrowing heavily in New York in order to have capital with which to tie up as much of the cotton market as possible.[8] Once established as a loan agent, Payne then proceeded to buy the plantations themselves.

Thomas Gilmour represented the other side of the equation. As a broker, the London-born Gilmour purchased cotton from cotton factors like Payne on behalf of interests in Liverpool, Hamburg, and other spinning centers. There were far fewer brokers than factors, but the 5 percent commissions and rapid market fluctuations created some large fortunes. A German competitor of Gilmour's once earned the equivalent of $1.2 million in three days.[9] Gilmour himself had been in New Orleans scarcely three years before he was able to build his comfortable Italianate home at 2520 Prytania Street.[10]

The keys to success for cotton factors and brokers alike were to establish close links with northeastern or foreign capital markets and to diversify into banking and real estate as quickly as possible. Walter Robinson was stunningly successful at both. This enabled him to build his exceptionally lavish home at 1415 Third Street.[11] Like many Garden District entrepreneurs, Robinson had come to town with his brother and established himself in cotton. Thanks to his background in Lynchburg, Virginia, Robinson knew the tobacco market as well and promptly cornered the trade on the rare Perique blending tobacco, which was and is produced exclusively in a small district in St. James Parish. In the end, however, it was neither cotton nor tobacco that established Robinson's fortune, but his credit operations. Through the Merchants and Traders Bank, of which he was president, Robinson built a financial empire that linked lower Louisiana and lower Manhattan.[12]

THE COMMISSION MEN

The second great source of Garden District wealth—wholesaling—owed its existence to the astounding speed with which America's trans-Appalachian heartland was settled. Within the span of only a few decades, millions of pioneers poured into the Mississippi Valley, traveling westward along a moving frontier stretching from Texas to the Dakotas. These settlers needed provisions of every sort, from dry goods to farm equipment, seeds, boots, and hardware. Eventually their needs were to be met by the merchant princes of Chicago, who capitalized on the new railroads that fanned out westward from their city to trade in distant markets. Still later, the improvement of the United States mail service opened the way for mail-order merchandising and the ubiquitous Sears Roebuck catalogs. But in the decades before the Civil War it was the Mississippi River system that provided the main channel for merchandising. New Orleans, with its shipping links with both the Northeast and Europe, was the natural home base for wholesale firms exploiting this opportunity. In the period lasting from 1820 to 1850 especially,

Henry Lonsdale, New Orleans' chief coffee broker (NEW ORLEANS
PUBLIC LIBRARY)

merchants as far afield as Illinois, Iowa, and Missouri purchased
their stocks from New Orleans wholesalers, thanks to the low
prices prevailing in the Crescent City.

All of this created a perfect environment in which an extraordinary group of merchant princes could thrive. Each of the new
giants of commerce was distinctive; whispered tales of legendary
achievements followed them all. To single out John Adams, the
wholesale grocer, or Henry T. Lonsdale, the coffee and gunnysack
magnate, is to speak of just two artists on a stage full of soloists.

John Adams's success was far more dramatic than the plaque
in front of his baronial cottage at 2423 Prytania Street suggests.
Born in New Jersey, Adams grew to maturity in the most primitive
frontier conditions, in Preble County, Ohio, where his family had
settled. With nothing more than a rudimentary education, Adams
headed back east in 1834. There he managed to learn the wholesaling business and then went south; within three days of his arrival in
New Orleans in 1842 he had established himself as a wholesale grocer.[13] After a few years, he was shipping salt, sugar, spices, and
other necessities to virtually every town in the Mississippi basin.

Henry Lonsdale's dual legacy to New Orleans was the modern
coffee industry and what was, in its day, one of the costliest homes in
the city, at 2521–23 Prytania Street.[14] Born in Brooklyn, New York,
in 1809, to English parents temporarily residing in the United
States, Lonsdale lived in England until he was nine. Then his family
moved to St. Johns, New Brunswick, Canada. Young Lonsdale eventually made his way to New York, where he found employment with
a merchant. Like Adams, he stayed in the Northeast only long
enough to learn the fundamentals of the wholesale trade, then left
for New Orleans, arriving there by ship in 1828. But his first efforts
to conquer the New Orleans business world ended in failure. He
then spent several years on the rivers and in Kentucky before
attempting for the second time to establish his fortune in the
Louisiana city. This time he knew the needs of the western settlers
and quickly cornered the gunnysack market. By the time of the 1837
Panic his jute sacks had become the standard means for packaging
all western produce. Utterly ruined by the Panic of 1837, Lonsdale
started over again in Louisville, returning to New Orleans some
years later. This time he established himself as the chief coffee broker of the city and hence of the American West.[15]

Grocer John A. Adam's baronial cottage, 2423 Prytania Street, 1860–61

There was nothing provincial about the wholesale magnates of New Orleans. In the early years of the century they brought their produce mainly from Philadelphia and Baltimore, but by the 1830s New York had become the principal source of supply. The legendary wealth of the Anglo-Irishman John Burnside, who eventually owned 2200 slaves and ten plantations, was based originally on dry goods brought from England on the return run of cotton ships. Lonsdale, of course, exploited Central American sources for his coffee. So dominant was New Orleans' position as a transshipment point that millions of tons of produce came to the city from upriver as well, only to be repackaged and shipped out again across the river system.[16]

By 1850 some of the biggest fortunes in New Orleans had been built on wholesaling, their profits rivaling even those of cotton. Among the Garden District's monuments to such fortunes are the residences of grocer George Sweet at 1236 Jackson Avenue; the commission merchant Hiram Anderson at 2427 Camp Street; the commission merchant Albert Brevard at 1239 First Street; the grain dealer John Rodenberg at 1238 Philip Street; the wholesale grocers Charles Eager and Luther Stewart at 1406 Seventh and 1208 Philip streets, respectively; the hardware dealer Lafayette Folger at 2508 St. Charles Avenue, now demolished; and the dealer in "western produce," John Wallis, at 2403 Camp Street. The operations of such tycoons were national, even international in scope, leaving their mark on the economic life of cities, towns, and remote farmsteads thousands of miles away from the Crescent City. Never before had so much commercial wealth been generated in any American city outside the eastern seaboard.

THE SUPPORTING INDUSTRIES

The twin engines of cotton and wholesaling that drove the economy of antebellum New Orleans also pulled along dozens of secondary businesses in their wake. With the exception of the insurance industry, which was desperately needed by cotton factors and western-produce men alike, this third sector of the economy did not produce towering fortunes. But it sufficed to enable many men to build in the Garden District and give it a social diversity that it might otherwise have lacked.

Every aspect of the mushrooming economy was fraught with risk, which the chief actors sought to minimize through insurance. The architect of the insurance industry in the West was Thomas A. Adams, no relative of the grocer, but an equally vigorous entrepreneur. Boston-born, Adams had mastered the intricacies of mutual insurance at its American source, the Mutual Safety Insurance Company in New York. Arriving in New Orleans in 1842, he founded the Crescent Mutual Insurance Company as a branch of the New York house.[17] So rapidly did his firm prosper that within seven years Adams was able to build his comfortable home on Prytania Street which, although long destroyed, will warrant close attention later.[18] Hard on the heels of Adams's Crescent Mutual came a series of other insurance firms serving both individual and corporate clients. Their founders made a career of prudence and independence, qualities that are accurately mirrored in the architectural tastes of such men as London-born Charles Briggs, whose Gothic Revival cottage at 2605 Prytania Street is as correctly formal in its plan as it is distinctive in its details.

Beyond insurance, the support industries were highly diverse. Henry H. Hansell of 3000 Prytania Street supplied the western market with saddles, while Joseph Maddox established his nest egg as editor of the *Daily Crescent* and built a handsome, columned five-bay home at 2507 Prytania.[19] There were also attorneys, such as the dynamic and politically active Charles Conrad, who lived on Prytania and First, or Levi Peirce of St. Charles Avenue.[20] But in that less litigious era lawyers were fewer in number and those who prospered derived their wealth from sources other than the practice of law. Conrad, for example, was a developer of urban real estate who amassed agricultural land on the side.

Fruits of a Vermont-born newspaperman's success: the Joseph Maddox house, 2507 Prytania Street, by architect John Barnett, 1852

[LEFT] *Gold-leafed parlor capitals of Daily Crescent publisher Maddox's handsome residence, by architect John Barnett and builder John R. Eichelberger, 1852*

[RIGHT] *Provisioner makes good. The iceman A.W. Bosworth's residence, 1126 Washington Avenue, by English-born architect Thomas Wharton, 1859* (THE HISTORIC NEW ORLEANS COLLECTION)

Meanwhile, others built their fortunes by owning and operating steamboats, as was the case with Captain Thomas Leathers of 2027 Carondelet Street.[21] In the heated economy of antebellum New Orleans even the ice industry could prove lucrative, as it did for A. W. Bosworth formerly of Skowhegan, Maine, and the owner of a simple but imposing home at 1126 Washington Avenue.[22] Bosworth's business thrived in tandem with that of the dealers in western produce since his ice was brought to the South as ballast in merchant ships. Anything that could render more comfortable the lives of the princes of commerce could generate a fortune sufficient to enable one to live comfortably in the Garden District. Thus Lewis Elkin's home at 1410 Second Street was built on money from oriental carpets and Samuel E. Moore's home at 2925 Coliseum Street on the profits from the importation and sale of crockery, china, and glassware; T. S. Waterman, who lived on Jackson Avenue, established his fortune by manufacturing soda water.[23]

"SOUTHERN YANKEES" AND ENGLISHMEN

Who were the men who hastened to New Orleans to reap profits from the cotton boom? Obviously they were entrepreneurs, quick to seize the chance for profits and self-betterment. The American West in the 1840s offered a cornucopia of opportunities, however, among which the New Orleans mercantile world was but one. Those who heeded Horace Greeley's advice to "go West, young man" and then proceeded to seek the end of their rainbow in New Orleans were a carefully self-selected group.

In their place of origin, for example, they offer a fairly consistent profile, and one that scarcely fits the image of the antebellum Garden District as a bastion of the Old South. Of some forty of those who built the largest houses, only three—Michel Musson, Antoine Jacques Mandeville Marigny, and the widow of Augustin Tureaud—were New Orleans-born or Creole.[24] Of these three, Mandeville Marigny had married an Anglo-Saxon woman, and Musson, who had not, quickly fled back to the city's Francophone center on Esplanade Avenue.

Even scarcer than Creoles in the Garden District were native-born Southerners. The two most prominent sons of the Old South domiciled there were Virginians, Walter G. Robinson and Charles Conrad. Robinson's lavish manner and Conrad's reputation as a duelist—he killed a man over a point of honor in his early years—gave them each the aura of *grands seigneurs* of the Old Dominion. Both, however, had been born in the hill country in the west of the state, rather than the more patrician Tidewater, and had come west early in their lives. In contrast, half of the civic leadership of New Orleans' rival port, Mobile, Alabama, were southern-born in the last antebellum decade.[25] Moreover, quite a number of Louisiana planters, men like John Randolph of Nottaway Plantation and Samuel Packwood of Myrtle Grove, boasted of their Tidewater origins.

Far better represented in the Garden District were the border states, especially Kentucky. Indeed, the Kentuckians included in their number several of the major architectural patrons. Henry S. Buckner, Colonel Robert Short, Wirt Adams, and Jacob U. Payne had all made their way downriver from the Bluegrass State during the 1830s and 1840s. Several had formed strong southern links in the process. Wirt Adams, for example, had spent years in Natchez,

Mississippi, before moving into his great house on Chestnut Street in the Garden District, now demolished. His Mississippi plantations and his career as a duelist certify his assimilation. Similarly, Jacob Payne had spent enough time in Vicksburg to acquire a plantation and meet his future wife before establishing himself on First Street in the Garden District.

If by the 1850s a few of the Kentuckians embodied what has become the stereotypical image of the Old South, the majority did not. Men like Robert Short were quick to exploit their upriver connections, but their closest financial link and the source of their business style was New York City. Indeed, the Garden District was more closely linked with New York than with any other city or region.

James De Bow, a New Orleanian who edited one of the most authoritative economic journals of the day, *De Bow's Review*, explained the situation in 1855. According to his statistics, the population of New Orleans included more natives of Maine than of any Southern state except Mississippi, and twice the number of New Yorkers than of Kentuckians and Virginians combined.[26] As the *Daily Crescent* observed in 1851, "A majority of the business men of this city [are] from north of Mason and Dixon's line."[27]

The Northeasterners set the tone in the Garden District. The life of Samuel H. Kennedy in many respects typifies the group. Born to a Massachusetts farming family, Kennedy cut his teeth as a businessman in Manhattan before making his way west to Alton, Illinois, where he established a wholesale grocery business. By age twenty-seven, having outgrown Alton, he set out in 1843 for New Orleans in search of broader territory to conquer.[28] Within a decade of his arrival there, he was in a position to enlist architect Lewis E. Reynolds to design for him a grandiose cottage on Camp Street, now destroyed. All the while Kennedy maintained close contact with his creditors in New York, visiting them periodically during the steamy New Orleans summers.

The lives of numerous Garden District grandees follow this same pattern, with only minor variations. The result was a commercial establishment solidly in the hands of Northeasterners and men oriented toward that part of the country. Northern shipping and merchandising houses controlled much of the exports and even most of the imports of New Orleans.[29] City directories and commercial guides of the period are full of advertisements by New York firms or their local agents, and the New England Society, of which Thomas Adams long served as president, surpassed virtually every other local club in the prestige and wealth of its membership. In antebellum New Orleans, the word "Yankee" carried no pejorative connotations. A locally published work of 1845 could speak admiringly of "the enterprising, calculating, hardy Yankees" of New Orleans.[30] Centered in the Garden District, these men were what a recent scholar has termed "southern Yankees."[31]

After the Northeasterners and Kentuckians, the third most important group of Garden District patrons was English or Anglo-Irish. There were other foreigners as well, notably Germans and Jews from Alsace, such as Manuel Goldsmith, a resident of 1122 Jackson Avenue, who immigrated from France in 1851.[32] The English and Anglo-Irish were by far the largest non-American element in the suburb, however, and enriched it with some of its most enduring architecture.

Robert A. Grinnan, a cotton broker and commission merchant, had barely arrived in New Orleans from London in 1850 when he hired architect Henry Howard to design his elegant villa at 2221 Prytania Street.[33] Scarcely less ambitious than Grinnan were Londoners Thomas Gilmour, whose Italianate house on Prytania Street broke new ground stylistically, and the insurance executive Charles Briggs, who lived in his Gothic cottage in the next block of Prytania from Gilmour. Henry Lonsdale, whose immensely costly mansion still stands near the Briggs and Gilmour houses, also had an English heritage. Even though a few of these Englishmen became Americanized, most, including Grinnan, Gilmour, and Louis de Saulles, builder of the distinctive Natchez-style home at 2618 Coliseum Street, retained their former loyalties and appear to have left New Orleans after making their fortunes.[34]

In contrast to the English and Anglo-Irish, the Irishmen who attained sufficient wealth to establish themselves in the Garden District tended to make a firm commitment to their new country. Driven from their native land by poverty, they were true immigrants, grateful for what they had and eager to improve themselves in their new environment. Peter Conrey, James Coyle, and John McGinty may not have been such adventuresome patrons of architecture as the English, but they all occupied important positions in the New Orleans community of the day.[35]

THE IMPORTANCE OF BEING EARNEST

After the Civil War the great homes of the Garden District were to be surrounded with a romantic aura that persists to the present day. Is it not true that the comfortable homes fairly exude a mood of patrician ease, indolence, and even Mardi Gras frivolity? Yet the patrons were distinguished in the eyes of their contemporaries by an entirely different set of values. Jacob Payne was singled out in a city directory for being "strictly attentive to the business interests of his house,"[36] while Henry S. Buckner, the great cotton factor, was said to have pursued a "cold-hearted policy" in the Panic of 1857.[37] Buckner was also described by contemporaries as "a man of great resolution, energy, and executive ability."[38] John A. Adams was renowned for having led "a simple, unostentatious life," and for having been guided by "puritanical principles of sterling integrity, determination of purpose, and indomitable energy."[39] Adams worked to the day of his death at age eighty-four.

Whatever their backgrounds, those who settled in the Garden District were self-made men who owed their positions in society solely to their own efforts. For the most part, they did not aspire to own a plantation or rural retreat. Charles Conrad and Jacob Payne were exceptions to the rule, as was Anglo-Irishman John Burnside, who owned the lovely Houmas House and nine other plantations in addition to his Garden District properties. Most knew too much about the insecurity of their upriver planter clients to yearn for the planters' style of life.

A strong streak of moralism also ran through the entire group. Jacob Payne, for instance, spent much of his time in Vicksburg mounting a vigilante assault on the sporting houses of that city. This moralism was supported by religious conviction. The genteel congregation of Episcopalians in Trinity Church was dwarfed by the more austere Presbyterians, who worshiped either with the old congregation on Lafayette Square or in their new church on Prytania Street.

If the antebellum Garden District was a tropical outpost of the Puritan ethic, its first article of faith was the value of hard work. As A. Oakey Hall wrote in his 1851 volume, *The Manhattaner in New Orleans*, "'Work, work, work' is the unceasing cry. Except among the Creoles, a man of leisure is a wonder."[40] Or, as a visiting French musician noted a few years later, "[New Orleans] is a world of commission men, speculators, and dealers who argue feverishly in the midst of their piled-up merchandise."[41]

After the 1850s the cult of work began to be leavened somewhat by a new interest in sports and culture. Yachting was already popular and rowing clubs with such Yankee names as "Knickerbocker" and "Locofoco" were organized.[42] Baseball and cricket made their entry into uptown New Orleans at the Delachaise Grounds at this time as well.[43] Amateur theatrical groups were also organized for the first time in the 1850s.

It was principally the younger men, rather than the middle-aged patrons of architecture, who indulged in such light-hearted activities. The great patrons worked unceasingly throughout the winter trading season and then left town as soon as hot weather descended. Most went north, not only to escape the tropical fevers but also to renew contacts in their home regions. When the "Can't-Get-Away Dramatic Club" was formed in the Garden District in the summer of 1855, it was considered a droll novelty.[44] It is no wonder that an observer of the Anglo-Saxon social scene in 1851 could conclude that "few and far between are they who cultivate within [New Orleans] a home feeling."[45]

Indeed, more than a few Garden District pioneers eventually left town and settled elsewhere. In addition to the Englishmen who have already been mentioned, George Sweet, Hiram Anderson, J. J. Warren, David Godwin, Joseph Maddox, and H. H. Hansell are but a few of those who, as one cynic put it, "after the gold hunt [was] over, returned home to spend it."[46]

MEASURING THE WORLD OF MAMMON

The Garden District was built by and for the men who amassed substantial fortunes. The extent of their wealth, however, is difficult to determine with any precision. Fortunately, the U.S. Census of 1860 included questions about each citizen's property holdings. The figures must, of course, be adjusted to account for the much greater value of the dollar then—well over twenty times its present worth. Since then, as now, citizens had no reason to boast of their wealth to the census taker, it can also be assumed that the reported figures understate rather than overstate the actual situation. With these cautions in mind, consider Henry Lonsdale, with his $250,000 in real estate and $211,000 in "other property." Or reflect on Jacob Payne, with his $318,000 worth of real estate holdings and $563,000 in "other property." For Thomas Gilmour comparable figures were $60,000 and $140,000, and for Lewis Elkin $40,000 and $7,500. Such men were very wealthy indeed, especially when one considers that by far their most valuable assets were their businesses. There were less wealthy neighbors, of course. Michel Musson reported only $70,000 total worth, including both real estate and other property, as did Edward Davis on Prytania Street. But these were exceptions. In an era when most home-owning New Orleanians had assets under $1500, the wealth of nearly all Garden District residents stands out prominently.

Garden District residences were not cheap during the 1850s. Albert Brevard's house at 1239 First Street was assessed at $13,500; the comparable figure for Hiram Anderson's house at 2427 Camp Street was $15,000. The Robert Grinnan and Jacob Payne houses were assessed at $19,800 and $20,000, respectively, while the tax value of Robert Short's famous villa with the "cornstalk" fence at 1448 Fourth Street was set at $23,750.[47] All these figures represent the tax assessor's judgments, which were notoriously low, rather than the market value of the properties; moreover, they must all be multiplied by at least twenty times to approximate present dollar values.

Surviving tax rolls for 1857 indicate that a few grandees had put vast sums into their residences. Henry Sullivan Buckner's showplace on Jackson Avenue at Coliseum cost $30,000. When Henry Lonsdale put $40,000 into his Prytania Street residence,

[ABOVE] *Residence of London-born Robert A. Grinnan, by Irish-born architect Henry Howard, 2221 Prytania Street, 1850* (THE HISTORIC NEW ORLEANS COLLECTION)

[RIGHT] *The Grinnan house hallway*

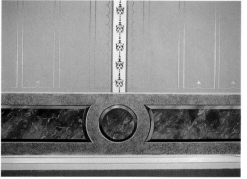

[ABOVE] *Faux marble at the Manuel Goldsmith house, 1122 Jackson Avenue. Irish-born Henry Howard and German-born Albert Diettel were the architects, 1859.*

[LEFT] *Henry S. Buckner's gallery looking out to Trinity Church, where Leonidas Polk preached. 1410 Jackson Avenue, Lewis E. Reynolds, architect, 1850*

cautious souls like the architect Thomas Wharton criticized him for vulgar ostentation.[48] James Robb's Washington Avenue mansion (destroyed) broke all records at $65,000, but Robb, as everyone knew, was in a class of his own.

Only three or four men elsewhere in the Crescent City had sunk as much into their homes as Messrs. Robb, Buckner, and Lonsdale.[49] All of these men, however, put no more money into their residences than was absolutely necessary. Few tied up as much as a fifth of their property in their homes, and a tenth was typically the norm. There were several sound reasons for this caution. New Orleans was ruled by harsh cycles of boom and bust. Even the richest Garden District residents enjoyed little or no security. Henry Lonsdale, as previously noted, had already gone broke twice in New Orleans before he built his coffee fortune. Thomas Toby of 2340 Prytania Street fell so deeply in debt in the 1830s that he had to appeal to the fledgling government of Texas, whose cause he had long supported, for repayment of his advances to the state.[50] James Robb carefully diversified his holdings but was still bankrupted in the national panic of the late 1850s. The Englishman Charles Briggs was unable to complete his Gothic-style cottage before mortgaging it to its builders, James Gallier and Company, in 1850.[51] New Hampshire-born Joseph H. Maddox, founder of the *Daily Crescent*, lost his handsomely galleried house at 2507 Prytania Street in 1854 through court seizure.[52] Lavinia Dabney, whose inheritance shrank precipitously in the recession of 1857, had scarcely a year to enjoy the home at 2265 St. Charles Avenue that James Gallier, Jr. designed for her before she, too, was forced to sell.[53] Writs of seizure and sale were a looming threat in the early Garden District. In the fairly mild recession of 1854–55 the architect Thomas Wharton noted that "there had been more large failures within the last few days and still more are expected."[54]

A further reason for the limited funds that patrons invested in their private dwellings is that New Orleans was starved for capital. This was a problem throughout the South, of course. Precisely because of this, the cotton factors plowed every cent they could into loans to planters. The commission merchants did likewise, investing in inventory as well. The more ambitious the businessman, the less liquidity he enjoyed, and the less discretionary cash he had to build his residence. This problem was the norm because nineteenth-

century Americans had to pay cash for their houses. There were banks, of course, but interest was high and the borrower was expected to pay back the entire amount, along with interest, in just three to five years. Only with the rise of the building and loan associations did this change, and then only gradually.[55]

Even a prosperous shipping magnate like Captain Thomas Leathers, owner of the steamboat *Natchez*, showed great parsimony, if not downright stinginess, in architecture. Meeting with his contractor W. K. Day, aboard the *Natchez* in 1857, Leathers confronted the projected cost of $20,000 for his house at 2027 Carondolet Street. The Mississippian accused his builder of being a spendthrift with his, Leathers's money. They argued. Finally, Day, in high sarcasm, played a gambit that he had earlier used with John Chillton when he was negotiating the construction cost of that man's home at 1506 Seventh Street.[56] Day told Leathers he was prepared to build either an ornate Episcopalian mansion, "a plain old-fashioned Methodist house," or a "solid Presbyterian compromise."[57] They finally agreed on the middle course, but matters did not end there. When the final bill came in above the $20,000 estimate, Day had to take Leathers to court to get his fee.[58]

Fortunately, Victorian architectural practice enabled patrons to cut costs at every turn. When Charles Conrad built his raised cottage in 1841, his contract called for the front door to be "grained in imitation of some fancy wood."[59] The contract for the impressive Forcheimer house at 2331–33 Magazine Street specified wood plastered and painted to look like masonry.[60] Lavinia Dabney upgraded the original plan for her house from wood to brick, but could not afford stone, and hence asked here architect to plaster and paint the brick to appear like stone.[61]

Throughout the Garden District, yellow pine was grained to look like oak, wooden mantles were painted to resemble marble, cemented brick foundations were plastered and painted to suggest granite, red cedar fences were painted to appear like sandstone, and facades were laid off in blocks to represent masonry.[62] These were, of course, the normal conventions—or pretentions—of Victorian architecture. By comparing prototypes in New York and Philadelphia with what was constructed in New Orleans, however, the Garden District variants stand out by their greater simplicity and lower cost.[63]

Captain Thomas P. Leather's "solid Presbyterian compromise," 2027 Carondolet Street, by architects Henry Howard and Henry Thiberge, 1857

A group portrait, if it is to be artistically convincing, must suggest why the particular people that it depicts came together at one time and place. To this point our group portrait of Garden District patrons is incomplete, for it has not touched upon the specific factors that led them, in the late 1840s, to establish their own suburb. The Garden District was created by and for a distinct group, united by background and economic circumstances. It is a curious fact, however, that before 1852 the largest mansions built there were owned mainly by resident English businessmen who retained their British citizenship, or by such American mavericks as Thomas Toby, the former Philadelphian who fanatically embraced the cause of the Texas revolution from his Garden District home, even to the point of naming a son "Texas." What, then, caused the building boom? Why did members of the new American elite suddenly rush into this large area and create a new type of American suburb? The answer, as is so often the case in New Orleans, involves politics. Other causes, of course, were also present, but it was the local political crisis of 1849–52 that most directly precipitated suburbanization in New Orleans.

Antebellum residents of the Garden District for the most part were able to express their strong political convictions successfully without actually standing for election. Of the four dozen largest property-holders of the District, fewer than six ever ran for public office; most considered it bad form to do so. Jacob Payne, for example, spent his whole life "carefully shunning the notoriety of public positions...."[64] One early city guide noted approvingly how Thomas Adams "uniformly declined any proposition of a political or public nature...."[65] Charles Conrad was a rare exception in that he served in the Louisiana state legislature, in both houses of the United States Congress, and as Secretary of War under President Fillmore before entering the first and second congresses of the Confederate States.[66] James Robb also served in the Louisiana legislature but declined a proposed nomination to the U.S. Senate.[67]

Members of the uptown elite avoided public office but were passionately interested in securing and exercising political power. As Anglo-Saxon businessmen in New Orleans, they were beleaguered on every side. Far from marching to easy victory over their opponents, as many historians have depicted them, they had to fight for every inch of ground they gained. Clear victory only came to view in 1852.

At the national level, wealthy merchants and traders had long been under assault from the heirs of President Andrew Jackson's democratic revolution. Tariff protection, strong centralized banking institutions, and a firmly united country were necessities to the mercantile class. In election after election the rest of the population indicated its hostility to these policies.

At the state level, the new cotton planters of north Louisiana were almost all Democrats as well, united in their antagonism toward their urban creditors down river. Finally, within the city the predominantly Creole areas below Canal Street were staunchly pro-Democratic. The Protestant Anglo-Saxons appeared to be gaining economic hegemony, but their political hold on the city was anything but secure.

The one national party behind which the future Garden District patrons could rally at every level was the Whig coalition forged by the venerable Henry Clay. Like Whigs in New England and elsewhere, the uptown Whigs of New Orleans were suspicious of the masses, protective of American banking, and supportive of a strong government that promoted the cause of property.[68] Virtually every major patron of architecture in the Garden District was a Whig.

During the 1840s the confrontation between Democrats and Whigs in New Orleans reached a peak. At stake was control of the city. The division of New Orleans into three separate municipalities had failed disastrously, leading to a political standoff. Neither party favored reunification on any terms but its own. To strengthen their position, the predominantly Creole Democrats successfully enlisted most of the new Catholic immigrants from Ireland and south Germany to their cause. This was accomplished through various means, not all of them legal. A typical method was to ferry voters from polling place to polling place along the Mississippi, thus enabling them to cast their ballots three or more times. The uptown Clay Clubs countered such practices with equally dubious procedures. For example, they would pay recruiters for every new voter they signed up for the Whig cause, the bounty in Lafayette being three dollars. The goal of such schemes was to turn Lafayette and the Garden District into a Whig bastion that could then be merged with New Orleans to form a fourth municipality, thus tipping the political scales toward the new mercantilists.

The battle was waged on practical and symbolic levels simultaneously. When the Anglo-Saxons above Canal Street brought in James Gallier, Sr., to build them a lavish Municipal Hall, the Creoles of the French Quarter and their allies responded with the Baroness Pontalba's impressive reconstruction of the Place d'Armes. When the Creoles then renamed the Place d'Armes "Jackson Square" and placed a statue of Old Hickory at its center, James Robb and his fellow Whigs responded with plans to erect a statue of Henry Clay at the foot of Canal Street, a goal they attained in 1860. Such sparring dragged on for years.

Finally the city council of Lafayette forced the issue. In 1851 the Whig coalition in that body threatened to establish the town as a free port unless the Creoles dropped their opposition to the annexation of Lafayette and the reorganization of New Orleans. Had it been enacted, this would have damaged the downtown shipping interests and crippled the Creoles economically. The mere threat of such drastic action forced the downtown Creoles to come to terms. The following year James Robb, soon to be the Garden District's richest citizen, introduced legislation in Baton Rouge annexing Lafayette to New Orleans. Even though it took a few more years for the new uptown leadership to consolidate its victory, the annexation of Lafayette marked the final shift in power from the old to the new elite.[69]

In one sense the uptown leadership had scored a Pyrrhic victory. Even as it gained ascendancy in New Orleans, the Whig party nationally was collapsing over the issue of slavery. It lost its narrow majority in the Louisiana legislature in 1852 and even in New Orleans it was rapidly evolving into a Native American (or "Know Nothing") Party. From the standpoint of the new mercantile group, however, the annexation of the City of Lafayette to New Orleans in 1852 was a momentous event. The Yankee businessmen of New Orleans were finally emancipated from what they felt had been their second-class citizenship in a city they had long controlled economically. Victory gave them new cohesion as a group, and, most important for architecture, emboldened them to cap their triumph by building a new suburb for themselves. Thanks to the political settlement of 1852, the construction boom in the Garden District was on.

The Whigs' response to local Jacksonians: the Clay Monument, now in Lafayette Park.

THE IDEAL OF A GARDEN SUBURB

The political triumph opened the way for the creation of a separate residential quarter for the new leadership. However, it had no bearing on the form that such a quarter should take. This was to be determined in response to a number of factors, some practical and others purely ideological.

Among practical considerations, health was by far the most important. The rich were as prone to yellow fever (known locally as "the strangers' disease" or "Bronze John") as were the poor, especially since the newcomers among them had yet to acquire immunity. Suffice it to note that James Robb lost his wife and a daughter to yellow fever, and the noted architect Lewis Reynolds lost six members of his family to the same scourge. There was little agreement on the causes of yellow fever. A particularly devastating epidemic in 1853 brought this issue to a head and with important consequences for town planning.

The epidemic appeared first on Adele Street, hard by the levee in the very heart of the Irish Channel, the old Lafayette riverfront section. By the year's end 7,248 cases had been reported, equal to half the population of Lafayette, including the Garden District. Over a thousand of these victims died. The detailed investigation carried out by the New Orleans City Council focused on the causes of the outbreak. The testimony of numerous doctors pointed toward four chief culprits: moisture, crowding, filth, and bad air.[70] All were present to an exceptional degree in the squalid riverfront wards of the town, which were in stark contrast to the Garden District to the north. According to the best medical knowledge available at the time, cities in general and poor neighborhoods in particular were breeding zones of death. Obviously, anyone who could afford to would seek a place of residence that was dry, uncrowded, clean, and wafted by fresh breezes. In the entire New Orleans area, the Garden District came closest to fitting this description. That many of its residents also died from yellow fever was less important than the fact that medical knowledge affirmed that such a garden suburb was likely to be safer than downtown.

A second practical consideration pushing the new leadership toward suburban life was crime. Robbery, muggings, and murder had long been commonplace in the port city on the Mississippi.

When New Orleans was designated the chief military depot for the Mexican War in 1847, the crime rate soared still higher. As the *Bee* put it a few years later, "Our city has been infested by a band of desperadoes who have shed innocent blood and spread terror and consternation among certain classes...."[71] Among those areas worst hit was the Faubourg Ste. Marie, where many of the American leaders had heretofore settled.

Pushed out from the city's center by pestilence and urban violence and propelled forward by their own economic and political success, the new leaders set about building their garden suburb. The basic grid plan had already been set, thanks to the efforts of Samuel Peters and his partners back in 1832. In its relentlessly formal design, the Garden District is a throwback to the earlier nineteenth century, when cities across the land were adopting the rigid grid system embodied in the Northwest Ordinance of 1785. Absent is the romantic ruralism that appeared in Victoria Park near Manchester, England, in 1837, and which made its American debut in the plans for Boston's Mount Auburn Cemetery in 1831, and later in Alexander Jackson Davis's 1852 scheme for Llewellyn Park, New Jersey, Philadelphia's Fairmont Park of 1855, or Glendale, Ohio, and Lake Forest, Illinois, both also of the 1850s.[72]

That the new suburb was to be served by steam and horsecars was also certain; Peters's own funeral was timed to enable mourners to arrive uptown on the five o'clock train on the St. Charles Avenue line.[73] That railroad, one of the earliest in the country, was to prove a powerful stimulus to uptown development, just as the Philadelphia-Germantown line, opened in 1832, gave rise to suburban growth outside the old Pennsylvania city, and new lines in New York (1837) and Boston (1838) opened these cities to suburban development.[74] Beyond this, it was clear that much green space would be preserved, which would be planted not in formal gardens, as had once been common in the French Quarter, but in lawns to be trimmed with the new mechanical mowers that had been invented in England in the early 1830s.[75] Again, the rigid grid asserted itself: the suburb would be more urban than rural, a *rus in urbe*, in the fashionable phrase of the day.

What was not clear was the balance to be struck between individual and communal concerns.[76] From the earliest days the collective impulse of the new patrons made itself felt in the absence of fences between lots. Moreover, the traditional high New Orleans board fence along the streets soon gave way in the Garden District to low cedar rails or, later, to cast-iron fencing. Such arrangements assured that passers-by would be restricted to the sidewalk but at the same time be invited to gaze at the splendor just beyond reach. Thus did privacy give way to a collective display and to a partially recovered sense of neighborhood.

In this respect the Garden District differed little from the first true American suburb established at Brooklyn Heights in 1819. An early real estate ad for that community could equally have served the Garden District:

Families who may desire to associate in forming a select neighborhood and circle of society, for a summer's residence or a whole year's, cannot anywhere obtain more desirable situations.[77]

If shared ideals are reflected in the Garden District's plan, the limits of the sense of community are no less evident. Except for the old Lafayette Cemetery there is no central place, no main square or even a principal axis other than Jackson Avenue. Churches sprang up virtually at random along the main streets. To this extent the new suburb manifested the individualism of its founding fathers. No less, it reflected the growing democracy among the self-made men who constituted the elite. In contrast to Beacon Hill in Boston or Fifth Avenue in New York, there was no evident pecking order among the various streets and blocks. The absence of a main and a central square made the sites for future homes and churches far more nearly equal in prestige than they would otherwise have been.

A large body of literature published in the pre-Civil War decade could have guided New Orleans businessmen as they carved out their new suburban lives. In William A. Alcott's *City and*

Country, published in Boston in 1839, they could have found an impassioned plea for the moral superiority of country life over the life of the city. From Andrew Jackson Downing's magazine *The Horticulturalist* and later from his *Treatise on The Theory and Practice of Landscape Gardening*, issued separately in 1859, they could have learned that fenced yards promote suspicion and unselfishness while unfenced yards foster cooperation, kindness, and civic well-being.[78] From Alexander Jackson Davis they could have discovered how people in the Northeast were using covenants signed by each property owner to protect the integrity of the neighborhood as a whole.[79] From Gervase Wheeler's *Homes for the People in Suburb and Country* they could have picked up homilies on the current fashion for asymmetrical and "natural" garden plans.[80] Or from Englishman Calvert Vaux they could have received endless advice on how "every young republican of means in America should aim to be aristocratic in its literal sense; that is, to be '*aristos*'—the very best."[81] Even though such books were widely disseminated at the time, there is no evidence that those who moved to the Garden District actually read any of them or that they felt the slightest need for instruction on how the rich should comport themselves. Such advice was for the insecure. Though they were assuredly parvenus, the new rulers of New Orleans were confident in how they wanted to live. Without reading the works of snobbish sermonizers they nonetheless absorbed their message, probably by observing the lives of business associates in the Northeast who had been directly influenced by such writers.

There were serious choices to be made. Among these, none was more important than the style of architecture appropriate to members of a triumphant class. On this issue genuine differences emerged. Since the outcome determined the very character of the Garden District, it is time now to address the issue of style.

Antebellum Style

THE WORD *STYLE* has about it a touch of old regime snobbery. Along with its first cousin, *taste*, it draws one away from crass mercantilism and back to the parlors of Georgian London.[1] To be sure, sophisticated Americans on the Atlantic seaboard and in the Midwest were acquiring great self-consciousness in matters of style by the 1830s. Even small rural weeklies in the Northeast carried art criticism on their pages.[2] The inveterate critic of New World mores, Mrs. Trollope, on her visit to Cincinnati, observed that Americans seemed more hurt when she disparaged their paintings than when she criticized their morals.[3]

Several factors held Anglo-Saxon New Orleans at some distance from such genteel notions of style. First, the city retained a touch of frontier practicality. Buildings were erected to be functional, not to indulge someone's aesthetic fancy. Second, even though Garden District patrons were politically opposed to Jacksonianism, they were, like Old Hickory himself, self-made men. Their education had been acquired on the job, and they were inclined to view an excessive interest in matters of taste as an effete indulgence. Finally, they were hard-driven businessmen, the very kind of mercantile Americans whom that arbiter of refined living, Andrew Jackson Downing, denounced for their "feverish unrest and want of balance."[4]

[FACING PAGE] *Philadelphia-born Thomas Toby's urbanized and Anglicized retreat, 2340 Prytania Street, 1838–42*

The local press did little or nothing to raise the level of architectural criticism. Its reviews noted merely that a structure had been built and at what cost. Up to the Civil War gross errors were common, as when the Daily Picayune in 1850 described Robert Grinnan's chaste Greek Revival home at 2221 Prytania Street as "a magnificent Italian villa."[5] Under the circumstances, the most stringent critiques of new buildings came not from the public but from the architects themselves, though professional discretion kept these assessments from the public eye. Thomas Wharton, architect and Garden District resident, judged Henry Lonsdale's Prytania Street home as "a huge tasteless pile of Brick, Marble, Iron, and Stucco...," but this did not go beyond his diary.[6]

How, then, did patrons select the styles in which their homes were to be built? Few were aware of the numerous handbooks published by designers in New York, Philadelphia, and Boston. They did not realize that these books were written precisely to help them make such decisions. Instead of consulting experts, they simply looked around them. James Gallier, the Irish-born architect who built many important buildings in both the Anglo-Saxon and Creole sections of New Orleans, considered this neighborly imitation an American trait, which he first observed in New York: "When they want a house built, they looked about for one already finished, which they thought suitable for their purposes; and then bargained with a builder to erect for them such another, or one with such alterations upon the model as they might point out."[7] In New Orleans, with its less developed architectural profession, this practice of building by analogy was even more widespread. Thus, when Thomas Layton ordered his residence in Lafayette, he asked the builders, Messrs. Wilson and Wirtz, to make his home "like the house on number 58."[8] That was in 1848. Three decades later, when the novelist George Washington Cable built his raised cottage at 1313 Eighth Street, he ordered his architect, Frederick Wing, to be sure the exterior paint would be "similar to that of Mister Flower's house at the corner of St. Charles and Seventh."[9] The process may have been unsophisticated and even crude, but it resulted in an impressively integrated architectural environment.

The antebellum decade was an age of eclecticism, with a cornucopia of styles from which patrons could choose. In practice, however, Garden District patrons tended to be somewhat con-formist in their selections, which contributed to the consistency of the District townscape. Had there not been among them a few men who took pleasure in architectural innovation, the Garden District might have suffered from monotony. Fortunately, these trend setters seem to have viewed the architecture of their homes as a symbolic extension of their own personalities.

The leading patrons of architecture wanted their homes to reflect every improvement in their fortunes. Edward Davis, for example, was in his mid-twenties when he commissioned architect William Freret to build a two-story brick house for him at the corner of St. Andrew and Coliseum Streets, now demolished.[10] Barely five years later, in 1858, Davis, now with two children, ordered a far more showy second residence with Corinthian columns, which still stands at 2504 Prytania Street.[11]

By nearly any measure the most unflaggingly zealous patron of architecture was the cotton factor Henry Sullivan Buckner. No sooner did he establish his fortune in the late 1830s than he bought a home in Alexander Thompson Wood's and James Dakin's Julia Row, in the Faubourg Ste. Marie. Among the first to be bitten by the taste for suburban life, Buckner in 1841 commissioned David Moore to build him a two-story pilastered brick home on land fronting St. Mary, St. Andrew, and Coliseum Streets, now demolished.[12] Meanwhile, he hired James Dakin to build a four-story commercial building for his firm on Gravier Street, and in 1849 commissioned another new residence for himself, this time on Coliseum Street, also demolished.[13] Each move represented another level of Buckner's prosperity. The Coliseum Street house, with galleries and columns on three sides was, for at least a time, the grandest in the District. The establishment of Buckner's partnership with Frederick Stanton of Natchez in 1856 drove him to new architectural heights. Stanton immediately hired a New Orleans architect, Lewis E. Reynolds, to design for him the grandiose Stanton Hall at the corner of North Pearl and High streets in Natchez. Not to be outdone, Buckner turned to Stanton's architect to build for him an even more opulent home at 1410 Jackson Avenue.

Buckner's architectural gourmandism eventually touched everyone around him. He presented his house at 1401 St. Andrew Street to his sister-in-law as a gift.[14] After the Civil War he saw to it that his son and daughter each were properly housed in a

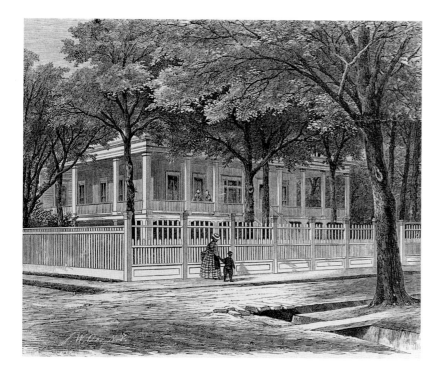

[ABOVE] *Moving uptown. Henry Buckner built his house at 1401 St. Andrew in 1849, but gave it to his sister-in-law, Mrs. Archie Allan Brand, in 1857, when he moved further uptown to the Garden District. David Moore, architect; now demolished* (THE HISTORIC NEW ORLEANS COLLECTION; ORIGINAL, NEW ORLEANS NOTARIAL ARCHIVES)

[RIGHT] *Henry Buckner's uptown palace, 1410 Jackson Avenue, by architect Lewis E. Reynolds, 1857*

Self-conscious architectural features on the façade, but bland functionalism on the side Samuel E. Moore built his house at 2925 Coliseum Street, 1853–58, with profits from the import of crockery, china and glassware

substantial residence at 2607 and 2627 Coliseum Street, respectively, both designed by architect William Freret and both now demolished.[15] Thus, Buckner was directly or indirectly responsible for five major Garden District houses.

Such confirmed nest builders as Davis and Buckner set the pace for their business colleagues. Granted that no one in the Crescent City demonstrated the *mania grandiosa* shown by such New York magnates as the merchants A.T. Stewart or Hart M. Schiff in those same years, local entrepreneurs still set the architectural tone for New Orleans. And not only for New Orleans. In dozens of cities and towns in the Mississippi Valley and Texas, people looked to the Crescent City for social and architectural cues. The stylistic preferences of well-known businessmen like Henry Buckner and his Garden District neighbors eventually shaped the tastes of the region's elite and middle class in the last antebellum decade.

To Buckner's credit, his many houses reveal a man whose stylistic horizons were constantly broadening, as seen in the following pages. More than that, they reflect the eye of a man who had a sense of the building as a whole, rather than of its separate parts in isolation. This was an exceptional gift. For most patrons, architectural style was something that pertained only to select parts of the building. Like the man who buys bland suits and gaudy neckties, these patrons thought it sufficient to demonstrate their concern for taste and style primarily on the facades of their homes. At best this produced baroque pyrotechnics on the street exposure. At worst it left the neighbors to stare out at the monstrous blank brick sides of their homes, shapeless and unornamented. A glance at the side exposure of the Lonsdale house or of the Moore house at Seventh and Coliseum streets shows how disagreeable this could be. Indeed, a normally quiescent *Daily Picayune* singled out this baneful practice for criticism in a post-Civil War critique of a new Garden District home.[16]

Inside the home, attention was concentrated above all on creating grand spiral stairways. This was an exercise in pure show, for the private family quarters of Garden District houses, like Victorian homes elsewhere in America, were strictly off limits to guests. The visitor was invited to be impressed by the staircase, or perhaps titillated by the thought of the boudoir to which the staircase might lead, but not to the point that he would actually dare ascend it. One inadvertently thinks of the deep décolletages common to gowns of otherwise stringently chaste ladies of nineteenth-century America.

The focusing of architectural attention on the part rather than on the whole produced further anomalies. Most Garden District homes had one or more outdoor cisterns to collect rainwater from the roof. The hulking cylinders, which frequently rose two stories in height, dominated the homes and gave them, in Mark Twain's words, "a mansion-and-brewery suggestion."[17] Strangely, this offended the sensibilities of very few patrons or architects. By the 1850s it had become fashionable to hide a second storage tank of some 500 to 2,000 gallons in the attic. The main cisterns, holding 4,000 to 5,000 gallons, remained in the yard, untouched by the niceties of design. Meanwhile, the eye of architectural fashion roamed freely, one year concentrating on ornate cast-plaster ceiling medallions and the next year on wooden lattice-work columns or intricately turned newel posts.

Even though they could be diverted by what may strike us as the superficialities of style, Garden District patrons knew what they wanted when it came to a choice of a basic house type. They were confronted with a bewildering array of clashing models, the polyglot architectural vocabulary of an eclectic age. Their selections among the competing stylistic types of homes show consistency and sureness of judgment. They may have been guided in their choice by instinct and prejudice, but the results constitute a distinctive communal style of architecture. By reviewing the responses of patrons to the prevailing house types of the day the logic behind their collective taste emerges.

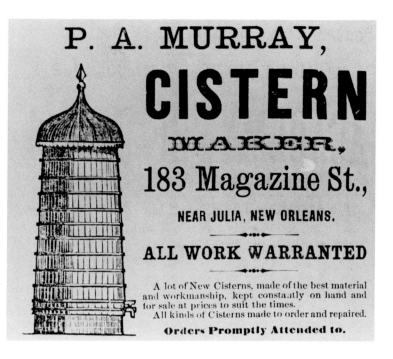

*Towering above the houses to give them "a mansion-and-brewery suggestion," said Mark Twain. Advertisement for cisterns in the 1874 City Directory (*NEW ORLEANS PUBLIC LIBRARY*)*

VERNACULAR STYLE: PLANTATIONS AND COTTAGES

When Yankee merchants arrived in Spanish California, they often hired local Spanish artisans to build them two-story galleried homes in the style of the region. Prosperous Yankees settling in uptown New Orleans likewise had before them practical local patterns in the Creole plantations. In the 1840s the old Saulet, Melpomene, Panis, and Livaudais plantations stood as successful models for comfortable living. Nonetheless, the newcomers rejected these tested prototypes out of hand. Indeed, Anglo-Saxon architecture influenced that of the Creoles far more than vice versa. The future pattern was set as early as 1832, when an Anglo-Saxon purchaser of the old Saulet plantation on Annunciation Street had it remodeled with a low roof and fancy balustrade in the Federal style to make it fit more closely his conception of what a proper residence should be. One of the very few instances of Anglo-Saxon assimilation of the French plantation style was a house on Urania Street

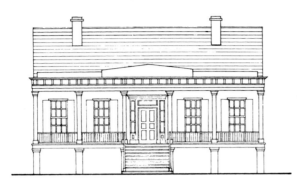

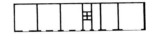

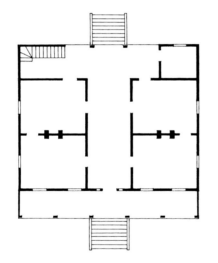

[LEFT] *Typical raised cottage with center hall*
(MCGILLIVRAY AND VILDOSTEGUI)

[RIGHT] *Typical cottage with Creole plan*
(MCGILLIVRAY AND VILDOSTEGUI)

between Coliseum and Prytania, but the addition of a Georgian balustrade on the roof kept even this home safely Anglo-Saxon.

The new Anglo-Saxon rulers viewed members of the Creole aristocracy, after all, as competitors. From the standpoint of Garden District Yankees it was splendid when a distinguished Creole, Antoine Mandeville Marigny, the youngest son of Samuel Peters's old rival, married into the Claiborne family and settled down in a proper center-hall cottage on St. Charles Avenue. That was considered to be influence in the right direction. The reverse situation would not have been so readily tolerated in the Garden District, given the low regard of many uptown Anglo-Saxons for the Creoles as a group. When Theodore Clapp, the Presbyterian minister, wrote admiringly of the generosity of Creole Catholics in the field of welfare, his New Orleans friends did not leap to emulate them.[18]

Several specific features of the Creole plantations made them unacceptable to the newcomers. First, they maintained the eighteenth-century concept of a series of rooms, each opening to the others, which offered maximum flexibility in function. The more orderly and conservative Anglo-Saxons found this practice quaint and bizarre. Second, the Creole plantation houses lacked halls, and hence privacy. The Yankee newcomers all hailed from a world in which privacy was important.

It is scarcely surprising that the Americans—at least until 1850—looked with greater favor at the upriver plantation homes built by their fellow Anglo-Saxons. When Thomas Toby of Philadelphia built his columned home at 2340 Prytania Street in 1838–42, he clearly had in mind a plantation residence of this type. Toby's unknown architect achieved a graceful and practical solution in the one-story columned house with service rooms below.[19] Henry S. Buckner, the tireless experimenter, probably had the same architect design his nearly identical home on St. Andrew Street in 1849.

Very few Garden District residences have as much regionalism in their genealogy as these. A handful of residences looked further upriver to Natchez. The house that Londoner Louis de Saulles built astride an entire block at 2618 Coliseum would be far more at home in Anglo-Saxon Mississippi than in French Louisiana, as would the modest but handsome three-room, six-bay structure at 3008 Camp Street, between Seventh and Eighth.[20]

The one exception to this rejection of local prototypes—and an extremely important one—is the raised cottage. Such structures were common in French Canada and the West Indies, as well as in South Louisiana. Yet there is nothing particularly French about these simple pitched-roof structures, with their galleried main floor lifted above rustic ground level. Remarkably similar houses were built in the Hudson Valley by the Dutch, and by Anglo-Saxons throughout the Mississippi Valley to Tennessee. Even if the raised cottage was not exclusively French, however, it had strong regional roots. Many prototypes existed in the French Quaker and especially in the other Creole faubourgs. Such cottages were simple to construct and, with the addition of columns or wooden ornaments, provided a hint of Palladian grandeur at a low cost. By 1824 the first raised cottage had appeared in Faubourg Lafayette, built for Francisco Canellas on Tchoupitoulas Street near St. Andrew, now destroyed.[21]

In its Americanized Garden District form, the raised cottage is a five-bay structure, the fifth bay having been introduced to accommodate a center hall separating the double parlors on one side from the bedrooms on the other. The process of assimilation of this building type was complete by 1841, the year Charles Conrad hired two Irish builders, James Sullivan and Patrick Joyce, to construct his large cottage at Prytania and First streets (demolished).[22] A virtual flood of cottages of various styles followed on the heels of Conrad's house. The earlier ones were as simple as any cottages in the Creole faubourgs downtown. For example, the raised cottage built at 1527 Washington Avenue by Lothrop Smith, a dealer in tarred cordage, is nearly devoid of ornament except pilasters.[23] Some early Garden District cottages show direct continuity with French prototypes. The house built by Edward Gottheil for William Haneman on St. Charles Avenue and subsequently absorbed into the Whitney house (demolished) retained typically Creole cabinets, or small office-like rooms at either end of the rear gallery.[24] A single cabinet is still preserved on a handsomely proportioned raised cottage from the early 1840s at 2120 Carondelet Street.[25] A homeowner at 840 Fourth Street remained loyal to the traditional Creole prototype by leaving out the characteristically English center hall.[26]

A grocer's palace, the John A. Adams house at 2423 Prytania Street house, said to have been designed by builder Frederick Wing, 1860–61

[CLOCKWISE FROM TOP LEFT]

Sophrone Claiborne Marigny, wife of Mandeville Marigny and daughter of Louisiana's first Governor, W. C. C. Claiborne, built this typical raised cottage in 1857, 2524 St. Charles Avenue

English-born cotton press owner James P. Freret's generous 14-room raised cottage, 1525 Louisiana Avenue, 1858–59

Alexander Harris house, 2127 Prytania Street, 1857–58

Corinthian columns at the Alexander Harris raised cottage, 2127 Prytania Street; James Calrow, architect, 1857–58

The raised cottage did not long remain simple either in style or form. Brick construction soon made its appearance, which in turn opened the way to plastered facades scored to simulate fancy stonework. At the same time the scale increased. The generously proportioned Mandeville Marigny home at 2524 St. Charles and the Lawrence P. Maxwell home at 1431 Josephine Street both represent what had become the average scale by the late 1850s.[27]

In a few instances the simple raised cottage was expanded to truly gargantuan proportions. Massachusetts-born Samuel Kennedy was a force to be reckoned with, both as commission merchant and Whig politician. Kennedy's Camp Street home, destroyed by the 1890s, might technically be classed a cottage, but even in the postwar era, when the wealthy demanded massive residences, it was considered "one of the most elegant houses in this city."[28] Almost ninety feet square, with a large service wing to the rear, the house sold for $22,000 in 1888, an enormous sum at the time.

The only other raised villa to achieve that same imposing scale was built by James P. Freret, the English-born cotton press owner, at 1525 Louisiana Avenue.[29] With fourteen rooms and seven bays on the street, the Freret home adheres rigorously to the traditional cottage format, notwithstanding its monumentality.

In the twentieth century one easily forgets that conservatism in taste can give rise to enduring art. The tenacity with which Garden District homeowners clung to the basic raised cottage format provides evidence for this notion. By the 1850s prosperous New Orleanians were seeking more flexible spaces than the traditional cottage afforded. Rather than embrace new styles or adopt new building technologies that opened such vistas of style, however, they and their architects elaborated on the old. The results were

some strikingly refined, if conservative, buildings. Among the best was the John A. Adams residence at 2423 Prytania Street, said to have been designed by Frederick Wing. The low elevation, the semicircular colonnade on the western side, and the restrained ornamentation all create a serene and laconic effect.

Farther down Prytania Street stands a still more ambitious variant of the raised cottage. Designed by James Calrow in 1857–58 for the cotton factor Alexander Harris, the house at 2127 Prytania has a deep portico extending to the garden front supported by eleven richly carved Corinthian columns. The interior plan adheres to standard patterns, but it is carried out with lavish woodwork and pilasters supporting Corinthian capitals.[30]

That most ambitious elaboration of the basic cottage is to be seen at the Jethro Bailey house at 1314 St. Mary Street.[31] Here the center hall is abandoned in favor of a large entryway on the right of the house, opening into a single large front parlor and double parlors to the rear. The rest of the area at the front of the house is given over to the gallery, which extends fully halfway around the structure on the left. This feature would seem even more pronounced today if it were not balanced by a large late-nineteenth century addition to the right of the gallery. The exceptionally open plan and the extensive galleries of the Bailey house reflect the owner's origins in Newport, Rhode Island, where such devices were common. Yet this 1858 house preserves a thoroughly traditional format. In doing so, it follows the fundamental rule of architecture in Anglo-Saxon New Orleans: to adhere to established forms whenever possible, modifying them as necessity dictates but preserving their familiar aspects so far as is feasible.

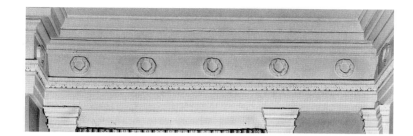

REVIVED GREEK REVIVAL

Greek Revival architecture reached New Orleans early and stayed late. By 1814, when Jean Baptiste Thierry built his Grecian-style home at 721 Governor Nicholls Street in the French Quarter, it was already taking root. In the early 1890s elements of the Greek Revival style were still appearing on new houses in the Garden District.

Those patrons wishing to indulge in Greek Revivalism need only to have looked around to find excellent patterns to emulate. Nationally known adepts of the style like William Strickland designed buildings in New Orleans. James Dakin and James Gallier, Sr., both built successful practices in the Crescent City by elaborating on the Greek Revival prototypes they had studied and, in Dakin's case, built in New York.

If a patron teamed up with a particularly knowledgeable builder, he might have been shown plates from the various design manuals featuring the so-called Grecian style. Whether or not the patrons saw these books, the builders consulted them. Asher Benjamin's *The Practical Carpenter* (Boston, 1830) and especially Minard Lafever's *The Modern Builder's Guide* (Newark, 1833) both left their mark on specific Garden District houses.

Back in New England and the old Midwest the Greek Revival was in full retreat by the late 1840s. Samuel Sloan of Philadelphia, for one, objected to the use of the same style for both public buildings and private houses.[32] Calvert Vaux, the pompous Londoner who dictated architectural tastes to New Yorkers in his book *Villas and Cottages* of 1857, found the Greek mode to be a "lifeless parody" whose "passionless repose . . . is not heartily sympathized with either by the American atmosphere or the spirit of this locomotive age. . . ."[33] New Orleanians, already habituated to this style, were not so easily dissuaded. The home that James Gallier, Jr., designed for Lavinia Dabney went up, without compromise, in the same year that Vaux issued his critique.

No single factor accounts for the tenacity of the Greek Revival in the Garden District. Surely the fact that so many residents had formed their architectural tastes in the Northeast in the early nineteenth century when the style was booming was of critical importance. When they obtained wealth, they wanted to acquire for

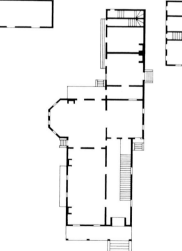

[TOP] *Minard Lafever's* The Modern Builder's Guide *applied, at the Jacob U. Payne house, 1134 First Street, 1849*

[LEFT] *Three-bay house with gallery. Architect James Gallier, Jr., designed this London plan dwelling for Lavinia Dabney, 2265 St. Charles Avenue, 1856. Instead of the usual large doorway between front and rear parlor, Gallier created two doors and expanded the rear parlor with an octagonal bay* (MCGILLIVRAY AND VILDOSTEGUI)

[ABOVE] *Unbroken columns on the Josephine Smeltzer house, between Camp and Magazine streets, 1856; now demolished*

[RIGHT] *Free planning within the framework of a London plan dwelling: Colonel Robert Short's house, 1448 Fourth Street, by Henry Howard, 1859*

[FACING PAGE] *The dining room in the octagonal bay at the Walter G. Robinson house, 1415 Third Street, by architect Henry Howard, 1859*

themselves the same marks of prestige that had prevailed in their hometowns when they were younger. Beyond this, New Orleans society had completely assimilated the London plan house, with its hall and double parlor. The popularity of this transplanted floor plan undergirded the continuing appeal of the Greek Revival style in which it was best embodied.

The one innovation introduced in New Orleans was the columned gallery across the front. While not invented there—it had already appeared on the Mordecai House in Raleigh, North Carolina, by 1824—the columned gallery quickly became part of the local idiom.[34] One of the earliest examples in the Garden District still stands at 1427 Second Street, the James D'Arcy house of 1844, which in its original form had Tower of the Winds columns placed in antis.[35] The basic form, the London plan, was standardized with variations occurring only in the details.

Yet such variations are visually significant. On the handsome Smeltzer house on Josephine Street between Camp and Magazine Streets, now demolished, the usual fluted Tower of the Winds columns were placed between sturdy paneled square pillars at the ends, giving a feeling of massiveness.[36] The distinction of the Smeltzer house lay in its columns running unbroken for two stories. It was far easier, however, to break the columns at the gallery, which in fact became standard practice. Those interested in economy could order simple square columns, as on a house on St. Andrew between Annunciation and Laurel Streets, now demolished.[37] The austerity could be relieved with a Greek-key doorway, as in another destroyed house on Laurel between Second and Third.[38] Luther Stewart, the wholesale grocer, took the same scheme one step further in his 1858 residence at 2120 Philip Street by having the square columns fluted.[39]

By the late 1850s a consistent approach to the gallery had emerged: whether at Albert Brevard's 1857 home at 1239 First Street or at the Stauffer mansion which once stood on Jackson Avenue, the formula called for square columns at the corners framing fluted columns with ionic capitals below and Corinthian above.[40] Only with the spread of lushly ornamented cast-iron galleries, as on the now demolished Luzenberg house on Chestnut Street, was this model challenged, and then only partially.[41] Just as often, a more lavish effect was achieved by employing elaborate

Corinthian capitals on all four columns, above and below. The widow Aurore Tureaud's house at 1220 Philip Street exemplifies this approach.

The three-bay Greek Revival home suffered from one serious shortcoming, however. It was too small. As with the raised cottage, several devices were employed to expand it. The easiest was simply to enlarge the scale, as occurred on the Stauffer, Luzenberg, and Tureaud houses. These larger residences all employed the so-called Philadelphia gable, in reality a Federal-style device common throughout New England and the Middle Atlantic states.

During the 1850s the social life of the Garden District became increasingly active, straining the bounds imposed by the basic plan of the three-bay Greek Revival dwelling. Many families were unable to accommodate their new needs merely by expanding the size of rooms. Particularly pressing was the demand for large, formal dining rooms. Houses built according to the London plan usually relegated this function to a small room carved from the narrow space behind the second parlor. The new sociability demanded more.

Architect James Gallier, Jr., proposed to J. J. Warren to add an octagonal bay on the right side of his house at 1531 Jackson Avenue.[42] Henry Howard did the same at the Robinson house. This solution was far from original, having been widely employed in New England over the previous twenty years. Original or not, it appealed to the Garden District sensibility because it preserved the basic scheme of the London plan while gaining the needed dining room. More commonly a bay was simply added to an existing house, as at Albert Brevard's house on First Street.

By far the cleverest solution to this problem was to broaden and enlarge the former service wing, and to push it forward into the center of the main dwelling. This simple device preserved the Greek Revival facade while vast spaces opened up in the interior; the appearance of formal order was maintained on the street, yet a form of free planning introduced within. The home built by John Rodenberg at 1238 Philip Street in 1853–54 is an early and very successful example of this technique.[43] With Henry Howard's mansion for Colonel Short, built at 1448 Fourth Street in 1859, it reached its fullest development.[44]

A far simpler though more radical means of expanding the London plan Greek Revival house was to double it, that is, to convert it into a center hall structure of five bays. This is precisely what Mrs. James D'Arcy did when she moved her 1844 house from First to Second Street. At the same time, she extended the gallery to cover the enlarged facade. Meanwhile, both Jacob Payne at 1134 First Street and his neighbor, Hiram Anderson at 2427 Camp Street, built five-bay columned homes with center halls.[45] These two fine residences, once identical, stand in the tradition of center-hall Georgian and Federal-style American buildings. By contrast, in the rich surviving interior moldings of the Payne house, based on plates from Minard Lafever's 1833 volume *The Modern Builder's Guide*, the Greek Revival element is clearly evident.

During the 1850s the center hall columnar house joined the three-bay London plan dwelling and the extended raised cottage as the third basic house type in the Garden District. The New Hampshire-born newspaper editor, Joseph H. Maddox, built such a house at 2507 Prytania Street in 1852, as did George Washington Squires in 1851–54, on St. Charles Avenue.[46] In 1860–61 Charles W. Wilson, a builder, adopted the same plan for his spacious residence at 1205 Louisiana Avenue.[47] Wilson's house is one of many center-hall dwellings with Philadelphia gables built in the Garden District, all of them being of a type that had made its local debut in the French Quarter as early as the 1830s. An almost identical house, built for H. H. Hansell in 1859–61 at 3000 Prytania Street, is in all likelihood also the work of Wilson. In addition to the Philadelphia gable, the stepped gable on this house also became popular, a type common in upstate New York in the 1820s.

None of the many center-hall mansions broke new ground in architectural design, nor was that the builders' intent. Rather, it was to accommodate an enlarged social life within familiar architectural forms. By this standard, Henry Lonsdale's towering residence, built in 1856, epitomizes this phase of antebellum New Orleans architecture. It mattered little that several other Anglo-Saxon immigrants had built almost identical homes in Tennessee, Alabama—especially Mobile—and Louisiana. Obviously, the well-ventilated, center-hall columned house made practical sense in the Deep South, and it flourished there.

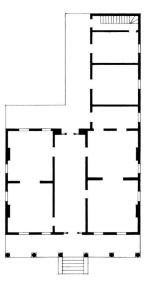

A five-bay center hall dwelling: the Jacob Payne house, 1134 First Street, 1849 (MCGILLIVRAY AND VILDOSTEGUI)

Stepped gables on Henry Lonsdale's towering residence, 2521–23 Prytania. Henry Howard, architect, 1856

❧ MISSISSIPPI GOTHIC

By all rights, Gothic Revival architecture should have flourished in New Orleans. As with the Greek Revival, it arrived there early. Imported to America from England in 1806, it reached New Orleans by 1815, thanks to the energetic Henry S. Latrobe, son of the great Baltimore architect Benjamin Henry Latrobe. In the years after he built his octagonal Gothic church on Canal and Bourbon streets, now demolished, the whole city was swept up in a kind of literary "gothomania," fed by Sir Walter Scott's *Waverly* novels. Dramatizations of Scott's novels were smash hits on the New Orleans stage through most of the 1820s.

And then it all subsided. In 1840 a single Gothic church was built—James Dakin's St. Patrick's Roman Catholic Church on Camp Street, now demolished—and a station for the Carrollton railway also essayed some Gothic motifs. Nothing more came until the 1850s. Dakin proposed a Gothic-style Commerce Building in 1842 and a Gothic Custom House in 1849, but both were rejected.

It is not that the antebellum architects of New Orleans were ignorant of the style. James Gallier, Jr., built a Gothic-style commercial building in Faubourg Ste. Marie on Tchoupitoulas Street in 1852; Lewis E. Reynolds featured Gothic ornaments in the advertisements for himself that he placed in the *Daily Picayune*; and the English-born Thomas Wharton practiced studies of Gothic molding, at the same time decrying "our pigmy efforts at Gothic."[48]

The Gothic ideals propounded by Lafever, Sloan, and others eventually found a weak echo in New Orleans, but not in domestic architecture. By the 1850s many of the same people who were building raised cottages or Greek Revival houses in the Garden District were ordering family graves ornamented with Gothic ironwork. Robert Stark was later to be buried in a Gothic-style tomb in Cypress Grove Cemetery, but he had James Dakin design his Annunciation Street house in the most refined classical style.[49] It was even permissible to add a Gothic gate to one's residence, as at Michael Hans's house at 2928 Prytania Street, built in 1866–70, but the house itself had to be in one of the accepted types and styles, in this case a classical raised cottage.[50]

How is one to account for the strange disinterest in Gothic architecture locally? It might be claimed that the Gothic style, with

The Gothic gate at groceryman Michael Hans's house, 2928 Prytania Street, 1866–70

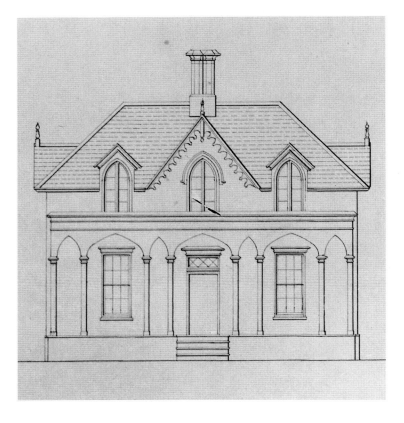

James Gallier, Sr.'s 1849 design of a Gothic cottage for Cuthbert Bullitt, 2423 Prytania. Not built (NEW ORLEANS NOTARIAL ARCHIVES; THE HISTORIC NEW ORLEANS COLLECTION)

its small windows, did not permit sufficient ventilation for the Deep South. Why, then, did a steamy inland town like Holly Springs, Mississippi, boast of such richly Gothic-style homes as Cedarhurst or Airliewood? Why, too, would the sugar planter Thomas Asheton Morgan have bothered to go all the way to Philadelphia to get architect William Johnston to design his Gothic-styled Orange Grove Plantation in torrid Plaquemines Parish, near the exposed delta of the Mississippi River south of New Orleans?[51]

Clearly the issue was not merely the style's suitability to the climate. Several other factors combined to discourage the use of Gothic Revival architecture in the Garden District. First, this style had become fashionable in the North after most of the local patrons had left their birthplaces in that region. Unless they encountered the style in their travels or through reading, it would have been unknown to them. Certainly it did not symbolize to the generation of the 1850s the ideal of success that the more conservative styles did. Second, local craftsmen were unfamiliar with the mullioned windows, elaborate brick work, and complex wood ornamentation the style required. Still more important was the religious factor: except among the Episcopalians, Gothic Revival architecture in Protestant America was widely perceived as being Roman Catholic. And it is rightly so. The first such building in the Republic was St. Mary's Catholic Seminary in Baltimore; the first book on Gothic architecture in America was written by John Hopkins, the Catholic bishop of Vermont. It is no wonder that the Protestant theologian Theodore Dwight asked, in 1834, "Why should [Gothic architecture] be introduced into America? There is not a feature of society here which bears the slightest affinity with it."[52]

Such objections to the Gothic Revival were all the more to the point in New Orleans, where the Protestant newcomers were on the defensive vis-a-vis the French Catholic establishment. It was considered mildly shocking, if not objectionable, when in 1849 the state legislature accepted a design for the capitol in Baton Rouge that called for a crenelated Gothic castle. The *Daily Delta* criticized the style as appropriate only to "the age of tyranny, of Baronial oppression, of monastic superstition, e.g., Catholicism."[53]

Just as the furor over the proposed state capitol was mounting, Kentucky-born Cuthbert Bullitt was thinking of building a house on the Prytania Street block that his wife, Eliza, had recently

Londoner Charles Brigg's proper Gothic cottage, 2605 Prytania, designed and built by James Gallier, Sr., 1849

Gothic bracket in the Briggs house

inherited. Bullitt was a gambler and the Beau Brummell of antebellum New Orleans.[54] Unlike most of his peers, he took a keen interest in style and cared not a whit for the kind of ethnic or theological nit-picking that led others to shy away from the latest fashion in architecture. In May 1849 Bullitt approached James Gallier, Sr., to design a house for him in the Gothic style. Gallier responded by drawing a design for a two-story cottage based on Plate II of Andrew Jackson Downing's *Cottage Residences*.[55] The pointed arches on the second-floor windows and on the veranda, the hooded moldings, and the chimneys all reflect a prototype that was proving popular from Ohio to Texas. Precisely this same prototype had been taken as the basis for Airliewood in Holly Springs, Mississippi.

Having commissioned so interesting a design, Bullitt then dropped it. The fact that at the same time he sold the Prytania Street property suggests that he may have experienced financial reverses. Meanwhile, farther out on Prytania Street, London-born Charles Briggs was contemplating a house of his own. In January 1849 he commissioned James Gallier, Sr., to design his classical revival house. The Gothic cottage for Bullitt was produced in May, and when Bullitt rejected it, Briggs apparently took it over. On the final version at 2605 Prytania the veranda is greatly simplified and the gingerbread work eliminated from the front gable. But the Elizabethan chimney stacks remained intact, having only been moved from the center to the outer wall of the house. Significantly, the inside is modified to accommodate a double parlor, needed for New Orleans socializing. The interior also features Gothic columns of bunched rods; Gothic roses are painted on the ceiling, and impressive Gothic brackets divide the main parlor into two. In few houses of the Garden District are exterior motifs carried through more successfully on the interior.

PICTURESQUE VILLAS

This survey of architectural styles in the Garden District under-scores a curious aspect of the bold businessmen who resided there, namely, their timidity in matters aesthetic. Gothic fantasies were rising across the country but the Garden District patrons abjured them. Perhaps they really did yearn for the picturesque, for a sense of movement, variety, and pleasing effect, but wanted a less alien idiom in which to express it. For such people there was readily at hand a "picturesque" style of architecture that would have exactly filled the bill. With pitched roofs and many rustic touches, including warm earth colors it was the very antithesis of the rigid geometry and cold formality of the Greek Revival that they embraced. It exuded English hominess and a wholesome moralism in architecture.

This utterly sane approach to home design found but one follower in the antebellum Garden District: Thomas A. Adams, the transplanted Bostonian who introduced mutual insurance to New Orleans and presided over the prestigious New England Society. In 1850 he set about to create a suitable residence for himself. The design he settled on was for a rambling house with deep gables on the front, quaint Jacobean chimneys, a small veranda, and ginger-bread under the eaves. This is all that is known of the original house, and this is known only thanks to a single rare photograph surviving from the 1850s. Adams's comfortable home evidently suited none of its subsequent owners, for by the time the next surviving photograph was taken a tall cupola and widow's walk had

[LEFT] Boston-born insurance pioneer Thomas Austin Adams, arrived in New Orleans in 1842, founded the Crescent Mutual Insurance Company, a branch of the New York house (NEW ORLEANS PUBLIC LIBRARY)

[RIGHT] Thomas A. Adams's picturesque villa, 2624 Prytania Street, 1848–49. Burned to the ground shortly before World War II, a rare photograph by Jay Dearborn Edwards showing the original 1850s house (THE HISTORIC NEW ORLEANS COLLECTION)

been added.[56] Shortly thereafter the gables were replaced with an ungainly columned facade to make the house (now destroyed) fit in better with its neighbors.[57]

The picturesque style enjoyed a brief vogue after the Civil War, but it died away quickly. Its progress was impeded by the fact that it required a patron who was prepared to ignore his neighbors and even to shock them. Adams belonged to the first camp, while Cuthbert Bullitt, the *bon vivant* who had toyed with the Gothic villa, belonged to the second. His picturesque house on St. Charles Avenue (now moved to 3627 Carondolet Street) must surely have shocked: it evoked a Swiss chalet.[58] It is notable that Bullitt built this residence at precisely the time when he was persona non grata with many of his neighbors due to his aggressively pro-Union sympathies during the Civil War. For the picturesque style to make headway, it needed more people of Adams's and Bullitt's independence, but they were few.[59]

[ABOVE] *Italian Renaissance at Michel Musson's house, 1331 Third Street. The diamond pattern on the Musson frieze of 1853 recalls ornament of Renaissance architect Giacomo da Vignola (1507–1573)*

[FACING PAGE] *Indecision. Greek and Italianate elements on the Lewis Elkin house, 1410 Second Street, 1858–59*

❧ NORMANS, PARISIANS, AND TUSCANS

Out beyond the settled heartland of raised cottages and three- and five-bay columned homes lay a welter of modern styles. In addition to the Gothic and picturesque modes, New Orleanians might have chosen the Norman style, with its richly ornamented round arches, or Napoleon III's Second Empire style, with mansard roofs and segmental arched doors and windows. Neither was to find any adherents in the Garden District until well after the Civil War. The self-made Whig oligarchs of the old Garden District were more concerned to be of the group than above it.

The one new fashion to make headway in the Garden District before 1861 was the Italianate style.[60] Like all the styles of the day, the Italianate was deliberately romantic. It strove to evoke exotic places and remote times. Its aim was to be "pretty as a picture," or, more accurately, "pretty as a picture of a picture." The pictures in question were the serene Italian landscapes by Claude Lorrain and his school, while the pictures of pictures were romantic landscapes by the young Englishmen and Americans who flocked to Italy in the early nineteenth century with hopes of learning to paint like Lorrain. Thus the Tuscan villa, with its deep eaves, spacious verandas, and square towers, became an ideal for dreamy clergymen in New Jersey and hard-driving traders in New Haven. Andrew Jackson Downing, who was among the first to make a career out of telling Americans they were boors, had promoted the Italianate style as being particularly suitable for the South on account of its open planning and large windows.[61] Soon Tuscan homes festooned with cupolas or robust towers were cropping up throughout the Southern states. The Kirkland house in Memphis or Minard Lafever's sprawling Annandale Plantation in Jackson, Mississippi, rivaled anything in the Northeast for immodesty and pretension.

The urban variant of the Italianate style fared better in New Orleans than the other new fashions in style. It appealed to those seeking a more expansive scale, more florid ornamentation, and freer planning than the Greek Revival afforded. In Lewis E. Reynolds's Campbell house, which formerly stood at St. Charles and Julia Streets in the Faubourg Ste. Marie, one can see that it fulfilled these objectives by means of evolution, rather than revolution.[62] George Campbell's house was among the most splendid in antebellum New Orleans and fully comparable, in terms of sheer opulence, with anything in Manhattan.[63] It is important to note that its innovations were concentrated in the ornamentation rather than the basic plan, however, which represents only a modest development beyond what was already being done to render more flexible the five-bay prototypes so common in New Orleans.

Its adaptability to the warm climate and its compatibility with earlier styles recommended the Italianate style to Garden District patrons. Yet like the Gothic, the picturesque, the Second Empire, and the Norman styles, Italianate architecture at first made only slow headway in New Orleans. Among the earliest manifestations was a house built by Isaac Thayer in 1853 for the English-born Thomas Gilmour. The Italianate element is extremely timid, however, being confined to round-arched windows to the right of the entrance. Otherwise, this house at 2520 Prytania Street is a standard center-hall five-bay dwelling. It is revealing that the building

CHAPTER THREE

[ABOVE] *Plain and fancy: a stage-set façade on Second Street*

[LEFT] *A sophisticated consensus on style: three- and five-bay houses along the 1400 block of Seventh Street*

[FACING PAGE] *Hooded door molding and Italianate brackets on Frederick Rodewald's house, 1749 Coliseum Street*

contract was altered in favor of the present facade rather than a cast-iron gallery with pillars only at the last minute, as if by an afterthought.[64]

Gilmour's neighbor, Lewis Elkin at 1410 Second Street, underwent a similar change of mind. Elkin's home of 1858–59 had originally been a lavish classical structure with fluted Corinthian columns. When he decided to alter the house, he apparently took his inspiration from Gilmour's residence around the corner, adding round-arched windows and rusticated quoining to the now improbable facade.

Both the Gilmour and Elkin houses incorporate Tuscan elements in otherwise classical buildings. This became the rule for Italianate structures in the cautious environment of antebellum New Orleans. Madame Tureaud pioneered the selective application of Italianate motifs when her builder added segmental arched windows and a curved parapet (rather than the standard Greek Revival box parapet) to her house at 1220 Philip Street. James Gallier, Jr., did much the same for J. J. Warren's house. Soon hooded moldings with hanging pendants at the corners were making their appearance everywhere. In 1853 the anonymous architect of Michel Musson's house at 1331 Third Street used the handsome diamond pattern common to the buildings of Giacomo da Vignola (1507–1573) and other Renaissance architects to ornament the frieze.[65] Bay windows, another Italianate feature, also made their New Orleans debut on the original facade of the Musson house, only to be removed when the cast-iron gallery was added in 1884.

Ornamented brackets placed under the eaves were the most widely adopted Italianate motif in antebellum New Orleans. Easily mass produced, such brackets—usually in pairs—became a fad in the 1850s. At some time after the completion of a standard six-bay columnar house on Jackson Avenue in 1855, paired brackets were added to it.[66] It was not assumed that brackets would be added to all new houses, however. Some years later, the widow Oury still found it necessary to add a general article at the end of her contract with architect Lewis E. Reynolds to assure that brackets would be added to her house on Second Street opposite Clay Square, now demolished.[67]

The alert visitor in the Garden District will notice dozens of homes with Italianate features. Nearly all of them were built after the Civil War, when the style had begun to fade in the North. In 1860 a series of double houses were built on speculation on the new Woodland Terrace in West Philadelphia. All were designed as vast Italianate villas. In the same year William Freret undertook his speculative double houses on Coliseum Street, but he clung to the expanded version of a Greek Revival dwelling. By early 1858 a Northern critic, writing in *The Atlantic Monthly*, could claim, "Even the Anglo-Italian bracketed villa has seen its palmiest days apparently, and exhausted most of its variations."[68] Anglo-Saxon New Orleans had yet to explore this fashion fully, let alone tire of it.

EXPERIMENTATION AND CONFORMITY

This survey of architectural styles in the antebellum Garden District invites one unflattering conclusion, namely, that the tastes of the patrons were hopelessly dated and their architects either too provincial or too deferential to enlighten them. Surely these self-made men were exactly what Calvert Vaux had in mind when he archly announced in 1857, "There can not, indeed, be a more unpleasant spectacle than to see active, intelligent men, with long faces, knit brows, incessantly sacrificing time, health, home, and peace of mind to the one old 'Moloch'—*business*."[69]

Yet the facts do not support such a conclusion for the Garden District. Notice the chronology. The first era of construction extended from the mid-1840s to 1853. During that era Charles Briggs built his Gothic cottage, Thomas Gilmour his Italianate villa, and Thomas Adams his picturesque gabled mansion. In these same years a profusion of raised cottages and three- and five-bay columnar houses were built, many exhibiting great variety in style, if not type. It was a period of experimentation, during which patrons and architects alike tested nearly all the prevailing architectural fashions of the day. They were cautious and learned more by studying built prototypes than books, but they were neither ill-informed nor provincial.

After 1852 a growing uniformity made itself felt. Its three basic components were the raised cottage, the three-bay London plan dwelling, and the five-bay center-hall house. All three featured galleries or verandas and all three gravitated towards the same basic types of columns.

One might charge that during the great urban boom of 1852–61 a bland uniformity dominated the pioneer suburb in New Orleans. This is surely evidenced in Manuel Goldsmith's three-bay house of 1859, which is virtually indistinguishable from others in the neighborhood that were designed twenty years earlier.[70] The charge is equally applicable to the imposing but utterly standard three-bay columnar house at 3031 Coliseum Street built for commission merchant Robert Hutchinson in 1859.[71] There were extenuating circumstances, of course. Goldsmith, a recent immigrant from abroad, was understandably eager to conform to the mores of his new environment, while the twenty-eight-year-old Hutchison would probably have been keen to fit into the environment of his elder Garden District colleagues. Nonetheless the growing uniformity of style is undeniable. One need only examine the house built at 1302–4 Jackson Avenue for the Spaniard Joseph Fernandez or the similar structure, now demolished, on First Street between Prytania and St. Charles, to confirm this. Both these pre-1852 houses feature side galleries, which are unusual for New Orleans.[72] Neither had any successor in the antebellum years.

Is this the result of some crabbed conformity or of a genuine consensus? It is pertinent to recall here the political situation. The dividing line between the period of experimentation and the era of greater uniformity was 1852, the year in which the city of Lafayette was incorporated into New Orleans. Not only was it the moment that the uptown Whigs finally gained control of the entire city politically, but it is also the time at which the Garden District's status as a suburb for the ruling elite was confirmed. Is it surprising, then, that the men who had accomplished this feat might feel some solidarity with one another, and that this solidarity might find expression in a consensus on architecture?

This explains another aspect of antebellum style, namely, the absorption of diverse elements within the raised cottages, three-bay columnar houses, and picturesque villas that constituted the three basic housing types of the Garden District. The adoption of Italianate brackets on the exteriors, the use of polychrome paintings on ceilings, the application of specific Greek Revival features in an architectural context that was otherwise losing its moorings in that style, and especially clever attempts to satisfy the social needs for large and free spaces by altering the scale and plan, all attest to the presence of an adventurous spirit among people who were otherwise proudly conformist. Together, the Crescent City's new elite groped toward a single composite style that manifested their collective identity.

Acknowledging all this, one must nonetheless take note of the rapidity with which a sophisticated consensus degenerated into cliche. This can be seen with depressing clarity in the rise of grotesque, even comical fake facades on the eve of the Civil War. In the Payne, Wilson, Maddox, or Luzenberg houses, the columned facades are well integrated into the building as a whole. When Mr. A. W. Bosworth, the ice dealer from Skowhegan, Maine, built his residence at 1126 Washington Avenue, he clearly wanted a facade that would outdo those of his neighbors. The result was a truly monumental stage set by the English architect Thomas Wharton, pasted uncertainly onto the front of an otherwise standard American house. The Garden District presents still more striking examples, such as the huge cornices rising weirdly above the rooflines of cottages, cheap strivings for effect that would be more at home in a Colorado mining town than in the exclusive suburb of one of the nation's premier centers of commerce. For the time being, though, New Orleans was also a boom town. The great magnates set the tone and their lesser imitators did what they could to keep up with them. This accounts both for the emergence of a stately and timeless urban style in the new suburban neighborhood and for the profusion of vaguely comical imitations amid the palaces erected by the new Whig rulers.

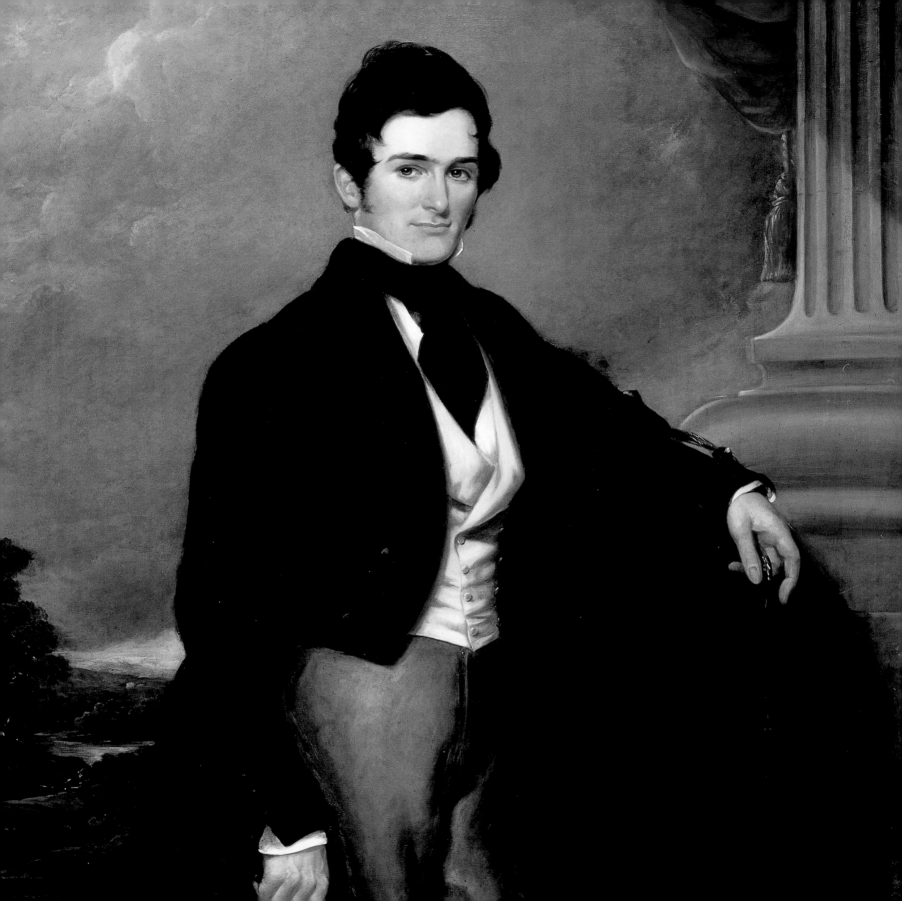

CHAPTER FOUR

James Robb, Magnate and Patron

O N ONE OF his frequent rambles through the Garden District in 1854, Thomas Wharton, the architect and diarist, watched workmen putting the finishing touches on James Robb's palatial residence. This "grand square mansion," he concluded, "is destined to take the lead of all competitors."[1]

Virtually every other observer concurred. As far away as Cincinnati it was known that Robb's Garden District mansion was "one of the sights of New Orleans."[2] Built in a severe palazzo style, the building looked out from a high grassy parapet over gardens embellished with costly vases and statuary. Beyond the grand stairway leading to the entrance was an art gallery with sixteen-foot ceilings and beyond that an octagonal study ornamented with huge mirrors in gilt frames, paneled doors of Honduran mahogany, and frescoes by Domenico Canova. Both house and grounds were executed with no thought to cost. Shortly after it was built, Robb's palace was assessed at $65,000, a vast sum in today's terms.[3] Until it was razed in the 1950s, it was the most opulent residence in a district known for its grandeur.

Robb had built his own life on the same scale as his home. Without a trace of false modesty, he later wrote, "I have been engaged in almost every branch of business, and made money until I did not know what to do with it. I have sat at the table with royalty, seen every phase of life, traveled the whole civilized globe and seen all its art treasures...."[4]

Such claims were not exaggerated. Robb's banking interests stretched from San Francisco to Liverpool and his investments reached from New York to Havana. He possessed the finest art collection west of the Alleghenies, and two of his four children married into wealthy and ancient families, including a branch of the royal house of Spain. A dedicated Whig and personal friend of Henry Clay, he was nonetheless so preoccupied with his banking interests that he turned down the seat in the United States Senate that Judah P. Benjamin later occupied.[5] Robb, in short, was the kind of man that Americans once named Mississippi steamboats after. The *James Robb* was a proud craft.

Robb's success was so thoroughgoing that he could scarcely be considered a typical representative of any group. Whether as businessman, citizen, or architectural patron, he burst out of the mold that produced the antebellum leadership of the Garden District. He was related to that pattern only in the way that symphonies of Mahler relate to those of Haydn: the elements were the same, but they were taken to gargantuan extremes.

❧ "WITHOUT THE AID OF A PENNY"

James Robb was born in 1814 in the rugged southwestern corner of Pennsylvania, at Brownsville, close to the present West Virginia line. His father drowned when James was five, leaving a widow, James, and two older children. His siblings had only modest ambitions, a brother ending up in the saddle business in St. Louis and a sister eventually becoming a schoolteacher in Mississippi. James set his sights higher, and as a youth of thirteen he set out on foot through drifting snow to make his way in the world. After trudging twenty-two miles, he reached Wheeling, now in West Virginia, and found work as a messenger boy in a bank. To his mother he wrote, "It may be that I may get seventy-two or a hundred dollars a year,

If I be a good boy And I hope it may be so."[6] Looking back to this moment some fifty years later, Robb wrote that "From that day to this my fortune has been pursued singly and alone, without the aid of a penny from anyone living or dead."[7]

Robb's career with the Merchants' and Mechanics' Bank of Wheeling began auspiciously. After moving up from office boy to cashier he was sent to apprentice in Pittsburgh.[8] By 1834 the twenty-year-old banker had sufficiently established his worthiness in the eyes of his superiors that they sent him on business to New Orleans.[9] Returning to Morgantown, (West) Virginia, young Robb worked for the local branch of the Wheeling bank, becoming a commission merchant on the side by trading in such items as cross-cut saws.[10] He also established himself in the field of stock trading.[11] Annual trips to New Orleans over the next few years exposed him to the financial center of the Mississippi basin and enabled him to refine his skills in all three of the fields in which he would gain his fame: banking, stock trading, and venture capital.

The year 1837 proved a turning point in Robb's career. The national banking crisis of that year would have created problems for the overextended Wheeling bank, even if its president had not made a series of bad loans for which he was dismissed. Robb offered to forgo his salary to help the firm weather the crisis, but it was clear by now that his future lay elsewhere.[12] Besides, he had long since gained financial independence, largely through active trading in western land and tracts in Mississippi.[13] With his own resources and his banking associates in Philadelphia as a source of credit, Robb settled in New Orleans, returning to Wheeling and Morgantown only to escape the torrid New Orleans summers and to check on his continuing interests.[14]

According to his anonymous earliest biographer, Robb established his financial empire by "buying and exchanging uncurrent money."[15] This he did by entering into partnership with Philadelphian John Bayard to form a brokerage business.[16] In the chaotic situation that followed the banking crisis of 1837, this form of speculation in the older currencies of regional banks proved to be extremely profitable. At the same time he became a commission merchant specializing in cotton. By the time the city's economy had fully revived, Bayard and Robb added a New Orleanian named William Hoge to their partnership, while Robb dropped Bayard

[ABOVE LEFT] *Thomas Wharton's 1855 sketch of the Robb mansion and grounds. It covered a city block, Washington Avenue, Chestnut, Camp, and Sixth Streets* (NEW YORK PUBLIC LIBRARY)

[ABOVE RIGHT] *Robb house, sans rooftop balustrade, c. 1857* (THE HISTORIC NEW ORLEANS COLLECTION)

from the firm soon thereafter. Under Louisiana law the bank did not have to be chartered, which left Robb with virtually complete freedom of action. Meanwhile he had been investing every cent he could in the New Orleans Gas Light Company, which he controlled by 1842. Thus by age twenty-nine, eight years after he arrived in New Orleans, Robb presided over both the burgeoning local utilities company and his own bank.

He soon bought out his partner, Hoge, who had disgraced himself in a duel over another man's wife. By 1845 Robb had extended his banking empire to include offices in St. Louis, San Francisco, New York, Liverpool, and, significantly for his later architectural projects, Philadelphia. He had also traveled several times to Cuba to establish the Spanish Gas Light Company, his principal co-investor being Maria Christina, the queen mother of Spain.[17]

All this time Robb had lived without ostentation in a house on St. Charles Street in the Faubourg Ste. Marie. He plowed most of his profits back into his three businesses or into land he purchased in the West, Midwest, and in uptown New Orleans. His only indulgence was fine art. There was nothing modest about Robb's taste in art, and his collection of old master and modern paintings grew with his fortune. From the Cincinnati sculptor Hiram Powers he purchased the *Greek Slave*, which now stands in the Corcoran Gallery in Washington, D.C.,[18] and Rubens's exuberant wall-sized

masterpiece, significantly named *Peace in Plenty*. As eclectic as he was lavish, Robb acquired major canvases by David, but also academic works on potboiler themes by such middlebrow American painters as Kellogg, Snyders, Roberts, and Leutze. When he learned that the collection of Napoleon's brother, Joseph Bonaparte, was to be sold in Bordentown, New Jersey, he traveled there and outbid all comers. Robb later admitted that the other bidders thought him mad.[19] So, it seems, did the great English historian Thomas B. Macauley, whose portrait Robb commissioned from a member of the Royal Academy. Macauley refused to sit for it.[20]

That Robb was motivated by a genuine civic spirit in his art collecting is suggested by his central role in the establishment of a grandiosely named "National Gallery of Paintings" in New Orleans in 1844. Situated on the upper two floors of a huge warehouse building on St. Charles Street in the Faubourg Ste. Marie, this institution aspired to assert the same national leadership in culture that New Orleans hoped to exert over the economy.[21] Robb loaned works to the gallery and generally labored to encourage art collecting among New Orleanians.

That Robb's instincts as a speculator and entrepreneur spilled over into his interest in art is beyond doubt. In 1847 he mounted a bizarre scheme to sell 380 paintings he had bought from the collections of Italian noblemen. Their purchasers were expected to turn them over for exhibition at the National Gallery on St. Charles Street, which would presumably enhance their value, as well as enliven the gallery. When purchasers failed to come forward, Robb had to auction off the entire stock.[22]

An even more questionable situation arose in his further dealings with sculptor Hiram Powers. In 1846 Robb ordered from Powers a statue, *Alard*, and, as Powers later claimed, left the sculptor free to exhibit the work for two years in order to earn sorely needed funds. Robb later denied that he had intended to leave the work in Powers's hands for so long while Powers, for his part, charged that Robb had not only let him show the work but had required him, Powers, to hide Robb's ownership of the piece, apparently to increase its value. After a considerable altercation Robb refused to pay and blamed Powers's Cincinnati agent, a Mr. Kellogg, for the mess, Powers being in Italy.

In January 1849 Powers vented his anger in a long letter from Florence, Italy, to his brother, Sampson Powers:

"He [Robb] gave me 600 pounds and he takes from me perhaps four or five times that amount, and he is rich too....So modest, too, is this Mr. Robb. He was afraid that it would leak out that he owned the statue lest the Editors should say, that it was 'a joint speculation of his and mine.' I was not to tell that he was the owner of it!!...What can I say but that I have been most shamefully *Robbed*. Yes, I will use the name [of Robb] as a just, a bye word for it belongs to everything that is unmanly and ungenerous."[23]

Powers never did settle his case against Robb, who counterattacked in what Powers called "a most insolent letter" and also in a pamphlet.[24] At the least, the affair revealed that in art, as in business, Robb drove a hard, even ruthless, bargain.

Robb met Powers while visiting a relative of his father's who lived in Cheviot, a western suburb of Cincinnati. About the same time, in 1844, Robb bought a large tract of rolling land in the same area on which he planned to resettle his mother, Mary.[25] There, near what is now Lora and Francis Avenues, he built a thirteen-room residence in the fashionable Gothic cottage style.[26] Unlike most of his business colleagues when it came to architecture, Robb cut no corners on this mansion. Rather than having the exterior plastered and scored to look like masonry, he used cut stone; instead of pine woodwork painted to look like oak, he ordered solid oak throughout. The Mary Robb residence survived to 1935.[27]

As his stake in New Orleans grew, Robb was drawn increasingly into politics. In 1845 the First Municipality, the American district in the Faubourg Ste. Marie, defaulted on a $150,000 loan that the bank of Robb and Hoge had extended. Robb rescued the government and went personally to Philadelphia to try to sell City of New Orleans bonds to cover the refinanced debt.[28] Robb blamed the Crescent City's financial crisis on the fact that the peculiar tripartite system of government left the community literally divided against itself. Accordingly, he spearheaded a campaign to consolidate the three municipalities into a single city and thereby reestablish its credit. He pressed this campaign during a term as alderman and continued to promote it thereafter as a private citizen. Meanwhile, as the owner of an unchartered bank, Robb also entered into combat with those politicians, mainly Democrats, who wanted to alter Louisiana's free banking laws. With equal vigor he also lobbied against all taxes on capital, another plank in the Democrats' program. Such positions made Robb a confirmed Whig. As late as 1850 this was still a minority position in New Orleans, and the local Democrats managed to kill every Whig-sponsored referendum to consolidate the three municipalities into one. In 1851, however, the Whigs edged out the Democrats in Orleans Parish. Robb and Judah P. Benjamin, among the local Whigs who shared in the victory, took their place in the state Senate. Taking advantage both of the Whig victory in New Orleans and of the divisions among Democrats elsewhere in the state, Robb was able successfully to introduce legislation in Baton Rouge to consolidate the divided Crescent City and annex Lafayette to it.[29] Thus James Robb single-handedly engineered the triumph of the uptown Whigs, the destruction of the Democrats' political stronghold in the French Quarter, and the annexation of Lafayette to New Orleans. It was a tour de force.

With the particular understatement that was the hallmark of the truest arrogance, Robb wrote that "had I yielded to the solicitation of friends [I] would have been selected as the representative of

*Robb house in a charcoal rendering by New Orleans artist Theodore Stark
Wilkinson, circa 1865* (MR. AND MRS. HUGH M. WILKINSON, JR.)

Louisiana in the Senate of the United States."[30] In fact, Robb had been personally importuned by Henry Clay, already mortally ill, to support S. W. Downs's campaign for reelection to the Senate. Clay had written that "his [Downs's] defeat would be a matter of exultation for the Abolitionists, the free-soilers, and those rash men in the South whose warlike counsels would have brought upon us all the horrors of a civil war."[31] Robb complied, supported Downs, and did not even bother to serve out his own term in the state senate. As soon as the consolidation bills were passed, he abandoned public office to promote his other great passion—railroads.

Amid the cotton boom, commercial New Orleans had blithely neglected the revolution that railroads were sparking in American life. James Robb was virtually alone in recognizing both the potential benefits of railroads to Louisiana and also the disaster the state would face if it failed to keep apace with railroad construction elsewhere. He reminded his fellow businessmen of the fragility of the local economy. In what must have seemed a staggeringly somber report, "The Condition of Things in New Orleans and The Remedy," delivered to a convention of prospective railroad builders in 1851, Robb spelled out the nature of the looming crisis: the Democrats' banking laws had shackled free trade; few ships serving New Orleans were locally owned; export was fostered at the expense of imports; and manufacturing of any sort was all but nonexistent in the city. Unless these conditions were reversed, New Orleans—and the entire South—would be doomed to the status of a backwater. The sole hope for salvation, Robb asserted, was through the promotion of free trade and the construction of railroads.[32] When the New Orleans, Jackson and Great Northern Railroad was organized the following year, the stockholders chose as its president James Robb.[33]

Thus in 1852 Robb emerged as one of the most powerful men in the political, economic, and cultural life of New Orleans and the South. He owned a large international bank and utilities companies in New Orleans and Havana; he was a major commission merchant; he had transformed the political structure of his adopted city; and he presided over the most ambitious railroad project in the region. It was at this moment that Robb decided to build his Garden District residence.

With characteristic flamboyance he staked out an entire city block, bordered by Washington Avenue, Chestnut, Camp, and Sixth Streets. In 1851 he moved his family from downtown to a rented house on the corner of Prytania and Third Streets so as to be able to watch the progress of his mansion only three blocks away.[34]

"A GRAND SQUARE MANSION"

The history of the design of Robb's palace has long been a mystery. Various writers have ascribed it to James Freret, to James Gallier, Jr., and even to anonymous architects from outside New Orleans. Documents preserved in the Labrot Collection at Tulane University[35] and in the Historic New Orleans Collection shed fresh light on this question. The trail leads back to England. The urbane Sir Charles Barry in 1836 had broken new ground by designing a building for the Manchester Athenaeum in the form of an Italian Renaissance palazzo. News of this innovative design soon reached America. A transplanted Scotsman in Philadelphia, John Notman, borrowed heavily from Sir Charles's scheme when he designed a home for the Philadelphia Athenaeum in 1845–47.[36] Notman, himself a member of the Philadelphia Athenaeum, proposed the same heavy rustication that Barry had used for the ground floor, but an even more severely unornamented facade for the second and third stories. Robb evidently knew of this building and probably had seen it in the course of visits to that city in 1847.[37] Its innovative design was certainly known among New Orleans cognoscenti, for James Dakin had borrowed heavily from it in 1847 in one of his several proposals for the new Custom House for New Orleans. Dakin, too, may well have examined the structure in situ during a visit to Philadelphia, for its influence on his architecture thereafter was evident.[38]

The idea of applying the austere and dignified palazzo style to domestic architecture was being pioneered in Philadelphia precisely in the years Robb was undertaking his New Orleans mansion. The

[ABOVE] *Young Philadelphia architect Richard Morris Smith's proposed elevation for the Robb house, 1853* (SOUTHEASTERN ARCHITECTURAL ARCHIVE, TULANE UNIVERSITY)

[RIGHT] *Façade of the Robb house, as built in 1855. James Gallier, Jr., probably refined young Smith's original design* (BRANDT V. B. DIXON, *A BRIEF HISTORY OF THE H. SOPHIE NEWCOMB MEMORIAL COLLEGE, 1887–1919*)

Rental property built by James Robb; his Washington Avenue palazzo in the back-ground (New Orleans Notarial Archives)

distinguished architect Samuel Sloan designed the Joseph Harrison house for Philadelphia's Rittenhouse Square in 1853, drawing inspiration for his Renaissance design not only from the Athenaeum but also from Italianate palaces of Russian grandees in St. Petersburg (Leningrad), where Harrison had long resided. The Harrison house, and also Sloan's house for brewer William Gaul on North Broad Street in Philadelphia, provided ready models for Robb's architect to draw upon.[39]

Why, then, did Robb not commission Notman or Sloan to design his house? Here one can do no more than speculate. Perhaps Notman and Sloan declined requests from Robb, either because they were too busy or did not want to repeat earlier designs. Robb almost certainly turned then to the famous Thomas U. Walter, also of Philadelphia. Walter, however, was tied up with work on the cupola of the Capitol in Washington, D.C., as well as other projects for the federal government, including the interior of the Customs House in New Orleans. This was probably not an insurmountable problem to Robb, however, who had a good idea of what he wanted and sought only a willing architect to adapt the prototypes of Notman and Sloan to his personal needs. Richard Morris Smith, a student of Walter, seemed up to this task.

Born into an established family of Burlington, New Jersey, Smith was twenty-five years old when he undertook the Robb commission. Unknown and untried, the young draftsman had been listed among Philadelphia's architects for a brief few months. He is known to have designed only three buildings during his career, not counting the remodeling of a Philadelphia interior.[40] Of these three, just one—Robb's house—was actually built, and then only after Smith's original proposal was substantially revised by other hands. Judging by his later writing, young Smith was a man of some culture, but he had only the most limited architectural training.[41] His two other designs besides Robb's house are both derivative of the work of the Philadelphia architect Samuel Sloan and of Smith's mentor, Thomas U. Walter. Nonetheless, there was no need to think that Smith could not meet Robb's needs.

Smith, whom Robb probably met in 1851 when he was in Philadelphia selling New Orleans municipal bonds, drafted his first set of elevations on 1 March 1853. A rear elevation followed a few days later.[42] The basic scheme of Notman's Athenaeum emerges: the three bays, the heavy rustication on the raised ground floor, and the smooth upper story framed by rusticated quoining. Only in the interior plan does Smith reveal any originality, by creating a central atrium to bring natural light directly into the rooms. By late May he had evidently won Robb's approval, so Smith began developing a series of detailed drawings of the front door, the elaborate front and rear marble terraces, and other decorative details. These, too, were forwarded to New Orleans, along with specifications for the actual construction.[43]

Even a cursory glance at Smith's original renderings reveals that they differ substantially from the final building. First, Smith called for a two-and-a-half-story structure; the Robb mansion was built on one floor. Second, Smith's design for the ground story facades are rusticated and the windows on the second story ornamented with Renaissance moldings; the main windows of the Robb house as built had neither rustication nor moldings, but very different windows in an Italianate style were added on the side and rear. Robb evidently had a change of heart.

The traditional explanation for the changes was that Robb had suffered sudden financial reverses and stopped work after one story.[44] Another variant has Robb making this decision as a result of the fact that two of his three daughters were growing up and about to leave home. According to this interpretation, Robb adapted to his changing family needs by reducing the planned mansion from three stories to one and by purchasing more land on Washington Avenue so that he could engage the younger Gallier to design the two identical houses that still stand there for the two Robb daughters and their future husbands.

The first theory is grossly overstated. Robb did indeed suffer grave financial reverses in the 1850s, but in 1857, a year after the Washington Avenue mansion was completed. While he was under serious financial pressure in 1852–54, it was far less than the crisis invoked to explain the shift in design, and different in character. The second theory must also be rejected. Not only is it absurd to think that someone as deliberate as Robb would have neglected to reckon with his daughters' ages when he planned his house, but there is no evidence that either daughter ever occupied the separate houses on Washington Avenue, which were in all likelihood conceived from the outset as rental properties.[45]

Why, then, was the Smith plan reduced to one story and otherwise cut back in scale and simplified? Lacking firm evidence, it is likely that Robb, eager to seize investment opportunities, found himself suffering from a short-term money shortage and simply lacked the cash during 1852–54 to pay for so grandiose a house as Smith had proposed. This theory is supported by several pieces of evidence. As early as 1850 a correspondent of Robb's reported that new western lands were being opened by Congress.[46] Robb proceeded to invest, but in early 1853 the same correspondent reported on the poor returns and by March of that year Robb was bailing out from some of these holdings.[47] About the same time, we find Robb maneuvering to sell slaves on a plantation in Reserve, Louisiana, and investing in large alotments of land in Texas and Mississippi.[48] He was also involved in a heavy flurry of correspondence with his Paris office, in all likelihood precipitated by the negative impact of the Crimean War on financial markets in the combatant nations. By early 1855, about the time the mansion was being completed, Robb's office instructed his agent in Havana to remit to Robb's account $100,000[49] to invest in land in Des Moines, Iowa, and Sheboygan, Michigan.[50]

Surviving documents are too fragmentary to permit a more detailed reconstruction of these transactions. It is evident, however, that in the early 1850s Robb engaged in complex maneuvers in all the major financial markets in an effort to shift part of his holdings from equities into land. Under such circumstances, Robb might have hesitated to plunge into the building of a residence that would have been several times more expensive than the small palace he actually built, even though the latter surpassed in price all previous houses that went up in the booming city of New Orleans. By scaling down Smith's plan, Robb maximized the capital he could pour back into fresh investments, always the strategy of Garden District barons in the flush antebellum years.

Was it Gallier, then, who reworked Smith's original design for the main house? The *Daily Crescent* stated unequivocally in 1856 that James Gallier, Jr., designed the Robb mansion. This is confirmed by the fact that the names of Gallier and his partner appear on the final floor plan.[51] Accepting this for the moment, it is clear that Gallier drew heavily on the palazzo style then in vogue in Philadelphia and on earlier variants for the mansion prepared by

Smith. The general layout for the rooms and the concept for the grand exterior entrance were executed much as the Philadelphian had proposed. Gallier also took over Smith's plan for the elevation of the structure on an artificial terrace and for lifting the main floor four more feet above the ground level to achieve yet more monumentality. The use of white marble for the facade, unprecedented in the Garden District, as well as soaring sixteen-foot ceilings in the receiving rooms, added distinction to Smith's proposal. All this, too, was incorporated in the Gallier design.

Nowadays such unacknowledged borrowing might be cause for professional concern, if not legal action, among architects. Such was not the case in nineteenth-century America, where architectural plagiarism of all sorts was common. Not until 1857, in fact, did the Supreme Court of New York find in favor of an architect who sued another for taking over elements of his project without recompense and even this decision had little practical effect for some years thereafter.[52]

Such elements of the Robb mansion as the handsome three-part rounded window on the rear exposure, the severe exterior moldings, and the elaborate balustrade on the roof had nothing in common with any of Gallier's work to date. Gallier may well have simply been moving into a more Italianate phase, but it is clear that he made this change exactly at the moment his patron, Robb, had brought to bear the influence of Philadelphia's fashionable new architecture in New Orleans.

The palazzo style exerted a continuing influence on Gallier's career. Twelve years after doing the Robb house, he built a wonderfully exuberant Renaissance palace on Leda Avenue off Esplanade for the wartime profiteer, Florence Luling. The influence of the Robb mansion is evident in the boxlike mass of the building, the plain exterior walls, the raised mound on which it sits, and the use of outbuildings. Here, though, the direct impact of yet another Philadelphian architect, Samuel Sloan, is even more apparent.[53]

Robb, on his side, clearly respected Gallier. After the Civil War, he turned once more to the young architect for the design of his Louisiana National Bank on Common Street. For this design, too, Gallier drew on the Philadelphia Athenaeum and even employed the same rounded Renaissance windows that first

Octagon room, Robb house (RICHARD KOCH, LOUISIANA STATE MUSEUM)

[ABOVE] *Front gate of Robb mansion, few guests passed through. Relocated to entrance of New Orleans Baptist Seminary, Chef Menteur Highway*

[FACING PAGE] *Roman-style fresco by Domenico Canova, Robb house*
(RICHARD KOCH, LOUISIANA STATE MUSEUM)

appeared in New Orleans when Smith introduced one on the garden facade of the Robb mansion.

The interior of Robb's mansion was executed in a style worthy of the first citizen of New Orleans. Most noteworthy was the large octagonal room at the rear of the house, which opened onto the gardens through the large Renaissance window. Glittering with mirrors that made the room seem to expand infinitely, the walls, as well as the ceiling, were ornamented with frescoes in the Roman style executed by Domenico Canova.[54] A relative of Antonio Canova, who had ornamented the finest homes of Beethoven's Vienna, Domenico had arrived in New Orleans in 1838 to cash in on his share of the building boom. He created frescoes for the old St. Louis Hotel, at San Francisco Plantation, and at Walter Robinson's Garden District home. Canova's frescoes for Robb were among his most extravagant, if not his best. Later, after Robb's business failure, architect Thomas Wharton commented acerbically about the frescoes being "wretched, badly drawn, worse in color."[55] The Garden District, however, had seen nothing to compare with them.

With his stately residence complete, Robb was ready to put it to its intended use: receiving the public. Even though reduced in scale, the mansion was large by any measure and what it lacked in sheer mass it more than made up for in the elegance of its interior fittings and furnishings. It was perfectly calculated to impress guests, be they railroad barons, visiting bankers, upriver planters, or art lovers. Yet this was not to be.

The Robb family installed itself on Washington Avenue in the late spring or summer of 1855, just in time for the family's annual departure for (West) Virginia to escape the New Orleans heat. Mrs. Robb, however, was gravely ill. "I sincerely regret to learn of Mrs. Robb's continued illness," a friend wrote, "but hope her health will soon permit leaving your sickly season, which would so greatly relieve the anxiety you are now suffering for her and your unacclimated Daughters."[56] It is not known whether the Robbs actually left town during that hot summer, but in late September yellow fever claimed the life of Robb's daughter, Louisa. Two weeks later Mrs. Robb herself succumbed to the disease, which had long debilitated her.[57]

Following this double tragedy, Robb took his three remaining children to Europe in the spring of 1856, leasing the Washington Avenue residence to his old Whig friend and sometimes fellow real estate speculator, Justice Thomas Slidell of the U. S. Supreme Court. While the family was in France, a Spanish nobleman-adventurer sought the hand in marriage of Robb's daughter, Isabella ("Bell"). Robb's social aspirations by now had bridged the Atlantic. He welcomed an alliance that had grown out of his own business contacts with Spain's queen—the very person after whom, presumably, he had named his daughter. The match turned out to be a disaster, however, for within a year the son-in-law sued Robb for his wife's inheritance as guaranteed under Louisiana's community property laws. Robb lost. Only many years later did Bell, now sans Spaniard, return to America and to the household of her aging father.

Meanwhile, the failure of a Cincinnati insurance company in the summer of 1857 triggered a worldwide panic.[58] Before Robb could return to his New York bank of Robb, Hollett and Company, it had suspended payments to his banks in Liverpool and San Francisco, which had to close their doors. The unliquidated liabilities of these three banks amounted to nearly $3 million dollars.[59] Back in Louisiana, Robb's New Orleans, Jackson and Great Northern Railroad also suffered grave reversals, further devastating his finances.

Anticipating several other Garden District residents who were to lose their fortunes during the Civil War, Robb resolved to sacrifice whatever was necessary to clear his name. He sold all his railroad stock, his holdings in the New Orleans Gas Light Company, his shares in the Bank of James Robb, and even his newly built residence. He moved quickly to stop work on the statues of Eve and Telemachus, which he had commissioned Neopolitan sculptor Gito Angelini to create.[60] He even consigned masterpieces from his art collection to the auction block, as well as several sets of fine china, crystal, and all the house's furnishings.[61] The same public that had swelled with civic pride over Robb's earlier triumphs now reveled in his demise.

The auction of his art collection in 1859 drew cynical remarks from more than one visitor. However, this was not to be "the last closing scene of this gaudy drama," as the jubilant Thomas Wharton predicted in his diary.[62] For these tragic events had the ironic effect of forcing Robb to liquidate most of his Southern holdings on the eve of the sectional war that would have claimed them anyway. He explored the possibility of establishing himself in San Francisco but abandoned that notion when he remarried, this time a widow from Athens, Georgia, with family ties in Pennsylvania.[63] By the time the first shots were heard at Fort Sumter, James Robb was in Chicago as the court-appointed receiver for the St. Louis, Alton, and Chicago Railroad Company. His fortunes quickly rebounded and he once more gained civic renown, this time through his work on Chicago's sanitary commission.

Robb's destiny was to be linked inextricably with the North. Even before he was forced to leave New Orleans, Robb had passionately opposed all talk of secession by the South. True, he was a friend of Jefferson Davis and a parishioner of Bishop Leonidas Polk, rector of Trinity Church on Jackson Avenue and later a general under the Confederacy.[64] There is even evidence that Robb owned slaves, although as early as 1838 and as late as 1855 he was actively involved with discussions on resettling freed slaves in Liberia;[65] on the eve of Sumter he declared slavery to be "illegitimate."[66] In spite of this, he consistently maintained that the best hope of New Orleans, and of the Deep South, lay in the modernization of its economy and its integration with the rest of the nation. Secession, he believed, was futile, for it pushed the region precisely in the opposite direction. As he wrote to his new father-in-law in Georgia, "the Union must be preserved at all cost."[67] Once it was ruptured, a military and political victory by the North was an absolute necessity.[68]

Such views recommended Robb to Lincoln's Republican administration, even though as a Whig he had long opposed the radical Abolitionists. In 1862 he was asked to serve as military governor of Louisiana, which he declined, just as he later turned down President Andrew Johnson's invitation to serve in his cabinet.[69] As ever, his goals were economic, not political. Accordingly, he returned to New Orleans in 1866, set up a new Louisiana National Bank, and hired James Gallier, Jr., to design its headquarters. The new bank rode the postwar boom, but misfortune once more befell Robb with the death of his second wife. The following year Robb departed New Orleans for the last time.

James Robb passed his last days in the Gothic Revival mansion he had built near Cincinnati for his mother, in the companionship of his large library and what remained of his art collection. Meanwhile, John Burnside, Irish-born dry-goods merchant and plantation owner who had bought Robb's Garden District home and the bulk of his art collection, maintained the great palazzo on Washington Avenue until his death in 1881. In 1890 Mrs. Josephine Newcomb purchased the property and added a second story to accommodate her newly founded Newcomb College.[70] In 1918 the Baptist Theological Seminary acquired the property, making further changes in the house and grounds. When the seminary moved to other quarters in 1955, the great house was razed and its ample grounds turned over to developers. Only a few giant oaks remain today from the Robb era.

CHAPTER FIVE

Architects and Builders

ONE DAY IN the late spring of 1857 the architect Thomas Wharton found himself in conversation with a New Orleans businessman who had just contracted with a local builder to design and construct a major office building for him. Upon being told that no architect was to be involved in the project, Wharton was indignant. "I made some very plain comments on that system . . . ," he noted in his diary.[1] But the client was unmoved.

That same year thirteen architects met in New York to form the American Institute of Architects. Its purpose was to enhance the status of architects as professionals and to assure they be paid and treated in the courts as such. However, it was one thing to declare in principle that buildings should be designed by qualified architects and quite another to find competent people to do this. James Gallier, Sr., complained that "During the practice of my profession at New Orleans, I could find no person capable of giving me much assistance in making drawings."[2]

Not only were there few architects, but throughout North America they were looked upon with suspicion, as purveyors of unnecessary luxuries.[3] Twenty years after the A. I. A.'s founding, a New York architect still had to defend his profession: "When a person is sick it is customary to seek the advice of a doctor; and, having confidence in his ability, it would be the height of folly not to follow

[FACING PAGE] *The house of John Turpin, who failed as an architect but prospered as a wine merchant: 2319 Magazine Street, by James Gallier, Jr., 1853-54*

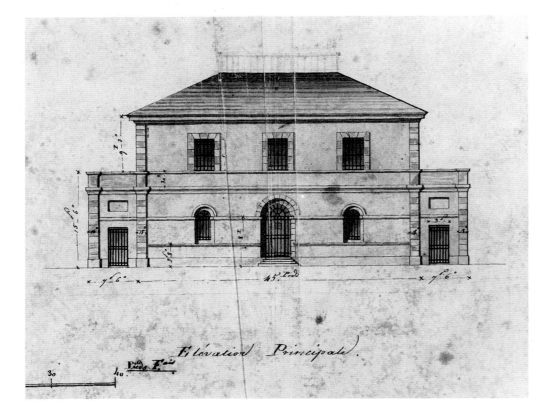

Highbrow architecture by local "surveyor" Benjamin Buisson: the Lafayette jail,
1836 (JEFFERSON PARISH ARCHIVES)

it."[4] To be sure, a growing number of Americans were more sympathetic to architecture. Only a handful of such enlightened patrons were in the Garden District, however. Hence, few specialized members of the new profession worked there.

The *New Orleans Directory* of 1858 includes some thirty-two people who identify themselves as architects.[5] The 1860 census enumerates far more. However, the frequent appearance in building contracts of these same men in the capacity of contractors or builders suggests that their transition to the specialized practice of architectural design was far from complete. Clients could get along without an architect but not without a builder.

Every aspect of the builder's work in New Orleans was fraught with problems. James Gallier, Sr., who identified himself as both builder and architect, complained about the weather, the mosquitoes, the construction materials, and about being "overwhelmed by difficulties in procuring the services of good workmen."[6]

Under such conditions, it was purely a rhetorical flourish when one John Barnett identified himself as the architect of a saloon built in Lafayette in 1853.[7] What counted to William McLaughlin, the barman, was that Barnett could see the job through to completion. It is no wonder that Edward Gotthiel, a competent designer, chose to present himself as the "superintendent" for J. H. Maddox's Prytania Street house rather than as the architect.[8] The point was to get the job done. Patrons were willing to pay those who could do this, without regard for their titles or degrees.

Architecture as an independent profession separate from government made its debut in England. The founding of the London Architectural Society in 1806 makes an important step in the creation of such a profession.[9] In France, by contrast, the practice of architecture had long been organized by the Crown, with architects often serving as "surveyors" for the government. The Creole Benjamin Buisson, designer of the Lafayette City Hall in 1836, stands directly in this tradition, for he worked as Lafayette's official surveyor rather than as a free and independent architect. Only when a remarkable group of British immigrants arrived in New Orleans in the 1830s and 1840s did the British form of practice supplant the French.

Among the first to come was the Irishman James Gallier, Sr. After learning the building trade with his father in Dublin, Gallagher, as he was born, apprenticed in London, where, not wanting to struggle against the liability of being Irish, he conveniently gallicized his name to Gallier.[10] In 1832 he emigrated to New York, where he found only one official architectural office, that of Ithiel Town and A.J. Davis. After a brief stint with them Gallier moved on to gain valuable experience as a draftsman for the great Minard Lafever. He arrived in New Orleans in 1834.[11]

Two Englishmen who followed the same route were Thomas Wharton and John Turpin, a London-born bookkeeper who became associated with the Gallier firm as a partner. Turpin's house, presumably designed by James Gallier, Jr., in 1853–54, still stands at 2319 Magazine Street.[12] George Purves, designer of several Garden District homes, including the Isaac Bogart house on Fourth Street, was the most prominent of several Scotsmen or Scotch-Irish who entered architecture and the building trades in New Orleans. Another was Samuel Jamison, who arrived from County Antrim near Belfast in 1830. Similar to other immigrants from the British Isles, Purves and Jamison both gained their first experience with American building practices in Manhattan.

Many other booming American cities attracted British architects in these years, from Chicago to St. Louis, even to Portland, Maine. In New Orleans, however, British immigrants seem to have dominated the field to a greater extent than elsewhere. In no other city did they earn the support of such major patrons and hence gain so many of the city's chief architectural commissions.

New Orleans also claimed a number of German builders and architects during the antebellum years. Edward Gotthiel, for example, had completely mastered the local vernacular by 1853, when he designed a raised, brick cottage with fluted columns for William Haneman.[13] Another German, Albert Diettel, had arrived in New Orleans in 1849, having fled his native Dresden after the abortive uprising there the year before. Diettel eventually joined forces with Jacob Wilhelm Thiel from the East Prussian village of Fischhausen. Thiel shared Diettel's liberal politics, having supported the 1848 Revolution. A thorough professional, he had published in Berlin a textbook, *Applied Projection Drawing for Masons and Carpenters.*[14]

Thiel was later to design the Gates of Prayer Synagogue on Jackson Avenue at Chippewa Street.

Together, these British and German immigrants brought to New Orleans architectural practice a level of professionalism far in advance of most of their talented but less worldly native-born colleagues. Wharton, Gallier, and Thiel had published important handbooks, while all the others had gained experience in major offices before their arrival in New Orleans.

What of the American-born designers? Only one, William A. Freret (1833–1911), was a New Orleanian by birth. The architect of several Garden District homes,[15] Freret was also the sole American-born Garden District architect not to have cut his teeth in New York City. Not that all the others were Manhattaners by birth. James Dakin, the famous designer of the Conrey mansion on Carondelet Street, now demolished, and the Slark house on Annunciation, also razed, was born in Dutchess County, up the Hudson River from New York City. Lewis E. Reynolds, designer of several grand residences in the District, came from further upstate, in Norwich. Frederick Wing, architect of at least six District homes, was born and trained in Philadelphia.[16] Dakin, Reynolds, and Wing all hastened to Manhattan to complete their training and perfect their skills. Henry Thiberge, among the youngest antebellum architects, was exceptional in that he was a Manhattaner by birth. Thus at some point between 1830 and 1840 virtually every Garden District architect, whether foreign-born or American, was to be found working in New York City. It was an architectural outpost of Gotham.

Like their clients, the Garden District's architects were self-made men. Samuel Jamison, for example, was a bricklayer and plasterer by trade, while Lewis Reynolds, James Gallier, Sr., Frederick Wing, and Henry Howard all came up through the ranks of carpenters. The backgrounds of these craftsmen stand in sharp contrast to that of Jacques Nicolas Bussiere de Pouilly, the favorite architect of the local Creoles and a graduate of the renowned École des Beaux Arts in Paris. The Anglo-Saxons lacked the formal training available in France but their greater experience in the crafts brought practical benefits. Jamison's skill as a plasterer is evident particularly in the graceful moldings on both the exteriors and interiors of his two houses at 1315 and 1331 First Street.[17] And

Lewis Reynold's mastery of the subtle geometry of stairway building—he had written a treatise on the topic—is attested to by his daring spiral stairway in the Bradish Johnson house on Prytania Street and by the now destroyed stairway in Henry Buckner's Jackson Avenue residence.[18]

Lacking specialized training and being remote from the centers of innovation in their field, architects working in the Garden District were especially dependent upon design books. Gallier assembled a collection of architectural books, and Lewis Reynolds also had a library, consisting of some 112 volumes.[19] Samuel Jamison borrowed the design of cornices for several of his postwar houses from Plate LXXXIX of Samuel Sloan's *The Model Architect* (Philadelphia, 1851), thereby establishing that he had access to the important work. Similarly, Henry Howard drew material from Joseph Gwilt's *Encyclopedia of Architecture* (London, 1843) in the design of Thomas Leathers's house on Carondolet Street.[20] New Orleanians used published handbooks to keep abreast of the times.

One should not picture Garden District architects spending all their spare time pouring over design books, however. Most of them were busy with some collateral business, whether to assure themselves the necessary materials for their trade or simply to make money. Several owned and managed sawmills or brickyards. Others speculated in Garden District land. James Dakin, for example, bought and sold lots on St. Mary Street in 1849, while the Galliers traded properties along Magazine Street in the 1850s.[21] Still others entered into development projects as planners, financiers, or salesmen. Such business opportunities enabled many architects and builders to thrive. Yet their extra-curricular interests compromised their collective status as professionals. Such side interests, as much as any other factor, retarded the development of a specialized profession of architecture in New Orleans.

That Garden District architects responded to entrepreneurial opportunity does not mean that their lot was an easy one. Samuel Jamison and his partner grew rich as builders, but most did not. William A. Freret undertook to develop—with financial backing from his father, William Freret, an architect and a former mayor—five freestanding, three-bay houses on Second Street, circa 1859.[22] Freret had no regular labor force of his own and would have had to draw on workmen from the rather expensive open market. This,

[ABOVE] *Architect William A. Freret's own house, 1524 Third Street, 1859*

[RIGHT] *Architect and builder Frederick Wing's house, 1429 Seventh Street, circa 1853–60*

combined with the low sale prices dictated by the competitive situation, kept Freret's profits small. When Freret then undertook to build a row of five single houses along Coliseum Street between Fourth and Washington, he hoped to reap more substantial gains.[23] The Civil War, however, interrupted construction work at the site. By the time work was resumed in 1865, the houses had already lost money and had been dubbed Freret's Folly, a name they still bear today.

With one or two exceptions, the life of Garden District architects was one of struggle. Lewis Reynolds advertised in the press to find clients and still died poor. Henry Howard, the Garden District's most prolific architect, managed to keep up a rented home in the Garden District that he himself probably designed,[24] but he never enjoyed more than a taste of the luxury known to his clients and neighbors—this, in spite of years of eighteen-hour working days. It is no wonder that James Gallier's bookkeeper and partner, John Turpin, decided in 1858–59 that he could do better in the wine business than in architecture.[25] Nor is it surprising that the talented James Calrow, architect of the handsome Harris home on Prytania Street and the stately Brevard house, left New Orleans after only two years. The Garden District was no bonanza for architects.

This condition was reflected in the very process of contracting to design a Garden District home. In spite of Reynolds's ads, most architects, including Reynolds himself, secured commissions only through laboriously developed personal contacts. This may well explain why so many of the architects and builders chose to live in the District. Frederick Wing, Henry Howard, William A. Freret, Charles W. Wilson, the prolific Robert Huyghe, William Day, George Purves, and William Thiel all made their homes in the fashionable new suburb.[26] The absence of zoning and the consequent mix of expensive and moderately priced houses in the area enabled even a struggling architect to reside there if it served his purposes.

It might have been easier for the architects if there had been open competitive bidding on jobs, but then, such was rare on public buildings and virtually unheard of for private residences. This is scarcely surprising in light of the apparent capriciousness of the bidding process. When the elders of the Gates of Prayer Synagogue on Jackson Avenue invited open bidding on construction work for its new temple in 1865, the highest bid was almost twice the

[ABOVE] *William A. Freret's speculative interests: five identical, free-standing houses, 1703–1719 Second Street, 1859*

[FACING PAGE] *Architect Lewis Reynold's daring stairway at the Bradish Johnson residence, 2343 Prytania Street, 1872*

amount of the lowest one. The contract went to the well known and highly regarded Maryland-born Robert Huyghe, who had not even deigned to submit a bid.[27]

With whom should one contract, architect or builder? This problem further complicated the architect's plight. As noted, only two Garden District architects confined their attention solely to the design, as distinct from the construction, of buildings. Henry Howard eked out a living from the $150 he received to design each house, but he did so only through sheer hard work.[28] James Calrow, who took a yet more lofty view, did not condescend even to work out detailed drawings for his buildings. In his contract for Albert Brevard's house he pronounced that "working drawings such as pertain to galleries, cornices, interior furnishings [are to be provided] at the expense of the builder."[29] It is little wonder that the builder, in this case Charles Pride, prospered, while Calrow soon left town.

The weaning search for clients and the low remuneration for design work per se repressed the specialized practice of architecture, elevated the status of builders, and transformed builders into architects. Samuel Jamison, Charles Wilson, Charles Hillger, and Abram Howell are but a few of the local builders who, during the prewar decades, began presenting themselves as architects while also retaining their foothold in the more lucrative construction industry.

Such dual roles were confusing. Howell referred to himself alternately as "architect" and "builder" within the same contract for Luther Stewart's house.[30] Charles Hillger only rarely identified himself as an architect during the 1850s. A decade later when he designed the massive Jackson Avenue mansion for Julius Weis, now demolished, he was fully established in his new role, but, ever the builder, he still insisted on maintaining "supervisory power" over the project.[31] In their gradual transformation from builder to architect, New Orleanians followed the same evolution as many carpenter-builders in the Northeast, but the process was delayed in the Crescent City by about a decade.

What did it actually mean to be an architect in the antebellum Garden District? The character of the building was determined by the initial plan, of course, but in equal measure it was also shaped by the detailed written specifications that architects were expected to submit. Whether the work of architect or builder, such specifications, sometimes running over twenty pages in longhand, counted as the test of a designer's worth. Included with the contract, they provided a means of assuring that the desired product would be produced. In the early days specifications had been very brief. When the builder Manuel Castein designed a typical Creole *brique entre poteaux* dwelling on Jackson Avenue in 1834 for Marie Christophe, a free woman of color, his specifications amounted to only a few pages. Later, specifications became more elaborate. Samuel Sloan of Philadelphia published advice for architects on preparing more detailed specifications for various types of buildings and the learned Gervase Wheeler issued minutely enumerated model price lists.[32] About this time we find the conscientious Thomas Wharton straining his eyes studying such model specifications by lamplight in his Garden District home.[33] Thanks to all this attention, the capacity to draft elegant and exhaustive specifications came to be equated with ability as an architect.

Virtually the only difference between specifications drafted by architects and those produced by builders is that the former permitted the patron less freedom of choice. Architect Henry Howard specified that the walls of Robert Grinnan's villa should be painted with four coats of "good English white lead in oil."[34] In contrast, Isaac Thayer, who was a civil engineer and builder by trade, permitted Thomas Gilmour personally to select the colors for his home on Prytania Street.[35]

If such detailed written specifications had any purpose, it was to provide a basis for estimating the cost of construction. Yet it was precisely in this area that architects and builders frequently missed the mark. Few erred as disastrously as James Gallier, Jr., in 1865, when he underestimated the cost of the Luling mansion on Leda Avenue by one hundred percent. Substantial cost overruns were by no means unusual, and they invariably led to serious trouble. When William Day exceeded his budget for Captain Leathers's Carondolet Street house by a mere fifteen percent, it resulted in an acrimonious lawsuit.[36]

[ABOVE] *Restored fresco by Petro Gauldi at Manuel Goldsmith's house, 1122 Jackson Avenue. Architects Henry Howard and Albert Diettel, 1859*

[LEFT] *Builder Waldemar Tallin's elegant capitals for Robert A. Grinnan's house, 2221 Prytania Street. Henry Howard, architect, 1850* (RICHARD KOCH, PHOTOGRAPHER; SAMUEL WILSON, JR., COLLECTION, SOUTH-EASTERN ARCHITECTURAL ARCHIVE, TULANE UNIVERSITY)

THE HUMAN FACTOR

Those who prefer to view architecture as an art are frustrated whenever master designers are forced to make concessions to reality. Yet in the antebellum Garden District, the successful architect or builder was the one who was best able to adapt his art to the practical constraints that prevailed locally. Many such impediments confronted him, but the most serious one was the shortage of trained craftsmen. Everyone complained about it. James Gallier's objections have already been cited. Thomas Wharton also grumbled about jobs not being completed on time "owing to the difficulty of obtaining hands."[37] Nor did the problems cease when the workers were secured. Craftsmen might disappear overnight to more lucrative jobs in the West; possibly abscond with the supplies,

as did one of the builders with whom Charles Conrad contracted in 1841;[38] divide their time between two projects, thus delaying both buildings; or simply produce faulty work.

Contracts for Garden District homes bristled with attempts to counteract these various problems. There were constant demands that work was to be executed in the best and most workmanlike manner, and that proper methods were to be employed. Every conceivable pressure was put on the builder or contractor to meet deadlines. When Philip T. Philips contracted with Peter Middlemiss to build the mercantile building still standing at the corner of Jackson Avenue and St. Charles, he imposed a penalty of ten dollars for every day the work was delayed beyond the five-month deadline.[39] Not dissimilar to the modern practice of performance payments at the completion of construction stages, Garden District contractors knew they would be paid only after successful completion of each phase of work. Thus Peter Middlemiss received payment on Mr. Philips's store in six installments, the first when the walls reached one story, the second when the second story was raised, the third when the roof was slated, and so forth. This practice, common throughout the city, was a necessary measure to keep builders on their toes.

The problems with craftsmen cannot be blamed on poor pay. A skilled tailor or cobbler might receive two dollars a day in the 1850s, but a New Orleans painter or cabinetmaker could demand three dollars.[40] The building boom had caused wages to soar. In 1841, when Charles Conrad built his raised cottage, he had had to pay his "mechanics" only thirty-two dollars a month.[41] A decade later the bill might have been fifty dollars or more.

Surviving papers from the 1850s of the contracting firm of Cook and Moorhouse reveal much about the labor problem.[42] These contractors built many of the major Garden District mansions, including those of Michel Musson and Samuel Kennedy. For months on end they were virtually paralyzed by the absence of laborers, and their teams frequently had to redo jobs, especially to correct faulty plastering and leaking cisterns. Judging by the firm's accounts, Cook and Moorhouse eventually came to live off repair work rather than original construction.

This is not to deny the presence of artisans of genuine talent. Waldemar Tallin, a woodcarver from Germany (or possibly present day Estonia), executed magnificent work on the capitals of Robert Grinnan's villa and at various other residences designed by Henry Howard. Domenico Canova's impressive frescoes at the Robb and Robinson mansions have been noted. Also, the flamboyant fresco work of Petro Gauldi (or possibly Canova again) at Manuel Goldsmith's house is noteworthy. However, such master artisans were exceptions to the rule. Most of the craftsmen who built the Garden District lacked such individual distinction and for that reason remain anonymous today.

ARTISANS, SLAVE AND FREE

It is often supposed that the antebellum homes of the Garden District were constructed by slave labor. Certainly the institution of slavery was omnipresent in New Orleans. Slaves constituted fully 12 percent of the city's population in 1860.[43] They worked in every kind of job, from drayman to bookseller, and the labor force of several major industries was composed largely of slaves.[44] It is quite likely that the building trades employed slave labor as well.

Indeed, James Gallier, Sr., who launched his career in England at the very time abolitionist agitation was mounting, owned a crew of slaves in New Orleans in the 1830s and employed them at his sawmill in Lafayette City. Benjamin Howard, brother of the architect, also owned a number of slaves and leased an entire building to quarter them.[45] While it cannot be proved that either Gallier or Benjamin Howard used their slaves in construction, it is likely that they did so.

No such doubts surround Samuel Jamison who, with his partner James McIntosh, was one of the most active builders in the Garden District. Census records from 1860 indicate that the partnership of Jamison and McIntosh owned no fewer than fifty-seven slaves, making it the tenth largest slaveholder in Orleans Parish.[46] The firm's ranking among its uptown peers was even higher: with five of the ten largest slaveholders in the parish being Creole and two of the remaining Anglo-Saxons being planters by profession, Jamison and McIntosh were among the three largest Anglo-Saxon slaveholders in the city.

In spite of these figures, there are practical reasons for thinking that most Garden District mansions were constructed by free labor. Construction in New Orleans slowed or even stopped during the hot summer months, but slaves had to be fed and housed whether or not they were working. More important, the uncertainty of commissions also meant that builders who relied on slave labor had to bear high fixed costs at considerable risk. Unless a builder functioned on the scale of Jamison and McIntosh, it was simply unprofitable, and unnecessary, to sustain such a burden.

An alternative was to hire slaves by the day. Unfortunately, surviving data from the Garden District and Lafayette do not permit any firm conclusions on the extent of this practice there.

Ledgers of the Cook and Moorhouse firm for 1858 list workers named Peter, August, Antoin (sic), and Russell. All were salaried employees, but were they also slaves? Whatever their status, they—or their owners—received two dollars per day, the going rate for semiskilled labor in construction. If Peter, August, Antoin, and Russell were indeed hired slaves, they did not enable Messrs. Cook and Moorhouse to achieve any economies.[47]

The bulk of Cook and Moorhouse's artisans and laborers were Irishmen, with names like Flynn, McCaffree, Murphy, and Hogan. Their daily wages were the same as those of Peter, August, Antoin, and Russell. This conforms to the observations of Frederick Law Olmsted, who visited New Orleans in 1853: "the majority of the cartmen, hackneycoach men, porters, rail road hands, public wait-ers, and common laborers . . . appear to be white men."[48] Inexpensive immigrant labor was shouldering out slavery.

The 1860 Census for the Fourth District of New Orleans pro-vides a detailed view of the men who made up the building trade in Lafayette and the Garden District.[49] Artisans from elsewhere in the city also worked in these neighborhoods, just as many of the crafts-men domiciled in the Fourth District worked on jobs elsewhere in New Orleans. But the census data give a clear picture of those arti-sans domiciled in the Fourth District. Over 600 people identified themselves as "carpenters." Of these, only two were New Orleans-born and eighty-four—13 percent of the total—were Louisiana natives; four out of five of the latter were free blacks. The rest of the 213 American-born carpenters came from elsewhere, half hailing from the Northeast, with natives of New York, Pennsylvania, and Massachusetts predominating. Together, carpenters from the northeastern states constituted the largest group of American-born members of this craft, with free blacks from elsewhere in Louisiana being the second largest group.

Against these 213 American-born carpenters was a group of 403 immigrant carpenters. More than eighty came from Ireland, while some forty more had arrived from England and Scotland. The French, in contrast, were barely represented, with only seventeen carpenters.

The single largest group of carpenters working in the Garden District were Germans who, with 228 members, outnumbered by nearly two-and-a-half times the second largest immigrant group,

the Irish, and almost three times above the third largest group, Americans born outside Louisiana. German immigrants were drawn from many of the states around the republic, but the largest group arrived from the Catholic South, notably from the states of Baden and Bavaria. While there were many Prussians, Saxony and the other states of the Protestant North were poorly represented. Together, these Germanic carpenters constituted well over half of the foreign-born majority and two-fifths of all carpenters in the uptown district of New Orleans. In addition to being more numer-ous than other groups, the Germans were also more cohesive. Unlike the British, not to mention the native Louisianians, they brought with them a strong tradition of guild organization and hence were quicker to organize themselves for enterprises capable of completing the major building projects. It is scarcely surprising that Germans dominated the all-important craft of carpentry in uptown New Orleans at the time the Garden District was being built.

Statistics on other artisans tell a similar story. Half the brick-layers were European-born, with Germans constituting over a third of the total. Two-thirds of the painters and over half of the masons were natives of Europe. Immigrants also figured prominently in the plasterers' trade but in this instance the Irish outnumbered the Germans.

These figures may somewhat distort the situation, for New Orleans craftsmen and workers took work in whatever area of the city it was available. Even a number of native-born craftsmen from the Creole faubourgs likely constructed houses in the Garden District. There were limits to such interchange, however. Builders and contractors hired the laborers most readily at hand, and work-ers from the immediate neighborhood resented the intrusion on their territory of workers from other neighborhoods. Balancing these various considerations, then, it is safe to assume the Garden District was constructed mainly by Europeans, principally Germans.

[LEFT] *Museums of exotic woods: the newel post at the Morris house, 1869*

[FACING PAGE] *Joseph C. Morris house, 1331 First Street, 1869. Designed and built by Scotsmen Samuel Jamison and James McIntosh, two of Orleans Parish's largest slaveholders*

An early balloon frame for the Garden District, 1847 (THE HISTORIC NEW ORLEANS COLLECTION; ORIGINAL, NEW ORLEANS NOTARIAL ARCHIVES)

THE MATERIALS

Maybe architects are never as free as they think. New Orleans architects and builders were constrained by their clients' whims and by the capabilities of the local labor force. No less important, they were limited by the materials available for their use.

Architects today concentrate on designing and assume that virtually any material they desire can be obtained, if the cost is right. Antebellum architects in New Orleans did not enjoy this luxury. Building materials were in short supply. As a result, architects were preoccupied with the problem of selecting and obtaining them. The ambitious architect spent much time pouring through reports on materials and where to get them, and prowling through the back rooms of local supply houses. Exacting details about materials filled the building specifications. Indeed, almost all of the twenty-two entries in Henry Howard's specifications for the modest Norton house at 1617 Fourth Street pertained to this subject.[50]

The geography of New Orleans complicated the situation. Swampy land produced little good building timber except cypress. There is no local stone and the alluvial soil is useless for the manufacture of hard bricks. Even nails had to be imported from iron-producing regions. So great were the problems of materials that early architects and builders made every effort to shift responsibility for their procurement to the patron or client. When Jean Murville Harang contracted for the construction of his twelve-room home on Tchoupitoulas Street in 1832, now demolished, his master builder, Hesechiah Thistle, insisted that Harang himself supply bricks and other supplies.[51] By the 1850s contractors were generally expected to furnish their own materials and to vouch for their quality. Yet as late as 1869, when the Blaffer house at 1328 Felicity Street was built, the owner was still required by contract to purchase the bricks.[52]

The most important building material for Garden District houses was wood. Frames, floors, most interior trim, and even columns were wooden. In the early nineteenth-century days before the rise of the so-called balloon frame, which made it possible to construct building with cheap mass-produced nails rather than laboriously hand-fitted wooden pegs, all structural wood had to be seasoned before use.[53] Demand for seasoned lumber was so great that it was imported into New Orleans from as far afield as Florida.

The introduction of the balloon frame in the 1840s transformed American building and quickened the pace of new construction in the Garden District during the 1850s. Houses could be framed with a simple, self-reinforcing structure of inexpensive 2 inch x 4 inch joists, held in place with wire nails. Details of this technique were set forth with great clarity in an 1847 drawing for a house on Magazine between First and Second Streets.[54] The draftsman was a free man of color, Joseph Chateau.

One frequently hears that old New Orleans houses are "built entirely of cypress." To be sure, when Charles Conrad contracted for the construction of his raised cottage, he specified that all exposed wood be cypress.[55] Similarly, in 1852 the wealthy planter Bernard Kock demanded cypress flooring for his house at 1206 Third Street.[56] But such lavishness was exceptional. While cypress was twice as durable as pine or white oak, it was difficult and expensive to obtain. The largest stands were in virtually inaccessible marshes. Moreover, the Louisiana State legislature imposed harsh penalties for cutting cypress trees on public lands. As a result the cypress industry did not really develop until the 1880s, after the construction boom in the Garden District had passed.[57]

Most wood used in the early Garden District was yellow pine shipped in from the rolling land across Lake Pontchartrain and from Mississippi. Manuel Goldsmith's house at 1122 Jackson Avenue, for example, was built almost exclusively of pine,[58] as was the later Blaffer house.[59] The 1859 contract for the Forcheimer double house specified that yellow pine be used not only for the frame but for the exterior siding and floors; only the front steps were built of lesser quality cypress.[60]

As if to compensate for such modesty in material, builders frequently turned the grand stairways into virtual museums of exotic woods. Mahogany was frequently specified for handrailings, preferably the closegrained variety from Santo Domingo. Oak, tulip, and other ornamental woods were employed for spindles.

The short supply of cut and seasoned timber accounted for the extensive use of boards from broken-up flatboats. Acute shortages of sash and millwork also prevailed. An undocumented local tradition claims that Thomas Toby imported all the millwork for his house from his native Philadelphia. When the St. Charles Hotel was constructed in 1835–37, much of the millwork was ordered from

[ABOVE] *Brick and flagstone paving, First near Prytania Streets*

[FACING PAGE] *The obviously expensive mantel at Manuel Goldsmith's house,*
1122 Jackson Avenue; architects Henry Howard and Albert Diettel, 1859

the Baghdad Sash Factory in Santa Rosa, Florida. The Hinckle Guild and Company of Cincinnati is also known to have shipped large amounts of its products to New Orleans in the years in which the Garden District was under construction.[61]

To remedy the various shortages, steam-powered lumber and sash mills opened in New Orleans and nearby towns in Louisiana and Mississippi during the early-nineteenth century. By 1854 the Bemard Lumber Company of New Orleans could boast that it had at hand a million board feet of yellow pine from Mississippi.[62] Waterman and Company operated at a comparable scale. Payroll records show that even the small and specialized Louisiana Sash Factory maintained a labor force of several dozen men, all of them working twelve-hour days, six days a week.[63]

It was a lucrative business. Throughout the mid-1850s the Brownlee firm, which supplied Peter Middlemass, Gallier and Turpin, and practically every other Garden District builder, paid 90 percent of its bills in cash for amounts up to $1,000.[64]

Until the expansion of the lumber industry on the eve of the Civil War, demand chronically outstripped supply. As James Gallier observed, "The sawmills were few in number, and the demands upon them so great, that buildings were often much delayed from this cause."[65] To remedy this, and also to capitalize on a good business opportunity, several architects and builders established their own lumber mills. Gallier purchased a sawmill covering three city blocks in Lafayette City. The former owner, banker Thomas Barrett, included a payroll of twenty-five slaves in the sale.[66] Another builder-architect, Captain John A. Muir, bought the Hard Times Sawmill. Both Gallier and Muir were convinced this would secure a steady source of essential building materials for their architectural work.

One might think that the rapid industrialization of the building trades would have been accompanied by a similar growth in the standardization of materials. While identical mass-produced Greek-key doorways, transom moldings, and other fittings appeared on many Garden District buildings, the variety of basic materials remained great. This was not due to the manufacturers but to the unchanged habits of builders and architects. When architect Abram Howell contracted to build Luther Stewart's house, his

specifications called for nine different sizes of wood: 8" x 10"; 3" x 12"; 3" x 11"; 3" x 10"; 3" x 7"; 3" x 6"; 3" x 5"; 4" x 6"; and 3" x 4".[67]

An equally bewildering diversity of materials was specified both for modest structures like McLaughlin's Bar at Jackson Avenue and St. Thomas Street and for such elegant residences as Lewis Reynolds's home for the widow Oury on Second Street opposite Clay Square.[68] Garden District building thus stood at the threshold between the ancient handcraft tradition and modern industrialization, its architects and builders lagging the progress of cut-wood products by commercial manufacturers.

During the early American period in New Orleans, immigrants from Baltimore and Philadelphia tried to replicate the sturdy brick dwellings they had known in those cities. Short of importing brick from afar, most local builders used the relatively durable fired clay bricks from the northern shore of Lake Pontchartrain. Soft "river bricks" or "batture bricks" produced by the sprawling Delachaise Brick Works on the Mississippi at Louisiana Avenue were inexpensive but of poor quality. More than one lawsuit arose when clients accused their builders of resorting to the cheaper product. During the construction of Walter G. Robinson's Third Street mansion, for example, the builder used soft *batture* brick for one of the six-thousand gallon cisterns. It soon burst, causing a flood that damaged the foundation of the main house.[69]

Because neither river brick nor lake brick withstood intense heat, all fire-resistant bricks had to be imported to New Orleans. Henry Howard, who never spared the wallets of his Garden District clients, invariably called for the best English firebrick in his contracts. Most architects widely used a less costly firebrick produced in Pittsburgh.

No less important than the quality of the bricks was the mortar used to bind them. The loam of New Orleans was useless for making cement. Masons knew that the quality of their work depended on the materials and went far afield in search of good lime and sand. The invariable favorites specified in building contracts for the most expensive Garden District houses were sand from Natchez or Horn Island, Mississippi, and lime from either Thomaston, Georgia, or Cape Girardeau, Missouri. During the forty years after his arrival from New York in 1831, tomb builder Newton Richards made a considerable fortune supplying these goods to the building trade.[70]

As early as the eighteenth century, only tiled roofs were permitted on buildings in the city's center by the Spanish city council (or cabildo) of New Orleans following several disastrous fires. During the Anglo-American build-up of the Garden District, slate replaced Spanish tile as the preferred roofing material. There being no slate in the region, New Orleanians had to look elsewhere. Through a curious chain of circumstances, practically every roof in the Garden District came to be covered with slate from Wales. The cause of this unlikely development lay in the circumstances of trade. Large ships bore bulky cargos of cotton from New Orleans to Liverpool. Rather than return empty, they were filled with anything that would find a buyer in the Crescent City. The firm of Lyall Davidson and Company made handsome profits by importing slate. The same firm also marketed the English ridge tiles that were de riguer everywhere in the Garden District.[71]

Flagstones for paving were another unusual item imported on the deadhead return run from Liverpool. During the cotton boom, hundreds of tons of flagstones were shipped to New Orleans from England and north Germany. Discriminating Garden District homeowners like Bernard Kock generally favored the greenish stone from Bremen for their pavements and sidewalks. Their judgment was sound, for Kock's sidewalk at 1206 Third Street is still intact.

As prosperity waxed, so did the desire of New Orleanians to encrust their homes with marble. A bevy of local businessmen rushed to meet the demand, importing marble from as far away as Italy. The cemeteries, of course, provided a steady demand for custom marble work, but it was the growth of the building trades that opened vast horizons for mass production and standardization. Such items as mantels, lintels, and window sills were standardized long before the Civil War. It was sufficient for an architect simply to specify in the contract the cost of an item in marble for the builder to know what was called for. The seventy-five-dollar mantels at Luther Stewart's house were indistinguishable from the seventy-five-dollar mantels elsewhere in the neighborhood, just as the expensive mantels at Henry Buckner's mansion are identical to the mantels at the Perkins house across Jackson Avenue.

Little hardware was produced in New Orleans. Local newspapers and most editions of the city directory featured advertisements by firms that imported hardware from the North. The main purveyor was the house of Priestley and Bern, which specialized in New York wares. Glass, too, had to be brought from the North, but if "American" glass was acceptable for inexpensive homes and outbuildings, architects invariably specified "French cylinder glass" for use in the major villas. Good examples of this almost flawless glass can still be seen in the houses of Robert Grinnan and Albert Brevard. After the Civil War, double-thick polished plate glass made its debut in New Orleans. At the Blaffer and Weis residences, plate glass made possible window panes far larger than commonly found earlier.

The nineteenth century, called the age of steam and iron, made one great contribution to the materials of architecture: cast iron. The most important achievements of cast iron in architecture, of course, were structural, permitting heretofore unimagined bridges, arches, and towers. Cast iron was also used for ornamental purposes, on commercial and domestic architecture.

One of the earliest manifestations of this new material in the Garden District can still be seen at Jacob Payne's house at 1134 First Street, where the capitals of the Ionic columns are of cast iron. Each is embossed with the date, 1848, and with its place of manufacture, New York. The earliest cast iron in New Orleans was imported from the North—Philadelphia, Pittsburgh, and Cincinnati, as well as New York.[72] Local demand was considerable, and astute entrepreneurs established local branch offices of national firms, the most important of these being Wood and Perrot Company of Philadelphia, which in 1858 joined with Charles A. Miltenberger of New Orleans to form Wood, Miltenberger and Company. It is to this firm that the Garden District owes its most famous example of cast iron, the cornstalk fence surrounding Colonel Short's villa on Fourth Street at Prytania. The fence was ordered from the catalogue issued in Philadelphia, which contained over fifty patterns.[73]

New Orleans acquired its own architectural iron foundries beginning in the 1820s.[74] Several firms founded in the 1840s and 1850s were particularly active. Jacob Baumiller, for example, produced the delicate two-story gallery at Captain Thomas Leathers's

[ABOVE] *Cast-iron fence at Captain Leathers's house, 2027 Carondolet Street. Henry Howard and Henry Thiberge, architects, 1857*

[LEFT] *Cornstalk fence from Wood, Miltenberger and Co., at Col. Robert Henry Short's villa, 1448 Fourth Street, by Henry Howard, 1859*

house in 1859, and in 1869 the spectacular gallery that dominates the J. C. Morris house.[75] John Armstrong's foundry created an equally impressive gallery for Mr. Armstrong's residence at 2805 Carondolet Street in 1869.[76]

Neither the Baumiller nor Armstrong foundries specialized in architectural ironwork. Both of them, and most of the others in the field, mostly built steam engines and boilers for riverboats and sugar refineries. Architectural ironwork was a sideline, albeit a lucrative one. Local firms were producing iron grates, carriage guards, and stoves by the 1850s, competing with similar goods manufactured in Louisville, Cincinnati, and New York and sold through Bernardin Nature's home furnishing store on Chartres Street in the Vieux Carré. By the late 1860s, mass-produced cast-iron fences from local foundries lined the Garden District, many of the same patterns being used to surround tombs in Lafayette Cemetery. By then, too, architectural ironwork from New Orleans foundries was being sent north, eventually finding its way to such distant points as Wooster Square in New Haven, Connecticut.

Mass-produced architectural ironwork became ubiquitous in New Orleans, but it was the custom-designed and specially manufactured two-story galleries that had the greatest impact on Garden District architecture. The Baumiller works produced the first such items in the 1850s. Not until the postwar years, however, and especially the mid-1870s, did they really become popular. Then the fashion spread rapidly. In quick succession the two small houses on Washington Avenue that formerly belonged to James Robb, the J. J. Warren home at 1531 Jackson Avenue, and Michel Musson's former residence on 1331 Third Street were all equipped with ironwork galleries. The same feature completely transformed the character of many other Garden District facades—some might say romanticized—at this time.

Close inspection of these elaborate cast-iron structures reveals that most were made up of standardized elements. Yet in each case these stock components were adapted to the scale and format of the specific house. The foundrymen who carried out this subtle work remain unknown. Yet their impact on the architecture of the Garden District was as positive as it was immense.

Many Garden District facades took on a more romantic look in the postwar years by adding a two-story ironwork gallery: the Carroll house, 1315 First Street, 1870s

Transformed, romanticized…and cooled by adding iron-work galleries: Musson house, 1331 Third Street

Reviewing the building trades in nineteenth-century New Orleans, it can be seen that they exerted a decisive influence over what was actually built. To succeed, an architect—and his patron—had to be willing to work closely with the builders, suppliers, and craftsmen and to acknowledge them as partners in a collective endeavor.

There were, however, two circumstances under which one of the three chief human actors in a building project—the patron, architect, and builder/craftsman—could take control. First, a determined patron could, if he were rich enough, substitute one of the "pawners" with another person of his own choosing. James Robb did just that when he brought in an outside architect and his own principal artisans. Second, a particularly creative and strong-willed architect could take command of the situation, forcing the patron and builder to accept the program he set for them. The undeveloped state of the architectural profession in nineteenth-century New Orleans made this a rare occurrence. However, there were two Garden District architects who were endowed with the such inventiveness and force of personality: Henry Howard and Lewis E. Reynolds.

CHAPTER SIX *Architects of Opulence*

ｒ

RARELY HAS NEW ORLEANS attracted master architects. Throughout the period of French rule the city was a pestiferous swamp, thoroughly uninviting to the architecturally ambitious. Ignace François Broutin, engineer to the king, produced a number of grandiose schemes for the city, but few were actually built.[1] The city prospered under Spanish rule, yet its character as a provincial trading center was only reinforced.[2] Were it not for the initiative of one man, Don Andres Almonester y Roxas, the city would have entered the period of American rule without a single major monument other than the Ursuline Convent.[3] Even with Almonester's munificence, Spanish New Orleans remained a pale echo of the great rococo centers in Havana and elsewhere in the Spanish New World. Nor did the situation improve markedly under American rule. New Orleans attracted a genuine master in Benjamin Henry Latrobe, the supervising architect of the United States Capitol, but he succumbed to yellow fever before he could leave a strong and lasting mark on the city.

The first substantial signs of change appeared in the 1830s, when James Dakin and James Gallier, Sr., arrived from New York. Thanks to these two men, the architectural ambitions of New Orleans began to match its economic achievements. In Dakin's Union Terrace (1834, demolished) and

University of Louisiana (1847, demolished), and in Gallier's City Hall (1850) or St. Charles Hotel (1837, demolished), New Orleans' architecture finally attained a national level of accomplishment. Yet for all their distinction, the New Orleans designs of Dakin and especially of Gallier are essentially conservative, the careful elaboration of ideas which they and other architects had developed earlier in New York. Perhaps it was only the French-born Jacques Nicolas Bussiere De Pouilly who created something unprecedented in North America, with his grandly formal St. Louis Hotel, built in the Vieux Carré in 1835. Even here he invoked the buildings of the Rue de Rivoli in Paris as his model.

Whatever the attainments of Dakin, Gallier, and De Pouilly, their careers did not extend into the great building boom of the 1850s. As a result, the Garden District emerged with a severe liability. There existed no sharply defined local school of architecture whose concepts could be applied to the new setting. Nor were there among New Orleans architects any towering figures that were predestined to dominate work in the new suburb. Of necessity, Garden District patrons were compelled to seek out fresh talent when it appeared.

Several promising young architects first developed their art in the Garden District. William A. Freret, for example, possessed a fluent command of the latest national fashions, as demonstrated in his own house at 1524 Third Street. James Collins, while less well known than Freret, also bears mention, particularly for his central role in formulating the type of five-bay columned and galleried mansion that became so typical of the new suburb. Continuing the pattern of nearly all New Orleans architects before them, however, Freret and Collins were essentially provincials, adapting and combining preexisting elements to form a graceful (albeit local) vernacular, rather than introducing fresh, new elements.

Only two architects working in the antebellum Garden District exhibited a measure of genuine originality: Henry Howard and Lewis E. Reynolds. At his death, Howard was eulogized as "one of the most accomplished and reliable architects this city has ever known."[4] Reynolds, in spite of his fitful efforts at self-promotion, was never as well known as Howard, although some of the District's most discerning patrons passed him from hand to hand like a rare treasure. Both architects were prolific. Henry Howard

designed over two dozen Garden District residences, while the list of Reynolds's known works in the District stands at ten and continues to grow with fresh research.

Whether by qualitative or quantitative measures, Howard and Reynolds were the premier architects of the antebellum Garden District. Curiously, however, both master designers dropped completely from memory within a few decades of their deaths. Nearly all Howard's finest works came to be attributed erroneously to James Gallier, Sr., a mistake that was perpetuated even by so eminent a national authority as Talbot Hamlin.[5] Reynolds suffered from similar misattributions, and in the case of his splendid Bradish Johnson house at 2343 Prytania Street, the mistake is enshrined on a bronze plaque.[6] Fortunately, the living testimony of the work of both architects speaks more truly and eloquently than does fickle memory. Their numerous surviving works establish Henry Howard and Lewis E. Reynolds as the architects of opulence in the Garden District.

PARALLEL LIVES

Fate employed nearly identical patterns in shaping the lives of the two men who stood at the apogee of New Orleans architectural life in the 1850s. They were born two years apart, Reynolds in 1816 and Howard in 1818. They were almost a generation younger than New York style-setters Alexander Jackson Davis and Minard Lafever. Howard was an Anglo-Irishman from County Cork. After training with his father, a builder and architect, he emigrated to New York in 1836, just in time for the economic panic. Reynolds came from a well-established family in Norwich, New York, but chose to make his own way in the world, moving first to Cincinnati, then to Louisville, and finally to Manhattan shortly before Howard's arrival there.[7]

Both men entered architecture through the crafts of carpentry and stairbuilding. They met in New York and the two young journeymen set out together for the booming West, reaching

Galveston, Texas, late in 1836. It took them only a few months to realize that New Orleans offered more fertile ground for aspiring carpenters than did Galveston. After an initial trip on the schooner *Flash* in March 1837, they returned a month later to settle permanently in the Crescent City.[8]

The fastest way an aspiring carpenter or builder could get ahead was to win the support of someone already established in the field. Howard and Reynolds were fortunate to join Edward Sewell, an English-born builder responsible for more major construction in New Orleans during the 1830s than James Gallier and James Dakin combined.[9] Judging by the number of projects by Sewell with which they were both associated, it is evident they were introduced to the peculiarities of New Orleans architectural life in his office.

Both Howard and Reynolds also made contact with the architect James Dakin. Howard claimed actually to have studied with Dakin, who fostered the young Irishman's career over many years.[10] Reynolds's tie with Dakin may well have dated to 1836, when Reynolds was briefly in Louisville and Dakin's renowned Bank of Louisville was under construction. They certainly met later in 1836 when Reynolds went to New York, where Dakin had his office, and stayed in touch thereafter. The New Orleans Public Library preserves a copy of Reynolds's *A Treatise on Handrailing* inscribed to James H. Dakin. The monograph was published in 1849 at a time when Reynolds served as "superintending architect" of the Custom House in New Orleans. In August of 1850 Dakin revised the initial plans and Reynolds, in a letter to his patron and friend, supported Dakin's proposals.[11] It is significant that both Howard and Reynolds gravitated toward Dakin, whose best work exhibits boldness and experimentalism, rather than toward the more stolidly competent Gallier. In the end the two younger men were to put Dakin's influence to quite different use, but they shared a common point of departure. Each learned, processed, and absorbed much from Dakin during several years as journeyman-draftsman. This exposed them each to still further influences, in Howard's case to the skilled and successful Prussian-born architect, Henry Molhausen.[12] The measure of the two young men's success as draftsmen is that Howard decided to concentrate solely on design rather than building, and Reynolds continued to draft for contractors throughout his later career.

Conventional and efficient: Julius Forcheimer's double dwelling, 2331–33 Magazine Street, by Henry Howard, 1859

Henry Howard's house for John Moore, 1228 Race Street in Coliseum Square, 1867; Frederick Wing, builder

During the half-decade before 1843, various schemes and projects took Lewis E. Reynolds away from New Orleans. Howard stayed put and succeeded in winning his first commission in 1844, the D'Arcy house, now moved to 1427 Second Street in the Garden District. Reynolds's first known commission came the following year, a two-story frame building with kitchen at St. Charles Avenue and Erato Street, now demolished.[13]

From this point on both careers flourished. The restlessness that had driven each man to New York, Galveston, and then New Orleans was by no means spent. Howard briefly moved his entire office to Thibodaux, Louisiana, after 1845 in order to capitalize on an anticipated building boom in the Bayou Lafourche area. Reynolds, who nominally kept an office at 31 Camp Street in New Orleans, continued to accept odd assignments from builders and contractors, and he might even have spent some time in Howard's office.[14]

The New Orleans careers of Howard and Reynolds rapidly gained momentum in the late 1840s. Once Howard captured the design work for Banks' Arcade on Magazine Street and helped complete and stabilize the rebuilt St. Charles Hotel, he became one of the city's most sought after architects for commercial buildings. Lewis E. Reynolds fared equally well, as a result of his work on Factors Row on Perdido Street, on Jackson and Manson's store on New Levee Street, on the Canal Bank on Camp Street, and on the St. James Hotel on Magazine Street. Nor was either man lacking in prestigious patrons. Both James Robb and Charles Conrad brought commissions to Reynolds, while Howard gained a virtual monopoly on designing the urban residences of planters such as Evans Jones McCall of Evan Hall Plantation and Charles Kock of Belle Alliance.

Then, as now, patrons hired the person as much as the architect. Howard's and Reynolds's commissions can be easily traced through whole offices of business partners. After Simon Forcheimer commissioned Howard to design his double house at 2331–33 Magazine Street in 1859, his partner, Manuel Goldsmith, engaged Howard for his home nearby at 1122 Jackson Avenue. In much the same way, Henry S. Buckner hired Reynolds to design his great residence at 1410 Jackson Avenue shortly after Buckner's partner in Natchez, Henry Stanton, had turned to Reynolds to design Stanton Hall in that city.

*William Perkins house, 1411 Jackson Avenue,
by Lewis E. Reynolds, 1853*

Is this a further example of the patrons' caution and coolness toward innovation? When contrasted to James Robb's resolve in bringing in an architect from the outside, this is surely the case. However, there is no surviving evidence that would suggest that Howard's or Reynolds's employment by closely linked business associates imposed artistic impediments on them. These two architects, at least, were fortunate to have attracted some of the most confident and supportive patrons in the Garden District. The major houses they designed endure as statements by the architects themselves and not solely the composite results of their patrons' whims.

Since both Henry Howard and Lewis Reynolds were very productive, it is no simple task to identify their finest designs in New Orleans or the Garden District. Any list would at least include Reynolds's now demolished residence for Samuel Kennedy on Camp Street and Henry Howard's exceptional home for John Moore at 1228 Race Street in Coliseum Square. To select is to exclude, perhaps unfairly. Nonetheless, three surviving houses by each architect

command particular attention because of their robust conception and their confident execution. No buildings in New Orleans more richly reward close study than Henry Howard's residences for Robert Grinnan, Robert Henry Short, and Walter Robinson, or Lewis E. Reynolds's houses for William Perkins, Henry S. Buckner, and Bradish Johnson. Whether viewed in the context of these architects' complete works or against the background of the architecture of the Garden District, of the city, or of the region, they are outstanding and enduring monuments.

The first major Garden District residences designed by Howard and Reynolds went up in 1850 and 1853, respectively. Both the Robert Grinnan house at 2221 Prytania Street and the William Perkins house three blocks away at 1411 Jackson Avenue date from the early period when Lafayette was being absorbed into New Orleans. The Garden District still retained its bucolic character, and social forms were still sufficiently individualistic to find expression in diverse architectural styles.

Superficially, at least, both the Grinnan and Perkins residences of 1850 harken back to the great age of the Greek Revival in America. The Grinnan house's one-story columned portico, with its exuberant Corinthian capitals, dentiled cornice, and cast-iron anthemia, stands in the direct line of descent from the strongest Greek Revival work of several decades before in the Northeast. Doorways, interior window frames, and moldings present a kind of exhibition of motifs in the style of Minard Lafever.

Due to "improvements" inflicted on the Perkins house to make it suitable for a nursery school, it is hard to discern its original interiors. They appear to have been far more chaste than those of the Grinnan residence, depending for their effect on sheer spatial volume than on any masterpiece of the plasterer's art. In its severity the Perkins house, too, owes a certain debt to the Greek Revival.

Although these two residences draw on Greek Revival ornamental conventions, their basic forms were up to the minute. Both are asymmetrical in plan, grouping the three main receiving rooms in ways that had never before been seen in New Orleans. The principal mass of the Grinnan residence is rectangular, and the proportions conform to none of the ratios that were considered appropriate by pedantic masters of the Grecian style. The basic rectangular mass of the main bloc is enriched by the addition of a large square element that is placed deliberately so as to heighten the freedom of the plan.

In much the same way, the two-story portico of the Perkins house is a misleading front for a notably free complex of rooms. Far from masking this innovation on the exterior, as earlier New Orleans architects would have done, Reynolds flaunts it, even to the point of imposing a prominent round arch to the left of the two-story portico and repeating the arch in a two-story gallery set back still further from the main entrance.

In all but its most sophisticated versions, the Greek Revival was a rectilinear architecture of two-dimensional facades. The Grinnan and Perkins residences, in contrast, are anything but, carefully conceived architectural masses that present interesting vistas on every exposure. Consistent with this more sophisticated approach, their architects took pains to prevent the servants' wings from being jarring appendages and hid the unsightly cisterns under the roofs.

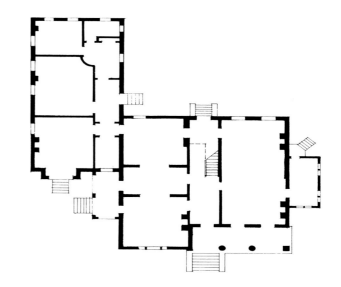

[ABOVE] *The Perkins house, by Reynolds*
(MCGILLIVRAY AND VILDOSTEGUI)

[FACING PAGE] *Minard Lafever's influence at Londoner Robert Grinnen's house, 2221 Prytania Street. Henry Howard, architect, 1850*

[LEFT] *Receding doorways, Robinson house*

[BELOW] *A five-bay dwelling built to grandiose scale for Walter G. Robinson, 1415 Third Street, by Henry Howard, 1859*

[FACING PAGE] *Howard's restrained doorway for the Henry T. Lonsdale house, 2521–23 Prytania Street. J. K. Collins & Co., builders, 1856*

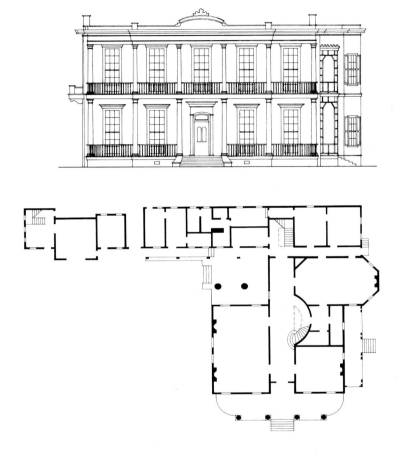

Robinson house, by Henry Howard (MCGILLIVRAY AND VILDOSTEGUI)

By these various means Henry Howard and Lewis E. Reynolds injected into New Orleans architecture a full measure of the sculpturalism, openness, and laconism that characterized Italianate revival design in America. To this extent, at least, Howard and others were justified in referring to Grinnan's house as a "villa." The Perkins residence, too, is a villa, but lacks the strong horizontality that is the style's hallmark. The rounded arches and the balustrade atop the roof were then fresh departures for New Orleans, even though they were executed with an almost shy restraint.

The Grinnan and Perkins residences are somewhat reserved in detail, while they introduced striking innovations in basic plans. It is emblematic of the fate of architectural design in New Orleans that neither house ever served as a prototype for other residences. True, Howard reworked certain elements of the Grinnan house into the 1858 residence of Shepherd Brown on Coliseum Street in the Lower Garden District.[15] Nonetheless, with this one exception, it is fair to say that these two great houses blazed trails that were not followed.

Following these lively projects, the Garden District architecture of both Howard and Reynolds became more measured. As earlier noted, Howard's villa for Colonel Robert Henry Short at Prytania and Fourth streets pays homage to the classic London plan house, with its three-bay facade, asymmetrical hall, and double parlors. Similarly, what little is known of Reynolds's house for Samuel Kennedy suggests that this large residence, too, retained the outer form of the simple raised cottage. The innovations in both cases were on the interior. The intensification of social life in the 1850s placed a premium on the large, open spaces that were created in both instances. The Short villa was by far the more original of the two, if only because of its placement on a corner lot with its formal facade on the cross street. As a consequence, one "reads" the house from the side, thus transforming it from an expanded but narrow town house to a rambling, asymmetrical, and grandly Italianate mansion.

In the last years before the Civil War, Henry Howard and Lewis E. Reynolds both found Garden District patrons whose architectural ambitions equaled their own, and whose wealth matched the task. It took little searching for either Walter G. Robinson or Henry S. Buckner to discover his architect. Each

Henry S. Buckner house, 1410 Jackson Avenue in the late 1850s, with belvedere. Lewis E. Reynolds, architect, 1850

patron had earlier lived within a block of a major residence by his future designer, and Buckner had an example of Reynolds's skill in the Perkins house, directly across Jackson Avenue from his own lot. Moreover, each architect was at the pinnacle of fashion, with Howard hard at work on Cyprien Dufour's magnificent residence on Esplanade Avenue and Reynolds occupied with Dr. George W. Campbell's imposing house on St. Charles Street downtown, now demolished.

Aside from their enormous scale, there would appear to he few points of similarity between Howard's Robinson residence of 1859 at 1415 Third Street and Reynolds's Buckner mansion of 1857 at 1410 Jackson Avenue. The one stands as the epitome of the five-bay columnar house, and the other, with its galleries on all sides, hints at a kind of classicized Creole mansion. Stripped of porticos and galleries, however, they are strikingly similar applications of the standard center-hall design. True, Howard's long salon completely absorbs the usual double parlors, which remain discrete in Reynolds's plan. Also, Howard placed his stairway at the center of the

hall, while Reynolds's stairs stood like a gigantic freestanding sculpture at the rear of the hall. Otherwise, the plans strongly resemble each other.

The chief difference is the same as in the Grinnan and Perkins houses, namely the horizontality of Howard's building and the verticality of Reynolds's. The airy galleries, with their system of columns extending from ground level to attic cornice, heightened this effect in Reynolds's design for Buckner. A belvedere, now greatly modified, reinforced it still further. In its original form the belvedere, like the Buckner house as a whole, recalls the strong vertical thrust of such classics of Federal-style architecture as the 1815 Hayes Manor of Edenton, North Carolina. Withal, the Buckner house gives the illusion of crowning a hillock, while the Robinson house, with its dependencies stretching horizontally around to the left side, is firmly planted on the alluvial plain.

These same qualities are paralleled once more in Howard's Dufour house on Esplanade Avenue in the Creole section of town and Reynolds's Campbell mansion in Faubourg Ste. Marie, both

[FACING PAGE] *Napoleon III's Paris on Prytania Street: Bradish Johnson house, 2343 Prytania; by Lewis E. Reynolds, 1872*

[ABOVE LEFT] *Stairhall skylight, Bradish Johnson house*

[ABOVE RIGHT] *Ceiling medallion, Bradish Johnson house*

[RIGHT] *Parlor doorway, Bradish Johnson house*

built in 1859. It is interesting to note, though, that each architect exploited a broader vocabulary outside the Garden District than he did for the Robinson and Buckner houses within it. This richer display outside the Garden District was not always better. If the Dufour house is fully the equal of the Robinson mansion, Reynolds's Campbell residence, with its unrestrained Italianate details, is less successful than the Buckner residence, notwithstanding the lavishness of its sweeping rosewood stairway. Is it possible that the emergence of stylistic harmony within the Garden District imposed a constructive constraint upon Reynolds that was lacking when he worked in the central city? If so, it reflects the general tendency of architects to produce their best work when limited by firm parameters, be they environmental, stylistic, or financial.

Both Henry Howard and Lewis E. Reynolds experienced personal hardship during the Civil War. Following the war, however, their architectural careers rebounded with renewed vigor. Howard designed five Garden District residences in 1867 alone. In the brief postwar prosperity, tendencies in each architect scarcely discernible in earlier commissions now came to the fore. One need only compare Henry Howard's imposing Coliseum Square residence for John Moore with Reynolds's now destroyed house for Lafayette Folger on St. Charles Avenue or his Bradish Johnson house on Prytania Street to see the difference.[16] Howard, it seems, remained loyal to his antebellum ideals, keeping Italianate design elements muted and confining the modestly scaled tower to the rear of the house. Reynolds, in contrast, permitted himself in the Folger mansion to indulge in a veritable orgy of fashionable Italianisms. In much the way the American-born Dakin had experimented more than the consistently solid Anglo-Irishman Gallier, New Yorker Reynolds now turned to the Second Empire style for inspiration. In the Bradish Johnson residence of 1872 he grafted the new French ideals onto the proven five-bay Garden District plan with great skill and élan.

It was Howard who continued to attract the lion's share of work, however, largely from the same grip of well-established clients whom he had served before the war. These were not showmen, and Howard served them well by deftly but cautiously manipulating familiar elements. His proven method, employed on his prewar design for Louis Meyer at 2331–33 Magazine Street, Howard now used in a series of postwar residences.[17] It is not that the architect was incapable of greater boldness: his remodeling of the Crescent Billiard Hall on St. Charles and Canal streets, now a private men's club, is a Renaissance palace worthy of a provincial capital in some old-fashioned and pretentious empire. In such postwar houses as the one for Charles Eager at 1406 Seventh Street or for George Sweet at 1236 Jackson Avenue, however, he chose no more than to dabble with the new gaudy fashions.[18] Apparently, both Howard and his old patrons emerged from the war more cautious than before.

This is in stark contrast to Lewis Reynolds, whose few postwar mansions are among the strongest architectural statements of the era. For Lafayette Folger, a recently enriched hardware merchant from Hudson, New York, Reynolds designed an exuberant mansion in the Italianate style. On this building of 1867–69, which formerly stood at the upriver corner of St. Charles Avenue and Second Street, the architect abandoned all restraint. The interesting plan features the same asymmetrical elements encountered in the Perkins house. Three significant stylistic changes include placing the door at the left of the facade rather than in the center, thus creating an anteroom to the hall; adding a semicircular and robustly columned bay at the left-rear corner of the house; and building a set of rooms behind the hall. These, plus the stage-set rustication, the quoining, and the deep overhangs supported by flashy sculptural brackets, give the building an arrestingly schizophrenic character, exuding pomposity and frivolity.

Reynolds's residence for Bradish Johnson at 2343 Prytania Street reveals an even more venturesome spirit. Here, for the first time, is a major New Orleans mansion designed in the full-blown Second Empire style. Now the Louise S. McGehee School for Girls, the Bradish Johnson house is ornamented with virtually every stylistic feature pioneered by Napoleon III's architects in Paris.

As a New Yorker, Johnson doubtless was more receptive to this new style than most of his Garden District neighbors, who were unaware of its immense impact on the Northeast. For all its superficial freshness, the Johnson residence fits squarely within Reynolds's work as a whole. The facade reverts to the symmetry of the Buckner residence, while the piers supporting the small gallery are drawn from that same source. The spiral of the stairway at the Johnson residence is also said to resemble that of the Buckner

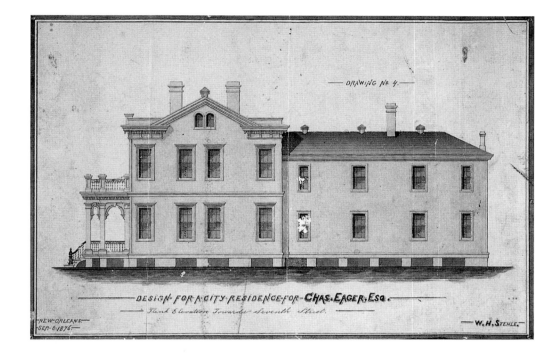

Henry Howard dabbles in the new Second Empire style for Austin Eager, 1406 Seventh Street. W. H. Stehle, draftsman, circa 1860–68 (VICTOR MCGEE)

house, although the latter stairway has long since been removed. Finally, the blocking of the center hall by a set of rooms to the rear is based on the precedent of the Folger house.

If the caution and refinement of Howard's urban residences call to mind James Gallier, Sr., Reynolds's restless quest for new approaches evokes the memory of James Dakin. Indeed, for all the similarities between their lives and their architecture, Howard and Reynolds present a study in contrasts. Howard, the specialized and sober professional, saw mankind as a mine of potential patrons. His social orientation favored the self-made planter who aspired to form a rural aristocracy. His aesthetic orientation, too, was appropriately conservative, with a strong dash of Regency England. Reynolds, in contrast, was an American polymath. Only part architect, he was equally a craftsman, pedagogue, philosopher, visionary, Yankee tinkerer, and crank. The distinctive aspects of each architect's work highlights how broadly the two men differed from one another.

[ABOVE] *Henry Howard goes Italianate: George O. Sweet house, 1236 Jackson Avenue. Frederick Wing, builder, 1874*

[RIGHT] *The Sweet porch…balmy breezes in a warm climate*

Reynolds's Second Empire mansion for Lafayette Folger, 2508 St. Charles Avenue, 1867–69, now demolished (THE HISTORIC NEW ORLEANS COLLECTION; ORIGINAL, NEW ORLEANS NOTARIAL ARCHIVES)

[ABOVE] *Architect Henry Howard* (ROBERT S. BRANTLEY)

[FACING PAGE] *Henry Howard's tribute to Sir John Soane on Third Street: the Robinson stables, 1859*

Henry Howard was above all a specialist. He abjured the role of builder, draftsman, and supervising architect in favor of that of designer. He received pay on the basis of a standardized price list, perhaps based on the one that James Gallier had called for in a publication he wrote and published in New York, prior to his move to New Orleans.[19] Confident in his own vocation, Howard did not hesitate to exert his authority in dealings with patrons. In one contract he loftily stated, "The owner [is] to be allowed the privilege of selecting the [iron] pattern."[20] It is doubtful that any New Orleans architect before Howard would have even thought, let alone actually dared, to permit the patron such freedoms.

Howard participated in the eclecticism of his age, but for his urban residences he worked from a consciously limited palette. Rarely did he match the venturesome spirit of his old mentor, Dakin. Far from being evidence of his limitations, however, his more classical tendencies attest to the rich possibilities inherent in the work of the English Regency masters to which he was exposed as a youth in Britain. Sir John Soane (1753–1837), John Nash (1752–1835), and George Dance (1741–1825) based their architectural design on a combination of clean geometric forms with a minimum of ornamentation. At a few points in his later career Howard did indulge in Victorian lushness, as in the richly decorative interiors of the George Sweet house. Even in these buildings, however, the restraint and refinement of his early classical training is evident. In fact, there are moments when Howard seems to have planted Regency notions directly into the Garden District, as in the exceptionally handsome stable buildings for the Robinson and Leathers mansions. These modest but elegant appendages are among the most perfect buildings remaining from New Orleans' golden age and attest to Howard's subtle creativity in adapting British prototypes to a new environment and new functions.

Whatever Howard's interest in design, it always remained subordinate to his concern for his patrons' comfort. Rooted in the Regency and Greek Revival styles, Howard's residences incorporate the most up-to-date planning concepts to assure the circulation of fresh air and fresh running water. Howard built homes for people, not mere sculptural monuments.

Howard's restrained classicism at the Robert Grinnen house, entrance stairhall, 2221 Prytania Street

Finally, Howard's fundamental orientation was more rural than urban. Raised in Ireland and England, his personality tended toward that of a country squire and sought out members of that class as patrons. This is not to deny, of course, that he designed buildings of every type. Indeed, his 1854 courthouse for Jefferson Parish on Carrollton Avenue, his Jewish Widow and Orphans Home on Jackson Avenue, now demolished, and his girls' high school on Chestnut near Jackson, also demolished, are all notable examples of urban design. Yet it was his plantations—the serenely classical Madewood (1846–48), the dignified Belle Alliance (circa 1848), the vast and ponderous Belle Grove (1853–55, demolished), and the sprawling Nottaway (1857–59)—in which his artistic abilities most flourished.

The urban residences Howard designed for the Garden District are the least interesting aesthetically, simply transplants from the congested downtown faubourgs. But when he enjoyed the space to think in rural terms, as in his designs for the Grinnan and Robinson houses, or the Archibald Montgomery residence at 1213 Third Street, Howard triumphed.[21] The pattern Howard established enabled the Garden District to retain its bucolic character, at the very time when rapid development might have transformed it into a neighborhood only slightly less densely populated than the central city.

REYNOLDS: UPTOWN VISIONARY

Where Howard was all focus and deliberation, Reynolds was the embodiment of restless, unfocused energy. Reynolds could not rival Howard's productivity. Yet his major homes are masterpieces, reflecting a desire to mold taste rather than simply to crystallize it in subtle designs.

In his published autobiography, Reynolds strives heroically to present his life as a carefully designed piece of architecture. He relates how he went to Louisville and New York to place himself "under the direction of distinguished architects." He reports on

"diligently pursuing a prescribed course of study, . . . uniting the theory with the practice of the Art of Design." Rather than establish himself as a working architect, however, Reynolds became a public lecturer. By his own account, he offered courses on building, architecture, and civil engineering at mechanics' institutes in New York, Philadelphia, Baltimore, and Washington. In this capacity he first visited New Orleans in 1833.[22]

Reynolds evidently felt a need to justify his long years as a traveling lecturer; after settling in New Orleans, he claimed in his autobiography to have pursued his new profession "with exemplary diligence and signal success." But this was not quite true. He continued to make lecture tours, and between 1847 and 1852 he never managed to design more than one or two buildings each year. His entire effort for 1848, for example, resulted in only two attached four-story brick buildings, on Gravier Street between Camp and St. Charles. His attention clearly was not on the daily practice of architecture. The contract for these brick buildings actually specifies that every element, from counting room partitions to staircases and shutters, was to be copied from earlier prototypes in the neighborhood.[23] Reynolds's best energies were invested in purely theoretical matters. He assembled a library on architecture that was by far the best in New Orleans at the time, adding to the literature his own *Treatise on Handrailing*, published in New Orleans in 1849.

Even during the busy 1850s Reynolds refused to focus his energies on any one point. It was at this time he entered business as a builder. He designed the now demolished Partee house at Lee Circle and at the same time supervised its construction.[24] By 1854 his name was appearing on numerous building contracts for stores, warehouses, and private homes. Three years later he tried again to make it as an architect, but in the late 1850s he was once more identified in several contracts as builder only.[25] During these same years he served as site architect for the splendid Story Building at Camp and Common streets, now demolished, a cast-iron structure designed by Tiffany and Bottom of Philadelphia and cast in Trenton in 1859.[26] Reynolds had become a wide-ranging enthusiast who lacked the spirit of professional specialization that Howard possessed and that was then on the rise in American architectural circles.

This is not to deny his consummate skill as an architect. In the very years when he was searching for his proper role, he designed

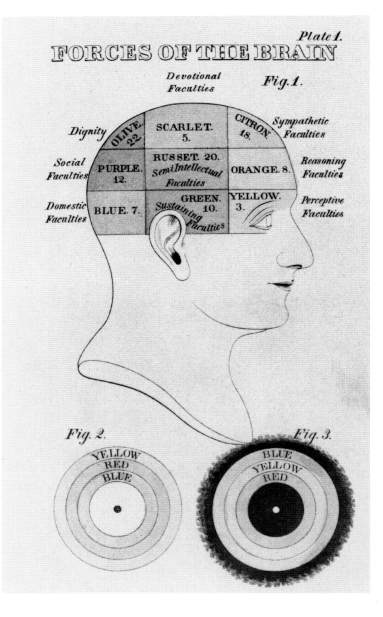

FORCES OF THE BRAIN

Plate 1.

Fig. 1.

Devotional Faculties

Dignity | OLIVE. 22. | SCARLET. 5. | CITRON. 18. | Sympathetic Faculties

Social Faculties | PURPLE. 12. | RUSSET. 20. Semi Intellectual Faculties | ORANGE. 8. | Reasoning Faculties

Domestic Faculties | BLUE. 7. | GREEN. 10. Sustaining Faculties | YELLOW. 3. | Perceptive Faculties

Fig. 2.

YELLOW RED BLUE

Fig. 3.

BLUE YELLOW RED

Lewis Reynolds speculates on the human brain

the Perkins, Kennedy, Campbell, Partee, and Buckner residences, all of them standing at the pinnacle of New Orleans architecture of the day. Nevertheless, Reynolds continued to devote much of his energies to more speculative concerns. His *Treatise on Handrailing* was in fact an entire course on geometry and trigonometry. Far exceeding the practical needs of any builder, it is an excursion into the pure realm of abstract Platonic forms. This interest was far more metaphysical and religious than practical. As so many of the greatest architects before him, Reynolds believed that God's presence in the world was most easily discerned in the perfection of abstract geometry. By manipulating such pure forms, the architect was, quite literally, doing the Lord's work.

Reynolds channeled this mystical turn of mind into Freemasonry. During the very postwar years when he enjoyed his most productive period as an architect, he was working on a thick volume, *The Mysteries of Masonry*, which he published in Philadelphia in 1870. His purpose was to demonstrate that geometry provided symbolic clues to the very nature of the universe. One could decipher these clues by ascending the spiritual stepladder of Masonic degrees. *The Mysteries of Masonry* purports to reveal the hidden design underlying all color, light, language, geometry, logic, music, astronomy, biology, and mineralogy. The keys to knowledge, Reynolds believes, lie in arithmetic, "the most important of all sciences."[27] He concludes his tract by demonstrating that the human brain precisely represents the inner structure of all creation and that the brain in turn is the model for the true Masonic temple. From math and metaphysics, Reynolds comes full circle to architecture.

Given the intensity of Reynolds's metaphysical interests, it is no wonder they were reflected in his Garden District residences. He uses the so-called golden section—a near-perfect ratio of approximately .61621—at crucial points on both the Perkins and Buckner houses. His stairways all conform to mathematically precise spirals, and proportions are based on geometric rather than purely visual relationships. This also true of the Bradish Johnson and Lafayette Folger residences, but in the latter case especially, the abstract geometry is overlaid with a thick encrustation of Italianate ornament.

FAILURE AND TRAGEDY

Henry Howard and Lewis Reynolds were the premier architects of the Garden District and of New Orleans in the 1850s and 1860s. In the context of American architecture as a whole, their work can be judged as highly competent, very extravagant, and even bold, though somewhat *retardataire*. Their fame was never national, nor was it purely local, since both set a standard for work throughout the region. Most important, they each made great contributions to one of nineteenth-century America's finest suburbs.

For all their accomplishments, however, Howard and Reynolds ultimately failed, and in an era when financial and social success was the expected norm. It is not merely that both were promptly forgotten after their deaths—more than a few American architects have suffered such a posthumous fate. Rather, failure was present throughout their working lives.

Howard's decision to specialize as a designer cost him dearly. In contrast to James Gallier, Sr., and the builder-architects before him, he was unable to cash in on his brief triumphs in the 1850s. His specialized professional practice was unable to support his wife and eleven children, with tragic consequences. His need to take commissions wherever they were to be found separated him from his family for long periods. Finally, during the Civil War, his New York-born wife, Caroline, threatened to move north and take the children with her. Only the intervention of friends dissuaded her. Shortly after the war she and Howard finally did separate, evidently with much bitterness: in city directories of the late 1870s she identified herself as "the widow of Henry Howard," even though Howard was still living.[28] Hard on the heels of the collapse of his marriage and of his health, Howard endured the profligacy of a son who, a drunken bully, met death in a highly publicized shootout at the Thalia Street firehouse.[29]

Reynolds suffered domestic grief when his wife died in 1865. For all his achievements, his assets at that point consisted of nothing more than his collection of architectural books, valued at only $28, and $235 worth of household effects.[30]

Both Howard's and Reynolds's architectural practices rebounded after the Civil War. Even as this renewal occurred, though, Howard had begun to suffer from a degenerative disease that eventually forced him into Charity Hospital. Poverty-stricken and alone by this point, Henry Howard died on 25 November 1884, leaving behind no significant estate.[31]

Some years earlier Lewis Reynolds had begun to suffer from what his Victorian contemporaries gruesomely called "softening of the brain."[32] He died on 9 August 1879, "leaving no property of any value in Louisiana."[33] Aside from $75 in cash, he left his second wife only "one old bedroom parlor set, and an old sewing machine." The court record of his succession, continues to note quite blandly that "all of [the] furniture being old, [it] did not have a value of $300." At the time of his death, Reynolds had been hard at work on a second philosophical treatise, this time revealing *The Mysteries of Creation*. Once more the book was to be dedicated to his beloved Masons. Later, the second Mrs. Reynolds reported rancorously to a New Orleans court that although the Masons had organized her husband's funeral, they had refused to pay any of the expenses.[34] She went to court in the hope of being declared indigent so the judge could turn her three children over to a guardian.

It is often rued that the most financially successful designers are rarely the most gifted architects. The bitter tragedies of Henry Howard and Lewis Reynolds suggest conversely that in nineteenth-century America some of the most talented architects were little recognized by their contemporaries and condemned to lives of professional and personal hardship.

CHAPTER SEVEN

The Culture of Comfort

V

ISITORS TO THE Garden District during its heyday were duly impressed by the stately homes, but they invariably saved their most extravagant praise for the lush plantings that gave the suburb its name. To be sure, the term *garden* in *Garden District* was taken in the English sense as meaning the entire yard. As the historian Kenneth T. Jackson notes, the British still often use the word garden to denote the yard surrounding a house rather than the garden itself.[1] When the District's own exacting English-born architect Thomas Wharton declared its gardens to be the best he had seen in America, after those in Brookline, Massachusetts, he was praising all aspects of the district's flora and fauna and not just the beds of flowers.[2]

Yet it is far easier to affirm the beauty of Garden District plantings than to characterize them with any degree of precision, so scanty is surviving information. Local notaries only rarely bothered to fill in the details of gardens in the otherwise precise watercolors of properties they registered. Surviving nineteenth-century paintings and photographs provide no more than a glimpse into the District's flora. Even the city maps issued nationally by the Sanborn fire insurance company after the Civil War ignore the grounds unless there are stone walls or other such prominent features to be

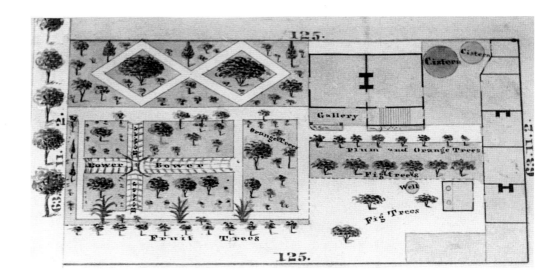

Axial planning on Josephine Street (NEW ORLEANS NOTARIAL ARCHIVES)

recorded. The best-documented garden in the District is probably that of the Goldsmith house at 1122 Jackson Avenue near Magazine Street. Still, the excellent photographs of it preserved in The Historic New Orleans Collection date from the turn of the century and record a replanting of that era rather than the original garden plan.

It is clear that local gardens adhered to both formal and informal design schemes in the middle and late nineteenth century. Examples of linear or axial planning are known to have existed at a now demolished residence on Josephine Street between Chestnut and Camp, at the charming Esquèrre house at 3232 Laurel Street, and, finally, at another residence, now demolished, on Fourth Street between Magazine and Camp.[3] The Esquèrre garden featured arbors and a trellis while the one on Fourth had herringbone brick walks and dense planting, suggesting that the planners of even these formal gardens considered them places for casual strolling and relaxation in verdant beauty. Every other garden of which we have any knowledge was designed in the informal English style, with meandering paths and picturesque natural plantings. Samuel Kennedy's raised cottage, for example, was surrounded by such a garden, which filled most of the available property.

It is by no means clear who designed these gardens or laid out the yards. Except for an Alsatian whom James Robb brought in to plan and install his gardens, no evidence has yet been found of landscape architects working in the Garden District, nor is there firm proof that the architects who designed the houses designed the grounds as well. In England after 1800 gentlemen homeowners often drafted plans for their own romantic gardens. This practice was slow to gain acceptance in America, where the first book on this subject, *The Art of Beautifying the House Grounds* by Frank Scott, did not appear until 1870 and then was explicitly promoted as a "commuters' manual."[4] There is no evidence that amateur landscape design spread to New Orleans or that men of the Garden District engaged in gardening at all. Novelist George Washington Cable, who once lived on Eighth Street, later launched an active campaign to draw men into the pleasant and uplifting hobby of gardening from his adopted home in Northampton, Massachusetts.[5] His former neighbors ignored him. Were gardens, then, a domain for solely women's initiative? Several guests in the antebellum Garden District mention being shown through the gardens by apparently knowledgeable ladies, but this does not suffice to prove that they were considered part of the women's realm.

In the absence of convincing evidence to the contrary, it is fair to conclude that the beauty of the district's gardens derived more from the lushness of the semi-tropical flora, which included orange

Rus in urbe. Fruit and banana trees, and fences too (NEW ORLEANS NOTARIAL ARCHIVES)

Elevation on Josephine Street

Lush plantings and formal gardens on Josephine Street (NEW ORLEANS NOTARIAL ARCHIVES)

trees, banana trees, and many imported flowering species, than from the design of the gardens per se. Rich green lawns spread across much of the area surrounding the houses and opened fine vistas on the exotic trees and plants, as they do today. These lawns almost certainly provided a venue for such popular nineteenth-century family games as croquet, archery, badminton, and horseshoes, at least during temperate periods of the year.[6]

Surprisingly, most, if not all, of these yards were closed to one another. A surviving photograph of Camp Street taken from the fire tower that stood near the corner of Washington reveals that in the period around 1856 that a picket fence divided each yard from its neighbor.[7] Such divisions directly violated the main principle propounded by Frank Scott in *The Art of Beautifying the House Grounds* and reveals another way in which the Garden District is rooted more in an early-nineteenth-century world of freely individuated properties than in the later Victorian notion of which a single, continuous garden encompasses the entire suburb.

Even the less formal plantings demanded constant tending, given the rapidity with which everything grows in the humid warmth. Far from being a task for genteel amateurs, gardening in New Orleans was a kind of war against proliferating vegetation waged by full-time professionals. If the landscape architects' identities remain unknown to us, the gardeners' do not. Nearly half the Garden District gardeners registered in the 1860 U.S. Census were immigrants from Germany, with another quarter from Ireland, and the rest from England, France, and Louisiana. The management of the District's gardens required not only a full-time labor force but also a considerable degree of organization within each household.

The same can be said of every other aspect of the great houses of the Garden District. Each suburban mansion was an independent economic unit, an autonomous republic within the larger neighborhood and city. This was a result of necessity, not of choice. In spite of its wealth, New Orleans was still poor in the amenities of urban life. Running water, sewers, and even paved streets were all but unknown in the antebellum era. Downtown, one could at least hope such municipal services would someday be instituted. In the new suburb it was safer to assume that they would not exist.

Water was provided through lead-lined cisterns of cypress wood. Some of these were truly enormous, standing two to three

Not yet the garden suburb: fenced-in yards in the 1850s (JAY DEARBORN EDWARDS, PHOTOGRAPHER; THE HISTORIC NEW ORLEANS COLLECTION)

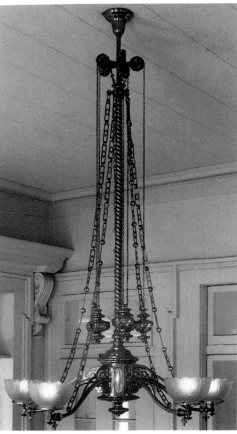

[LEFT] *Drainage ditch on Chestnut Street, now destroyed*

[RIGHT] *Gaslight chandeliers in Henry S. Buckner parlor, 1410 Jackson Avenue, by Lewis E. Reynolds, 1850*

stories high.[8] Even after Mississippi River water was pumped to Garden District houses in the late 1850s, the municipal supply could not compete in quantity or quality with rain water.[9]

With no municipal sewers, all drainage flowed into slab-lined ditches in the street. In the 2500 block of Camp Street one can still see ditches so deep that they have to be bridged. At the widow Oury's house on Second Street opposite Clay Square there were not even street ditches, so all bath water was emptied directly onto the yard.[10]

The impressive mausoleums in Lafayette Cemetery for members of the volunteer fire companies might lead one to think the brigades to have been both proud and efficient. Evidently, though, few persons trusted them. Most of the larger houses, such as Lafayette Folger's, had large iron tanks under the eaves to store water to be used in the event of fire. Each household in effect became its own fire station. Spratt's Lightning Rods could be obtained from Bernardin Nautre's home furnishings store in the

Vieux Carré. Another safety measure was to use gas lighting rather than candles. Available in English villas by the 1830s, gas lighting was installed in the Garden District on the eve of the Civil War, but the supply was erratic.

Fresh market produce was readily available in Lafayette City. If Garden District residents no longer maintained cows, as Jean Harang of Tchoupitoulas Street had done in the 1830s, even the greatest houses continued to raise their own chickens through the late 1850s. The sounds of the poultry house at Robert Grinnan's villa must have added a touch of realism to the semirural atmosphere. Kitchen gardens reinforced this aura. So important were these that James Robb took an active role in assembling seeds for the vegetable garden at his new mansion.[11] Admittedly, such activism by the man of the house was exceptional, but many did not hold back from investing in greenhouses. Robert Grinnan and his neighbor, Bradish Johnson, were only two of the many residents who maintained large greenhouses at their homes.[12]

Municipal services in the Garden District were primitive, but life was comfortable nonetheless. Numerous visitors remarked on the residents' passion for the most modern conveniences. Indeed, in terms of private amenities, the Garden District equaled or surpassed any other suburb in the country. Virtually every human need was catered to, without regard for expense.

There was nothing more urgent than to soften the effects of the summer's heat and to fend off the winter's damp cold. Even before David Boswell Reid published his *Ventilation in American Dwellings* (New York, 1858), uptown New Orleanians had opened up the circulation of the traditional London-plan house with larger doorways, higher ceilings, and tall windows. At the William Wright house at 1240 Sixth Street, the lower sashes were designed so that the windows could fully retract into the wall.[13] Adjustable shutters, venetian blinds, and gauze-like curtains may have given salons a gloomy look, but such features permitted the circulation of air without inviting mosquitoes.

New Orleanians assault on summer heat required ice. This was hauled by ship in great quantity from as far afield as Maine. Demand was so keen that several entrepreneurs, including A. W. Bosworth at 1126 Washington Street, became rich through the ice trade. Once it arrived at a Garden District house, the ice had to be stored. Grocer John Adams at 2423 Prytania Street built a round icehouse lined with a double layer of brick beneath the cistern, extending nine feet underground.[14] This arrangement would have been impossible in most lower-lying areas of the city, but the higher elevation of the Garden District enabled it to be common practice.

During the winter double shutters and heavy drapes provided insulation, while ventilating flues in chimneys assured the circulation of fresh air. Hot-air furnaces were common by the late 1850s, with devices such as the Chilson New Conical Patent Furnace being applied at up-to-date establishments like Shepherd Brown's house in the Lower Garden District.[15]

Hot and cold running water were all but universal in large Garden District houses by the 1850s, although the introduction into the city's more modest dwellings took several more generations. Typically, water from external cisterns was carried by

Louvred shutters in the reception parlor of the Walter G. Robinson house, 1415 Third Street. Henry Howard, architect, 1859

wooden pipes into the large copper tanks hidden under the eaves on the second or third floor. This was fed by gravity into a large boiler above the kitchen stove and was then force-pumped to bathrooms throughout the house.[16] With the spread of hot and cold running water, bathrooms grew in size and acquired the last word in appointments. In keeping with this trend, by 1857 architect James H. Calrow and builder Charles Pride were installing mahogany washstands with marble tops and silver-plated fittings in all four principal bedrooms of Albert Brevard's house at 1239 First Street.

In no area of domestic life did uptown New Orleanians exhibit a more single-minded fanaticism than in their search for the perfect bathtub. The portable tin variety was *degradare* by the 1840s, requiring a replacement with the ideal stationary. The breakthrough came in 1842, when Adam Thompson in Cincinnati installed the first indoor tub with running water in his house.[17] By the end of the decade, cast-iron bathtubs had made their debut. Gas burners underneath, these fearful contraptions seemed more appropriate for steaming seafood than bathing people. Fortunately for uptowners' complexions, they soon gave way to better types of tubs. Robert Grinnan's villa featured two lead-lined bathtubs by 1850, which upstaged the nearby residence of Thomas Gilmour, who had but one. Grinnan made his triumph complete by installing one of the city's first showers, or "rainbaths" as they were then called.[18]

All this was but a prelude to the achievement of worldly Edward Briggs of Coliseum Street. In one of the grandest gestures of the post-Civil War boom era, Briggs reportedly built a large sunken marble bathtub that could be reached only through a trap door in the bathroom. Architect William Freret's eclectic design for the residence as a whole pales in comparison with this extravaganza.[19]

The one issue on which uptowners evinced more zeal than for bathtubs was for the latest in toilet facilities. Back in 1841 Charles Conrad had settled for an outdoor privy—a double-holer—for his large raised cottage at Prytania and First streets, now demolished.[20] Yet by this time so-called tower privies had come into use. Known in England since Elizabethan times, these brick chimneys let seats at each floor level. While they were fairly common— three known examples were in Thomas Gilmour's house at 2520 Prytania, at Pope's Pharmacy at Jackson and Prytania streets, and

[ABOVE] *Trend-setter John Blaffer's house: black walnut toilets and the Garden District's first urinal, 1328 Felicity Street. Charles Hillger, architect, 1869*

[FACING PAGE] *Deep rooms and rich earth tones create pools of shadow even on a hot sunlit day: Frederick Wing house, bedroom, 1329 Seventh Street, circa 1853–60*

Advertising the latest cast-iron stoves: B. Nautre & Co. of Conde Street (NEW ORLEANS PUBLIC LIBRARY)

in Edward Ogden's residence at 1213 Fourth Street—tower privies had the disadvantage of requiring constant cleaning lest they become completely noxious.[21]

Up in the Northeast, Harriet Beecher Stowe and other sanitation reformers were promoting the products of the Earth Closet Company of Hartford, Connecticut, and even lauding the virtues of night soil.[22] By 1850 water closets were installed in all the better dwellings of uptown New Orleans. Exposed pipes running from floor to floor or room to room was a common sight in earlier residences upgraded with a "modern" water closet, and even in newly built houses. Besides being simpler to install, exposed pipes were defended by sanitation reformers as a means of facilitating access by plumbers and hence speeding quick action against the widely feared and supposedly deadly "sewer gas."[23] The water closet rapidly passed from the realm of utility into the higher sphere of beauty. At Robert Grinnan's villa, these commodes were crafted of the best Santo Domingo mahogany.[24] John Blaffer went still further and asked his builder to install locks on the covers of his fine black walnut toilets. Blaffer's right to the title of pacesetter in this domestic realm was assured when in 1869 he installed a urinal in his dressing room.[25]

The quest for comfort took many forms. Professional bell hangers installed elaborate systems connecting the principal rooms of most Garden District mansions. Central panels in the servants' quarters were a kind of Rube Goldberg fantasy of wires and mechanical bells. At Lavinia Dabney's St. Charles Avenue house the system extended out to the front gate.[26] Underground cold storage facilities, used as a means of preserving food and chilling wine, served such homes as the Jethro Bailey house on St. Mary Street and John Adams's home on Prytania Street. An area where the hand of modernity was particularly evident was the stove. One of the last open-hearth fireplaces in the District is still to be seen at the Ogden house at 1241 Fourth Street.[27] By the late 1840s almost all of these had been replaced with large cast-iron ranges. The new ranges facilitated the work of servants—a major consideration—as well as providing hot water for baths, producing far less ash and dust, and releasing less heat in the summertime than open hearths.

Where did this lust for comfort come from, and who promoted it? How did the American home become, as it remains to this day, the testing laboratory for every newfangled gadget that caters to our animal comforts?

To arrive at even the most tentative answer to these questions, it is necessary to recall the motives of the parties involved. Businessmen and speculators established the Garden District, with little evident participation by their wives. Having enriched themselves early—by their fortieth year in most cases—the men were ready to reap the benefits of success. They sought respite from the city for their families, if not for themselves. They aspired to neighborly proximity to other successful men who shared their outlook on the world. Their suburban homes were to be showcases where visitors could stand in awe before the conjugal union of money, morality, and good taste. The admiration of the public would confirm the owner's new role in the community.

This simple formula not only laid great stress on the domestic entertainment of guests but gave that activity a distinctively male flavor. The diaries of Miss Louise Dugan, whose father had purchased the old Thomas Toby house in 1859, provide intriguing insights on this point. A very sociable young lady in her late teens, Miss Dugan confessed a "love of pleasure . . . so strong that I cannot resist."[28] She records her experiences at boating parties, picnics at Spanish Fort, theater parties, and twice-weekly visits to the opera. Her mother, Mrs. Thomas S. Dugan, is frequently on hand, not only for outings but also for grand parties such as one at which an artificial fountain spewing cologne caught fire. Mr. Dugan, by contrast, is almost never present for all this gaiety at other people's homes. When he put in an appearance at a performance of *Hamlet*, it was cause for note by his daughter, for Thomas Smithfield Dugan was an antisocial man.[29] Nonetheless, he emerges clearly as convention's arbiter for formal receptions and assemblies at his family residence, the old Toby house at 2340 Prytania Street. In this role, for which he was so ill suited by temperament, Dugan went so far as to launch a campaign within the family in 1876 to sell their residence on the grounds that it "wasn't fit to entertain in."[30]

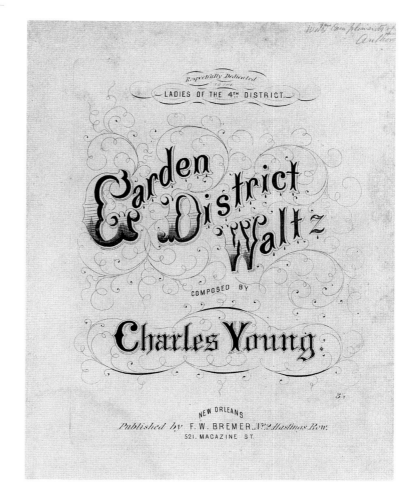

Worldly pleasures: Charles Young's "Garden District Waltz" (PRIVATE COLLECTION)

Between Mr. and Mrs. Dugan, as in other families, there seems to have been an informal division of labor, in which the husbands mounted grand and formal receptions and the wives and daughters organized more intimate gatherings. This arrangement directly affected the manner in which the great houses were actually used. A tradition passed down to the present owners of James P. Freret's raised cottage on Louisiana Avenue holds that the formal reception rooms on the main (second) floor were the domain of the master of the house and used primarily for business-related functions. His

wife is said to have found those rooms so stilted and inconvenient that she and the children spent most of their time in the comfortably informal quarters on the ground floor. In this regard, the Freret family followed a pattern familiar in Great Britain and Europe in the nineteenth century.[31]

The male dominion over the main public areas of the house found expression in the pompously appointed receiving rooms and also in the so-called libraries. In keeping with the men's inclinations, few libraries actually housed books. New Orleans author Grace King, writing in the late nineteenth century, venomously described a Garden District party at which "there were enough papas in attendance to fill up some card-tables in an adjoining room, which, in virtue of a writing-table and a bookcase, was called and thought to be a library."[32] It must be granted that several inventories list books or bookcases in the big houses, with collections of several hundred volumes not unknown. Granted, too, that a true library was added to a house at 2328 Coliseum Street in the 1870s. These were exceptions, however. The Coliseum Street house was outfitted as the manse for the Prytania Street Presbyterian Church and graced with a library on the assumption that ministers were readers.[33] Typically the *library* was in fact a smoking room, equipped with fancy brass-lined spittoons of oak, walnut, or mahogany beside the library table. Billiard rooms were another manifestation of the dominance of male interests. Few men in the 1850s failed to include such a room in their mansions, and the Antognini firm on Conti Street advertised vigorously to sell billiard tables to the local gentry.

Left to their own devices, women would probably have had neither smoking rooms nor billiard rooms and would have favored instead a series of more intimate rooms rather than the coldly formal parlors. This plan is embodied in the twin houses that James Robb built on Washington Avenue. Both have three smaller rooms on the ground floor rather than the customary double parlor and four adjoining bedrooms on the second floor. When Thomas Dugan fell ill, the ladies of his household promptly transformed his smoking room into "the most comfortable of bedrooms" for him.[34]

After the Civil War, women came increasingly to dominate the management of Garden District households. Billiard rooms were turned over to more feminine uses. Where they remained, as at the Dugan house, they became places for women as well as men. Smoking rooms were adapted into cozy family rooms. Even before such changes occurred, the feminization of Garden District households was well advanced. The men had abdicated this larger role when they moved their households to a suburb that was beyond an easy walk from their offices, now the place where they spent the better part of most days. This made the women responsible for day-to-day supervision of the residence and the large staff of servants.

The authority of women was the more absolute because they seldom shared it with in-laws or grandparents. While extended families were common on plantations, nuclear families prevailed in the city. The typical Garden District household recorded in the 1860 census consisted of 4.1 individuals; fewer than a third of all households claimed six or more members. Neither figure had risen by the time of the 1870 census.[35]

Increased ownership of property by women paralleled their mounting authority in the new suburb. When Samuel Palmer Griffin bought his property at 2702 St. Charles Avenue, he did so with the "separate funds" of his wife, Emily.[36] Mrs. Whitney also purchased the great Whitney property with her separate funds.[37] To some extent the habit of placing property in the wife's name was a strategy for preserving one's home in the event of bankruptcy. Yet this could have been accomplished without making the purchase with the wife's own money, as so frequently occurred in the Garden District. By the 1860s many women had inherited substantial capital from their fathers, who were the founding generation of the Garden District, and the suburb was becoming feminized economically.

Even free women of color participated in this economic feminization of the district. Winnefred ("Winny") Hubbard, a free black, commanded a considerable fortune. Even though illiterate (she signed all documents with an X), Winnefred Hubbard owned Peachtree Orchard Plantation on Bayou Barataria and built the house, now replaced, at 3116 Prytania Street.[38] Her endless legal wrangles only served to underscore the power that property gave her.

The postwar rise of women's prominence in the life of New Orleans was later demonstrated in the Cotton Centennial Exhibition of 1884 and in the establishment of Newcomb College two years later.[39] Many in the city and region were astonished at the civic leadership uptown women demonstrated in these two projects. Yet these abilities had been developing for many years in the private arena of the suburban home. The emergence of women into public life was a national trend, to be sure. Eliza Jane Nicholson and other Garden District women drew inspiration from such women in the Northeast as Julia Ward Howe, Eliza Peabody, and Harriet Beecher Stowe, whom they knew through widely read books and, later, from direct contact when several of the latter visited New Orleans for the Cotton Centennial Exposition. Efforts organized by women on the home front during the Civil War had stimulated this movement among American women everywhere. Its particular strength in New Orleans may have been due to the fact that little new wealth was being created after 1872 and much of the older wealth passed gradually by inheritance into the hands of women. With the depressed economy reducing the sphere of male initiative, women found their position in society enhanced in both absolute and relative terms.

[ABOVE] *Mixed hues and textures in the dining room of John Adams's house, 2423 Prytania Street Attributed to architect-builder Frederick Wing, 1860–61*

[FACING PAGE] *Double parlor of the Joseph Morris house, 1331 First Street; dining room in background.*

✏ FURNISHING THE SUBURB BEAUTIFUL

Here, reported without literary niceties, is a list of interior furnishings, drawn at random from the published inventories of a number of Garden District homes confiscated by the Federal government during the Civil War: marble-topped tables and bureaus; wax flowers under glass domes; mahogany card tables with ormolu; tufted ottomans; gilt-framed pictures; gondola chairs; potted plants; large-figured wallpaper; damask bedspreads; plaster casts; giant rosewood armoires; horsehair sofas; velvet portieres; campeachy chairs; faience vases filled with palmetto fans; rose wood rockers; heavy crystal and bronze-*doré* chandeliers; étagères; marble clocks; palms; fruitwood commodes; and bric-a-brac.[40]

This selective list reveals an interesting dichotomy. Garden District interiors were far more ornate and flamboyant than the exteriors. In architecture, New Orleanians yielded to fashion and adopted new styles, albeit with deliberate caution and restraint. Not so for the interiors. Here all the great civilizations of the past contended in a boisterous cacophony of form and color. Any one room might, by 1860, have sported a selective array of furniture in such styles as Renaissance revival, neo-Grec, Egyptian, Gothic, rococo revival, and Second Empire, not to mention traditional American pieces from earlier eras. Sixteen-foot ceilings invited furniture of formidable scale, which exaggerated every stylistic detail.

Outside, the colorful ochers that had been favored until the 1870s gradually gave way to a chaste white paint, which was the rule by the time Mark Twain visited the Garden District again in 1880.[41] Inside, however, a riot of richly pigmented colors prevailed. The ledger of the John Benson Company in 1859 lists paints in chrome yellow, black, West Indian red, ultramarine blue, brown, bronze, amber, sienna, Paris green, bronze green, and gold bronze.[42] If an architect wanted woodwork painted white, he often had to underscore it in his contractor's building specification.

The difference in the values exhibited in the architecture and the furnishings of the Garden District was so great as to cause one to wonder whether entirely different people were not responsible for each. This was in fact the case. Architectural design in mid-nineteenth century America was a male enterprise. With few exceptions, men designed buildings for male patrons. Even when Garden District women used their financial resources to pay for a house, they invariably turned to a husband, brother, or father to negotiate with the architect and sign the building contract. Lavinia Dabney stood as one of the rare exceptions to this rule.

Wives exercised control over the interior furnishings, however, and they did so with little apparent regard for cost. Whereas the men hesitated to tie up vast resources in the construction of their houses, women seemed determined to do whatever they considered necessary to render their homes attractive and fashionable. The U. S. Marshall's valuations of Garden District properties confiscated during the Civil War reveal that furnishings often constituted one-fifth the value of the house, and sometimes a third or two-fifths.[43] One need only apply this ratio to the cost of an expensive contemporary house to appreciate the scale of this investment. This sum would only cover the cost of furniture—not wallpaper, chandeliers, gilding, and other built-in decoration.

It is not surprising that the women were far more advanced and venturesome in their tastes than the men. As nonvoters, they were less directly concerned with maintaining the political and social solidarity of uptown society than were their menfolk and hence were less protective of the stylistic uniformity with which that solidarity was expressed in architecture. Besides, as Calvert Vaux and other contemporary writers testify, it was still considered slightly effeminate for men to evince too keen an interest in aesthetic matters.[44] Women, in contrast, had access to *Godey's Lady's Book* and other periodicals that whetted the appetites of feminine consumers.[45] The rise of such magazines and their wide distribution through the improved United States mail service quickened the pace by which new fashions could appear, be disseminated, and then replaced by yet newer fashions. Local furniture dealers had no choice but to keep abreast of this hectic process and to make known that they were doing so by means of advertisements in the daily press. Such ads were targeted at the feminine market. Small wonder, then, that even in the Northeast, architectural practice lagged half a decade or more behind tastes in furniture. In New Orleans the lag time was even greater.

The fainthearted consumer could always resort to interior decorators. The Royal Street firm of Henry N. Siebrecht enjoyed a lively business catering to precisely this clientele. Such commissions made Siebrecht a rich man. The small number of firms in the field of interior decorating, however, suggests that most New Orleanians were more confident in their taste and in their own ability to stay abreast of national fashions in furniture.

Ladies with more nerve dealt directly with the many home furnishing stores in New Orleans. In the antebellum era the firm of C. Boye on Royal Street specialized in walnut and cherry bedsteads and case pieces, Joseph Bruno did general cabinet work, while Bernardin Nautre on Chartres Street provided porch and garden ware. Better known was the Royal Street furniture shop of Prudent Mallard, who was born in Sevres, France, and had been in business in New Orleans since 1838. Mallard eventually took over the clientele of another French cabinetmaker in New Orleans, François

Seignouret, a former wine importer who sold furniture until 1853.[46]

Such firms had skilled cabinetmakers in their employ. The United States censuses for 1850, 1860, and 1870 reveal that most of these craftsmen were German- or French-born. At their best, these local artisans produced works of exceptional richness and vigor of design. Magnificent bedsteads and case pieces from the local ateliers of Siebrecht, Seignouret, McCracken, and Mallard found their way into the Garden District's great houses. Tables, armoires, prie-dieux, bookcases, and dining room suites furnishing local residences have been traced to New Orleans cabinetmakers. Such pieces invariably command the very highest prices when they appear in area auction houses today.

The popularity of Siebrecht, Seignouret, Mallard, and other expensive dealers stemmed not from the distinctiveness of their designs but from their ability to keep abreast of the latest fashions in New York and Europe, especially France. To meet such cosmopolitan tastes, these firms crafted and also imported large quantities of fine pieces from the North and from abroad. The successful Royal Street firm of Flint and Jones, for example, did not even bother to employ cabinetmakers of its own, so great was the response to such advertisements as one that appeared in the city directory of 1858 declaring that the firm had at hand the "best and most varied assortment of cabinet furniture ever offered for sale in the South."

The status of northern furniture in the Garden District reveals much about the cultural orientation of the elite there. Most posh suburbanites in the Crescent City were more akin to the propertied classes of eighteenth-century Virginia, who went to London for their furniture, than they were to the rich of Massachusetts who preferred the local product.[47] However fine and numerous locally crafted pieces in Garden District houses, the source of the greatest quantity of Garden District furniture was New York. Philadelphia was a remote second. This fact is obscured by the tendency of many nineteenth-century New Orleans retailers to place their own marks on pieces they imported, a practice that was common in many other fields of retailing. The great furniture houses of Manhattan fully acknowledged the importance of the New Orleans market. When the New York furniture manufacturer Joseph Meeks died in 1868, his obituary noted that he was the largest manufacturer of furniture in America

and "supplied the markets from Boston to New Orleans with the most expensive, elegant, and durable cabinet work made in America."[48]

Even the renowned Prudent Mallard imported furniture from France and Manhattan. Having spent nine years in New York before coming to New Orleans, he had personal contact with the leading cabinetmakers there. Through such links, Garden District ladies ordered custom-made pieces from the best Manhattan makers or from abroad. Mallard provided them with up-to-the-minute examples of the massive rococo and Renaissance revival pieces that were so much in vogue and complemented the popular Belgian carpets and wallpapers from Philadelphia.[49]

Besides the great manufacturers and importers of furniture on Royal Street, many small cabinetmakers worked in the Irish Channel and other parts of town, specializing in inexpensive pieces. Increasingly, they faced tough competition from the large-scale manufacturers in Cincinnati, St. Louis, and, eventually, Grand Rapids, Michigan. The Cincinnati firm of Mitchell and Rammelsberg, which employed 260 workers by 1854, could afford to maintain a New Orleans showroom, as well as outlets in Memphis and St. Louis.[50] By the close of the Civil War, cabinetmaking in New Orleans remained a cottage industry. Local craftsmen lacked the resources to compete with such modern and aggressive firms and were driven out of business.

PLEASURE, CULTURE, AND WORK

What were the cultural horizons of Garden District families? During the boom years the men for the most part were busy at their work. The women were avid socializers. Novelist Grace King, who was raised near the neighborhood and made a career out of describing its mores, rarely depicts her women in constructive roles, even though she wrote in a later era when Garden District women had become relatively emancipated. Uptown New Orleans in the Victorian era produced far fewer philanthropic societies, voluntary associations, and even church-related charitable groups than cities in the North and East. Cultural life was not deeply developed, except as a consumer endeavor. Few homes had music rooms, and even Walter G. Robinson's great house, which had ample room for staging musicales, had only an old upright piano by Pleyel rather than a grand piano increasingly preferred by the musically discerning.[51]

There were only a few great art collections in the District. Mrs. Charles A. Whitney assembled so vast a collection of Oriental and European art that she had to erect two wings on her residence on St. Charles Avenue to house it.[52] But this was quite exceptional. Until the formation of the I. M. Cline and Seebold collections later in the century and of the Hunt Henderson collection in the early 1900s, the only other significant art in the Garden District was that assembled by James Robb at his Washington Avenue palazzo.

An alternative to major works of art might have been family portraits. In the older cities of the eastern seaboard and those of the Midwest, leading families built up collections of ancestral portraits. This was not yet possible for the self-made folk of the new suburb, although quite a number of them, including the Brevards, Conrads, Conreys, Gilmours, Kennedys, Leatherses, Johnsons, Paynes, and Tobys, commissioned local and nationally known painters to create family portraits.[53] The rarity of ancestral portraits in the antebellum Garden District stands in sharp contrast to their popularity among downtown Creole families as early as 1800. Only with the second and third generations did new rich of uptown New Orleans boast of family portraits in numbers comparable to the older Creole families. By the late nineteenth century, however, such local artists as George David Coulon and Paul Poincy regularly painted portraits of Garden District residents.

Lacking major art of ancestral portraits, many of the new suburbanites contented themselves with inexpensive genre paintings and daguerreotypes. The Buckner house included such gems as *The Last of the Red Men*, valued at $50; *Reubens and His Wife*, valued at $5; *Saturday Night*, valued at $20; *Cupid*, valued at $15; and *Uncollected Bills*, valued at $40.[54] What little art the Federal Marshal confiscated during the Civil War was usually grouped on auction lists with such items as towel racks, bric-a-brac, and spittoons.

Before condemning these American elites for their limited cultural horizons, it would be well to recall the claims their station made upon them. In their early years the men worked ceaselessly to maintain their businesses without the benefit of limited liability or corporate security. The women not only had to dress day and night in high fashions that were inappropriate to the climate, but they had full responsibility for maintaining a way of life that was equally ill suited to the semitropical environment. To be sure, they had servants to carry out the actual manual labor. However, it was not the custom in suburban New Orleans to have a major domo or steward to supervise the staff. This crucial role fell to the lady of the house.

The sheer volume of work required to maintain upper-class life in a Victorian-era American suburb was staggering. Each May the entire house was reorganized for summer. Carpets were cleaned and rolled up with peppercorns or tobacco leaves to thwart insects. Sea grass mats were placed on all floors. Turpentine was painted on baseboards in a vain attempt to eradicate cockroaches, and camphor was hidden in the folds of furniture to discourage moths. White muslin slipcovers were readied and placed on all furniture, and gauze wrapped around chandeliers and picture frames to protect them from flyspecks and the filth that wafted in from open windows. Each spring mosquito netting had to be fitted on all beds, and summer fireplace covers were brought from the attic and fitted in place.

All these tasks, which were reversed each September, had to be accomplished without disrupting the normal housekeeping routine, let alone the family's calendar of entertaining. This encompassed regular cleaning and dusting, and systematic cleansing and maintenance of kerosene and gas lamps, chandeliers, coal grates, commodes, privies, tower privies, and cisterns. Then there was the sewing of clothes for daily wear; the washing and ironing of all clothing; the purchase, preservation, and preparation of food for the family and staff; the providing of common medical care for all members of the household; the maintenance of horses, harnesses, and carriages; almost daily work in the yard and garden; and the procuring of all tools and utensils necessary for these tasks. Stressing again that all this occurred in a viciously humid climate that shortened working days and threatened to engulf the entire domestic establishment in a cloud of mosquitoes, cockroaches, mildew, and rot, one can well understand why those responsible for maintaining the way of life—the women—enjoyed little time for philanthropic work or broader cultural endeavors and instead gladly fled into the pleasures of society whenever the chance presented itself.

The one mitigating factor in women's lives, and an important one, was the presence of servants in the households. To them fell all the tasks enumerated above. An ample labor force thus freed ladies from the need to engage in manual work, but at the price of time-consuming duties of management and what today would be called "personnel administration." The lady of the house had to supervise the servants down to the last detail.

This is not to say that Mark Twain's eyes deceived him when in *Life on the Mississippi* he reported on white-gowned ladies lolling ornamentally on Garden District galleries in the late afternoons. Still less does it imply that the lot of Garden District ladies was a tough one, especially by comparison with that of the slaves and retainers who toiled on their behalf. It does explain, however, how members of an ostensibly leisured class, through their management of what was in effect a small business with a half dozen or more employees, might have developed the decisiveness, strength of character, and leadership abilities that so frequently impressed visitors. The development of such managerial skills was the paradoxical result of the decision by antebellum businessmen to relocate their families to a semi-rural, bucolic suburb.

James Gallier, Jr.'s parlor in the French Quarter, girded against summer
(HERMANN-GRIMA / FALLIER HISTORIC HOUSES)

CHAPTER EIGHT

Slaves, Servants, and Retainers

THE GREAT HOMES of the Garden District could no more have functioned without servants than the suburb of today could operate without electrical appliances. The day began when servants lit the fires and prepared breakfast. It ended when servants turned down the gaslights, adjusted the shutters, and laid out the bedclothes they had washed. Even to send a note to a neighbor or to pick up wine for a party required servants. Full-time retainers were, in short, the backbone of the nineteenth-century suburb.

How large a staff did Garden District homes maintain? Various writers have left the impression that residents were served by veritable armies of retainers. Eliza Ripley, who grew up in the old Faubourg Ste. Marie, recalled two maids holding candles while she dressed.[1] Madame Marie de Grandforte, visiting from France, elaborated further: "In every wealthy family in New Orleans or even in those which merely enjoy moderate competency, there is a servant for every department of labor: for the kitchen, the washtub, the care of the children, the mending of clothes, chamber work, dressing the hair of the mistress, taking care of the carriage, going on errands...."[2] If we take Madame Grandforte at her word, one might conclude that staffs of eight or more were the rule.

[FACING PAGE] *The servants' separate building at the Michel Musson house quartered most of his eight slaves, 1331 Third Street. Servants building, circa 1850; stable, circa 1884.*

Even the owner of a small cottage in Lafayette at Chippewa Street required slaves and servants, and had to house them

Fortunately, several less impressionistic sources of information on the number of slaves in Garden District households exist. The United States Census in 1860 enumerated all slave inhabitants of Louisiana, by parish and ward.[3] More useful still are the tax rolls of New Orleans and those of the city of Lafayette. Since both municipalities relied on property taxes for revenue, local authorities believed it was vitally important to know the nature and value of each citizen's holdings in slaves.

Such sources reveal that among Garden District slaveholders, several possessed staffs sufficiently large to fit Madame Grandforte's description. Hiram Anderson owned seven slaves and Jacob Payne owned eight in 1857, as did Michel Musson and Robert A. Grinnan. Madame Tureaud and Thomas Gilmour had nine slaves each. The largest slave owners appear to have been Samuel Newman of First Street and Mrs. S. Duncan, who owned ten and eleven slaves, respectively.[4]

However impressive, such large staffs as these were exceptional. Far more common were those Garden District residents that owned three to five slaves, which included owners of some of the largest houses. John Rodenberg, Benjamin Horrell, and William M. Perkins each had five slaves. Staffs of only two slaves maintained many impressive houses. Neither Thomas Adams nor Thomas Toby, both of Prytania Street, exceeded this modest number.[5]

Even if few Garden District residents owned large numbers of slaves, the total number of chattel servants was large and presents a striking anomaly. It has long been maintained that slavery was gradually dying out in all the major Southern cities. This theory applies well to New Orleans as a whole, for the number of slaves in the city declined after 1840.[6] Yet in uptown and in Lafayette slavery continued to expand in absolute numbers, from 614 to 1,539 to 2,301 in the decades between 1840 and 1860.[7] While some of these slaves belonged to owners on the riverfront and even in the Irish Channel, it is clear that in the last decade before Emancipation, the Garden District became a center of urban slavery in the South.

Figures of the slave population underscore a frequently overlooked aspect of American nineteenth-century elite communities: their population consisted almost equally of servants and homeowners. On the strength of only thirty-six of the largest slave-holding Garden District households, three or four servants served four to six family members. In a few homes the staff outnumbered the family. Jacob Payne's household of five members was attended by eight slaves, while the four members of the families of Hiram Anderson and Thomas Gilmour had seven and nine slaves, respectively.[8] Quite commonly, slaves and masters resided in equal number.

The significance of the servant population to Garden District homes can be measured in other ways as well. About one-third the floor area of Walter G. Robinson's mansion was devoted to the servants' working and living space. At Albert Brevard's house the comparable figure is one-quarter; at other mansions the typical servants' spaces averages within these ranges.[9]

Who were the people who owned these staffs of chattel servants? Northerners who had immigrated to New Orleans were just as likely to own slaves as those who had moved from states where slavery was legal. Nor did British laws affect the behavior of Queen Victoria's subjects in the Garden District. Even though slavery had been outlawed in Great Britain in 1828, two of the Garden District's English-born residents were also its largest slave owners, Thomas Gilmour and Robert Grinnan. The decision to own slaves was a personal one, and most residents opted to do so. And yet there were many exceptions. For all their wealth, neither James Robb nor Henry Lonsdale kept domestic slaves, nor did Albert Brevard or the British Charles Briggs.

Why did some people own no slaves, and many others so few? No doubt, their religious and moral opposition to the institution of slavery motivated some. There were also strong economic reasons for not buying household slaves. King Cotton steadily drove up the demand for slaves and hence their price. Slaves were expensive in 1850s New Orleans, with price tags of $800 to $1,000 being commonplace. John Wallis sold "Charles," age 34, and "Tom," age 26, for $825 each in 1851.[10] His neighbor, Bernard Kock, bought a 27-year-old slave named Alexander Brown in 1852 for $800.[11] While these prices may appear low to the modern reader, the average cost of a small house in Lafayette during the same period ranged from $800 to $1,000, and when John Norton built his Fourth Street cottage in 1846, he did so at a cost of $1,260. It is no wonder that even the wealthy Bernard Kock took out a loan to purchase Alexander Brown.

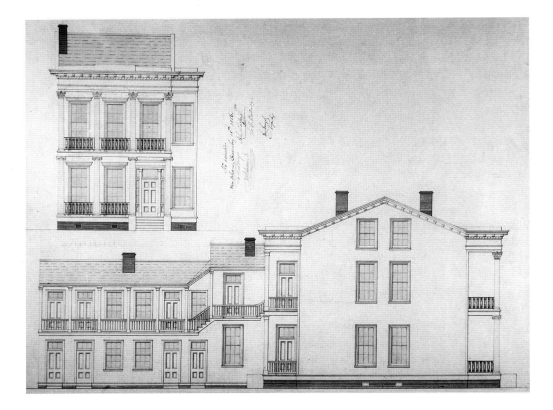

Façade and side elevation of Lavinia Dabney's house, showing servants' wing to left, 2265 St. Charles Avenue. James Gallier, Jr., architect, 1856 (SOUTH-EASTERN ARCHITECTURAL ARCHIVE, TULANE UNIVERSITY)

Slave quarters above Captain Thomas P. Leathers's stable were quite generous in scale, 2027 Carondolet Street. Most servants' quarters in stables were typically smaller than those in a main house. Henry Howard and Henry Thiberge, architects, 1857

Nearly as formidable as the direct costs were the hidden expenses of urban slavery. The slave owner ran a small welfare state of sorts. He maintained his human property in sickness and in health, during both productive and declining stages of life. Thanks to these benefits, urban slaves in domestic service enjoyed better living conditions than most free blacks.[12] The very inefficiency of the system must have raised hackles among businessmen who otherwise would have had few scruples in the matter. Such economic factors prevented slavery in the Garden District from expanding more than it did.

The easiest alternative to slave labor for a Garden District resident was to hire another person's slaves. Such labor was ideal for spot jobs and piecework industries, but it was ill suited for domestic work, which required greater continuity. A second alternative was to hire free blacks, but this, too, presented problems. The free black population of New Orleans dwindled rapidly between 1840 and 1860, leaving such labor in short supply.[13] Also, since many free blacks had mastered a variety of trades, they had little need or desire to hire themselves out as domestics and could demand high wages. There is no evidence that either hired slaves or free blacks were regularly employed in any Garden District homes for domestic services.

The best alternative to slave labor—and economically a very attractive one—was to hire recent immigrants from abroad. The rising number of Irish and German immigrants to New Orleans in the 1830s and 1840s settled in Lafayette as well as in the Faubourg Ste. Marie; downriver, the new European arrivals dramatically changed the labor market. Many Germans arrived with marketable skills and immediately entered the crafts and professions. Other immigrants, including most of the Irish, had no recourse but to compete with free blacks at the bottom of the economy. This was not simple, because, as one traveler observed in 1860, "The Negroes have decidedly the preference, and readily obtain much higher wages."[14] Yet over time the Irish successfully penetrated the labor market. As early as 1840 the Irish had driven blacks out of the lowly profession of draymen, and a decade later they constituted a majority among cartmen, hackney coachmen, porters, railroad hands, public waiters, and common laborers.[15]

Those Irish who aspired to work as domestics in the big houses faced formidable cultural and political barriers. Having been driven to America by famine, they rarely possessed the skills necessary to become cooks. Thomas Wharton of Coliseum Square recorded in his diary: "I took our new cook [to the market] and was pleased to find that she understood the choice of meats, which is an important quality and difficult to find among the Irish."[16] Nor did it help that the Irish and most of the Germans were Catholics in a Protestant suburb, and that they voted Democrat. In contrast, the registry of a slave ship reaching New Orleans in the 1830s indicates that this large shipment of slaves came from Virginia, North Carolina, and Maryland.[17] Unlike the Irish, such slaves were safely Protestant, conveniently familiar with Southern-American cuisine, and disenfranchised politically. Nor were they so likely to become infected with the spirit of democracy, although the presence in New Orleans of large numbers of free blacks worked constantly to erode the discipline of slaves there.

No wonder the Irish viewed their black competitors with fierce jealousy. The blacks reciprocated with disdain. Landscape architect Frederick Law Olmsted, upon observing to a black domestic slave in Alabama that many positions formerly filled by slaves were now filled by Irish, received the following reply: "Yes! And what kine of servant is dey? Ha! All de Irishmen dat ever I see haden so much sense in dar heds as I could carry in de palm of my han."[18]

The main advantages of Irish domestics were that they required no outlay of capital upfront and their monthly costs were low. Irish chambermaids, unlike slaves, required no loan and imposed no obligations beyond the moment. At discount prices, they also spared their owners the opprobrium of being slaveholders. This was important to at least some Yankee businessmen in the Garden District. Such considerations brought the C. K. O'Hara Agency of Camp Street a brisk business in the 1850s placing immigrant girls as domestics.[19]

Census figures from 1860 reflect the immigrants' successful invasion of the domestic market formerly monopolized by slaves. They also reveal that nearly half of all white domestics were Irish-born, with Germans constituting another third.[20] In the Garden District, as elsewhere in America, Irish domestics were on the verge of becoming the stereotypical servant on the eve of the Civil War.[21]

As the white invasion of the servants' quarters progressed, racial animosity also intensified: Garden District families could either buy slaves or hire immigrants but not both. In spite of this polarization, Garden District employers seem to have viewed the two groups as functionally interchangeable. The architecture of servants' quarters in houses built for slaveholders is indistinguishable from that of residences that employed immigrants. Any difference in the treatment of the two groups of domestics probably favored the slaves.

It is one thing to acknowledge that slavery and the exploitation of cheap foreign labor supported Garden District households and quite another to establish just what that meant in practice. Documentation on the treatment of domestic help is very elusive. Servants were illiterate and left few traces of either their suffering or their joy. Masters and mistresses in the Garden District almost never kept diaries, and those who did rarely touched on their relations with servants. Thus, to penetrate the issue at all, one must rely on indirect and incomplete evidence.

The treatment of domestic servants was shaped in part by the age and gender of the servants themselves. Census information and records of the sale of slaves in New Orleans confirm that a great majority of them were female.[22] Most, in the 1850s, at least, were very young. A slave or servant in her teens or early twenties would usually find herself directed by the lady of the house, who would be in her thirties or forties. The mistress's task was to educate servants to roles for which they had not been prepared. The natural posture for the mistress under such circumstances would have been one of firmness, maternal solicitude, and pedagogical condescension. Similar to students in school, the servants studied habits of cleanliness and upper class order, not to mention the rules of Victorian etiquette. Only when they had mastered such skills were they allowed to play a visible role in the family's domestic life.[23]

LIVING QUARTERS: PROXIMITY AND DISTANCE

The effectiveness of the lady of the house could he measured by her success in such training. This dictated that servants and house slaves, to some extent, lived lives that were scaled-down versions of their masters'. Far from being shunted into crowded hovels, members of the staff were given fairly generous quarters. While the room size varied somewhat, each servant's room was generally about 200 square feet, which far exceeds the federal minimum standards for contemporary public housing and compares favorably with the less than 200 square feet per employee specified for standard federal offices. Many rooms for servants or slaves were spacious indeed. The largest servants' rooms at the Robinson house measured 18 feet x 18 feet, while those at the Payne and Brevard houses measured 17 feet x 17 feet and 14 feet x 17 feet, respectively. Even the smallest quarters for servants or slaves at these mansions were at least 10 feet x 16 feet.[24]

The question arises whether these rooms domiciled more than one slave or servant. The evidence suggests they did not. In all but the most heavily staffed houses there were more rooms designated for servants' use than there were servants. Also, room-by-room lists of household furnishings confiscated during the Civil War rarely mention more than one bed in the servants' rooms. This same source also provides detailed information on the contents of servants' rooms. In George Sweet's house, the servant's room over the kitchen contained: a bed and mattress; a marble-topped bureau; a work table; a marble-topped washstand; an engraving; a woolen curtain; one carpet; a footstool; an armoire; an armchair; and one rocking chair, broken.[25]

Servants' living quarters were almost always segregated by sex and often by rank. While males lived in their section of the servants' wing of the main house, yard workers and stable hands lived in the all-male domain of the stable. These rooms were decidedly more primitive than those in the main house. A typical stable room at the residence of George Sweet, for example, contained a bedstead, mattress, table, and "one lot of sundries," while another contained a bedstead, an armoire, and a washstand. Male stablehands and gardeners were clearly not seen as requiring such civilized refinements as rugs and pictures on the walls.[26]

Three-story wing for slaves at the Buckner residence, 1410 Jackson Avenue, is visible from the main house's gallery and rear windows. Lewis E. Reynolds, architect, 1850

The domestic circumstances of Garden District servants contrast starkly with the environment from which they came, whether it was the teeming hovels of the Irish Channel or the slave quarters of a rural plantation. To be sure, rural slave owners had every interest in protecting the health of their human investments, especially in Louisiana, where the price of slaves was so high. Yet the separation of the living quarters of master and servants on plantations permitted a loose and laissez-faire attitude toward the slaves' daily habits. In the city, by contrast, master and servant shared the same domestic environment. Servants had no choice but to accept the same standards of cleanliness, order, and efficiency the Yankee businessmen set for themselves and their families.

Still other factors helped shape the relationship between servants or slaves and the master and his family. In the European old-world order, interaction between master and servant had been constant. In the novel *War and Peace*, Leo Tolstoy depicts Russian planters and their children socializing with their serfs on holidays. In England after 1800 this relationship became more formal and aloof, leading eventually to the "upstairs-downstairs" situation described in the novels of Galsworthy.

A few Americans in the Victorian era tried to follow the British trend. One such case in the Garden District is the generous cottage of Benjamin Horrell at 2627 Coliseum Street, where the servants' quarters were completely separate from the main house.[27] Reflecting the same distant formality, a photograph of the Joseph W. Carroll house at 1315 First Street in the 1870s shows black servants outfitted grandly in livery.[28] Such aloofness was not common in New Orleans, however. Most of the masters had grown up in the North, where the scarcity of domestic servants required that the few there were in a household live in the main residence. In most instances, it simply was not economical to have the architect build separate servants' quarters apart from the main house. Calvert Vaux, in his popular tract of 1857, *Villas and Cottages*, declared, "There is in this country a perpetual necessity for compactness of plan, however large the house may be, because…it is invariably difficult to get efficient servants."[29] Vaux goes on to criticize both Gothic and Italianate architecture as inappropriate to America, because they included too many hallways. Thus the architecture itself kept master and servants in close contact.

Servants' quarters atop the stable building: Joseph W. Carroll residence, 1315 First Street, 1870s

Liveried servants at the Carroll house, 1315 First Street, 1870s (GEORGE D. HOPKINS, PHOTOGRAPHER; THE HISTORIC NEW ORLEANS COLLECTION)

No less important as a force driving masters and servants together was the democratic bias of many of the Garden District's Yankee businessmen. As self-made men who had started at the bottom, they were still at ease with simple people, whether slaves or immigrants. They shared common experiences with servants on the farm, where hired hands worked side-by-side with family members. These people felt no need to segregate servants, even slaves, in separate quarters. This was in sharp contrast to three Englishmen who resided in the Garden District—Thomas Gilmour, Charles Briggs, and Robert Grinnan of 2520, 2605, and 2221 Prytania Street, respectively. At all three of their houses the servants' quarters were originally separate from the main dwelling and only later connected through the addition of closed hallways.

PRIVACY AND CONTACT: THE SERVANTS' WORLD

A typical Garden District mansion consists of a main block with a service wing and servants' quarters extending to the rear or side. Doorways at two levels connect the wing with the main house, the lower ceilings of the servants' quarters necessitating short stairways at the junction between the two units.

How much privacy from the master and his family did slaves or servants enjoy under this arrangement? An interesting insight is the fact that many homes, as originally built, had no separate stairways for servants, nor were stairways included in many service wings. While the 1859 Robinson and 1854 Rodenberg houses separated the servants' stairs, the practice of segregating them in the plan was quite rare until the 1870s and was by no means usual thereafter. This meant that servant and master met constantly in the main house and that, by extension, the notion of the invisible servant was not readily applicable in the old garden suburb.

Even so, virtually every antebellum service wing can be entered directly from the street. This assured the servants at least some degree of privacy and freedom. This design practice contrasts sharply with New York and Philadelphia townhouses, in which servants lived on the third floor, where the lady of the house could easily monitor their comings and goings, even if separate servants' stairs existed. It is possible that this reflects the indifference of New Orleanians to the Victorian custom of supervising their servants' morals. At the very least, the physical layout of Garden District houses made it more difficult for masters to exercise moral tutelage over the help.

Other aspects of the architecture reinforced the communal character of the household. The servants' wing featured outdoor galleries supported by square columns, a design feature common throughout the Ohio and Mississippi valleys. Had the architects and patrons been concerned with promoting privacy in the servants' lives, they could easily have faced these galleries away from the house or otherwise separated them visually from the main building. Yet Lewis Reynolds and Frederick Wing invariably placed the galleries so that they would be readily visible from the rear windows of the main house. Their motive was probably aesthetic: to create a picturesque two- or three-sided courtyard, not unlike those in the Vieux Carré. Whatever the architects' intention, though, the result was to render the lives of servant and master more readily visible to one another.

The relatively small number of slaves or immigrant domestics in each household further reduced their private realm. Typically, only two to four females were housed in the servants' wing and one or two males in the stable building—scarcely enough to constitute a separate society of servants. With little autonomous existence within the house to sustain servants, the human relations between slaves or immigrant servants and the master's family took on all the more significance. Unfortunately, the very subtlety of such relations makes them all but impossible to recapture after the passage of time. The more lurid tales often endure longest. One recalls with revulsion the story of Madame Delphine Lalurie, a mentally deranged Creole who is said to have tortured slaves in the attic of her Vieux Carré mansion. Yet to generalize from such tales is no more warranted than to do so on the basis of the many sentimentalized accounts of tearful partings of masters and slaves at the time of Emancipation.

One custom is evident: masters considered it to be in their interest to provide for slaves in such a way as to reflect well upon the household. Charles Raymond, a former New Orleanian, recalled the Sunday dress of domestic slaves as it existed on the eve of the

Civil War: "The younger 'girls' were dressed in pretty, French-looking costumes," he wrote, "many of them exceedingly tasteful. The 'boys' sported kid gloves, glossy beavers, patent-leather boots, and were many of them quite exquisite. This was the Sunday costume of house servants, clerks, porters, etc...."[30] As part of the same policy, slaves were given pocket money to meet their personal needs. An English traveler of clear abolitionist sympathies who visited New Orleans in the 1850s marveled, "When masters or mistresses want change, it is a common occurrence for them to apply to their negroes, who have almost always silver about them."[31]

Far more revealing about the true nature of the master-slave relationship in the Garden District are the records of slave sales. Although it is impossible to determine the precise frequency with which masters sold house servants, it was not an uncommon practice. Charles Kock, one of the District's few antebellum plantation owners, sold slaves with some regularity. John Wallis did so as well, although the timing of his several sales suggests that he was forced to do so for financial reasons.[32] Whether slave or free, Garden District servants were rarely permitted to raise families within the household. The slave Emilie, who belonged to Nathaniel Williamson, had a daughter, who lived with her in the servants' quarters of the Williamson home at 1226–28 First Street. When the daughter reached the age of five, Williamson sold off both mother and child.[33]

In contrast to such instances of callousness is the evidence of kindness and genuine solicitude on the part of slave owners. An advertisement in the *Daily Picayune* of 25 March 1850 announces the sale of a 28-year-old female domestic slave. Whatever his motives in selling the woman, the owner declared he would accept no offer at any price unless "I am satisfied that the girl is getting a good home." Even more striking is the case of an otherwise unidentified northern-born slaveholder in New Orleans who freed one of his household servants then sent him at his own expense to Oberlin College in Ohio, where in 1850 the former slave became one of the first blacks in the world to obtain a college degree.[34]

One of the reasons individual slave owners could afford to be lenient in disciplining their chattels is that New Orleans municipal law entrusted broad disciplinary powers over slaves to the city authorities.[35] The following observation, written by a staunchly abolitionist but reliable British observer of Crescent City life, provides chilling insight into this practice: "Nothing is more common than for the masters and mistresses of slaves, either male or female, when they wish them to be punished, to send them to the prison, with a note to the gaoler specifying the number of lashes to be inflicted. The slave must carry back a note to his master telling him that the punishment has been inflicted."[36]

How extensive was this brutal practice? This one reference, dating from 1833, may well describe practices that had diminished by mid-century when the Garden District began to flourish. If the number of slaves who chose to run away from Garden District masters is any indication, the abuse of slaves was rare or nonexistent. Of some 198 slaves who ran away from Orleans Parish masters in 1850, thirty-nine had escaped from plantations outside the city. Of those who fled from the city, 103, or two thirds, were males. It is impossible to determine how many of the fifty-six remaining females came from the Garden District. Since there were approximately 11,000 female slaves in the entire city at that time, however, the number could not have been great. The numbers may in fact have been smaller than raw statistics suggest. Garden District slaves, after all, enjoyed relatively good living and working conditions. Far more prone to escape would have been the large number of female slaves owned by middle- and lower-middle-income tradesmen and shop people. Living on the edge of poverty and working in hourly contact with their masters, such slaves constantly sought paths to freedom. Another group of slaves who were likely candidates for escape were those employed by New Orleans industries. Realizing the disloyalty of his slaves, the English-born James H. Caldwell, founder of the local gas works situated in the Lower Garden District, "erected a fifteen-foot brick wall and first-class set of iron gates to insure the affection of his chattels."[37] No such walls surrounded Garden District homes, although walled service areas were the rule in many urban houses elsewhere in the South.[38]

The evidence is admittedly circumstantial, but the generally comfortable situations of young Garden District slaves and their easy and constant access to the world beyond their households surely left them among the least dissatisfied members of the slave population as a whole and the least prone to escape.

*Nine servants, nearly a record for the Garden District, maintained Thomas
Gilmour's handsome establishment, 2520 Prytania Street, 1853*

THE PARADOX OF EMANCIPATION

Would slavery have died out on its own in the Garden District? The question is purely hypothetical and can no more be answered than the question of Europe's fate had Hitler died in the first attempt on his life in 1938. Yet intriguing possibilities present themselves. Slavery flourished as the great residences of the new suburb were built in the 1850s. At the same time, Irish and other immigrant labor made substantial inroads into the Garden District staffs on the eve of the Civil War. Indeed, New Orleans by 1861 had the largest number of white domestic servants of any southern city.[39] If the price of cotton had stayed high enough to maintain the high cost of slaves, one can readily imagine that free labor would have continued to erode the slaves' hold on the servants' wings. As this occurred and as the new immigrants' skills at handling domestic chores improved, the Irish might well have driven slaves out of the domestic market as surely as they had already usurped their places on the staffs of hotels and restaurants.

Emancipation halted this process before its ultimate extent could be known. Now the question became whether Garden District households would be staffed by whites or by free blacks. The abolition of slavery alone did not determine the outcome. As it was, the Civil War destroyed the plantation economy and transformed the world cotton market, driving tens of thousands of black plantation laborers into New Orleans in search of work. The competitive cost advantage of immigrant domestics evaporated over-night. Henceforth, blacks would completely dominate the domestic labor market, leaving the immigrants to seek better berths in the city's economy. Paradoxically, the popular image of southern mansions staffed by large numbers of deferential blacks more accurately fits the portrait of the postwar Garden District than it does the antebellum era there.

A further paradoxical consequence of Emancipation was to assure that Garden District grandees could continue to maintain the same size staffs to which they had become accustomed before the Civil War. Far from increasing the value of human labor in the city, emancipation decreased it by swelling the pool of unskilled labor. No longer did owners of the great houses have to invest the equivalent of $100,000 or more in today's dollars just to fill the servants' wing. Naturally, they hired whatever servants their households required. As a consequence of this ample supply of inexpensive domestic labor, there was one servant for every three households in New Orleans by 1870. By comparison, in Baltimore the ratio was 1:4, in Chicago 1:5, and in St. Louis 1:6.[40] Far from destroying the favorable labor market in which the great residences of the Garden District had flourished before the Civil War, the abolition of slavery transformed and improved that market in such a way as to guarantee the perpetuation of the suburb's way of life for several generations to come.[41]

[FACING PAGE] *Englishman Charles Briggs's free servants lived separately from the main dwelling, 2605 Prytania. James Gallier, Sr., architect and builder, 1849*

CHAPTER NINE

A *Neighborhood War, 1861–1865*

THE YEARS 1860 and 1861 were flush times on the lower Mississippi. The climate, usually capricious, for once cooperated with planters. These years saw the largest cotton yields in Louisiana's history, and bumper crops in sugar and rice as well.[1] It was all shipped to the Crescent City.

The commercial classes of New Orleans bustled to take advantage of the surge. Even before the cotton was picked, factors expanded their credit to the booming countryside. At the same time, they enlarged their brick warehouses along the riverfront to increase their inventory capacity and be able to hold out for the most favorable prices abroad. With money pouring in, many merchants broadened their activities. These were the years when Walter G. Robinson, who formerly specialized as a broker, expanded his operations into banking. Like James Robb before him, he capped his triumphs in banking by building a veritable palace in the Garden District beginning in 1859. Robinson was not the only one to gather the windfall, nor was he alone in expecting the boom to continue. Robert Short's factorage house also flourished to such an extent that he, for the first time, had enough liquidity to commission a sprawling residence for his family in 1859.

[FACING PAGE] *Freret's Folly, 1861. William Freret's speculative venture, five double houses in the 2700 block of Coliseum Street went bankrupt*

Neither Robinson, Short, nor many of their Garden District neighbors seems to have suspected that these years of ostensibly boundless prosperity would soon become "the good old days." Short, for example, was still buying slaves—a 20-year-old woman named Susan—in the late autumn of 1860 and taking slaves as collateral for loans.[2] Surely neither Robinson nor Short imagined they would have to wait over four years before settling into their new houses and that during these years the nation would be in the grip of a civil war. Walter Robinson did not move into his Third Street home until 1867, eight years after starting, and Robert Short did not accept his builder's work as completed until 1866 (although the Fourth Street house was at least habitable by 1862).[3]

That both these gentlemen were Southerners by birth was a significant factor in their buoyant outlook. Many members of the Garden District's Yankee majority, in contrast, were more cautious. The collapse of James Robb's fortunes in 1857–58 had sent a chill through the business community that had close ties with northern creditors. Thomas Wharton observed in his diary that "times are getting darker and darker and the financial clouds bred at the North are beginning to throw gloomy shadows over us here."[4] The impact of this gloom was felt far beyond the executive offices of entrepreneurial owners. At the very time the fortunes of Robinson and Short were waxing, Lavinia Dabney was forced to sell her newly completed Garden District house.[5]

The real estate market began to reflect mounting anxiety. When the Creole planter François Saulet died in 1859, his heirs barely managed to find a buyer for the family's venerable plantation house on Annunciation Street between Melpomene and Thalia in the Lower Garden District. The new owner, however, was unable to find someone to occupy the large domicile and soon sold it to the Sisters of Charity, who opened a girls' school there in 1861. Much later during the second half of the twentieth century many other great houses of the Garden District would suffer a similar fate as the Saulet Plantation.

When a brief panic in 1860 forced some thirty New Orleans factorage houses to suspend operations, only the most die-hard optimists ignored that trouble might well be afoot. The housing market responded by a pronounced shift toward less expensive multiple dwellings. It was in this climate that William A. Freret became something of a speculative venturer. A row of five single houses on Second Street served as a prototype for the five doubles on Coliseum Street that Freret developed in 1861. Unlike almost all later double houses, these galleried and columned dwellings between Fourth and Washington streets preserved the characteristic three-bay format, the apartments being divided horizontally rather than vertically. It was a clever idea, but a failure. As the national crisis deepened, construction work at the site had to be suspended; from the brickwork on the interior face of the chimneys one can still see that the work stopped abruptly, as if the men simply laid down their tools and left. The misfortune drove the elder Freret to the brink of bankruptcy.

Long before the election of Abraham Lincoln in November 1860, the subject of secession was being debated over the dinner tables of uptown New Orleans. Just what was said became the subject of some debate in later years. For half a century after the Civil War it was an article of faith locally that the community had supported secession. As John Smith Kendall, an eminent chronicler of the city's history, claimed in 1922, "a majority of the population of New Orleans unquestionably favored the withdrawal of the State from the Union."[6] This assertion, dubious at best for the population at large, is surely not true of the business elite. Bankers and factors had no desire to sever their vital credit links with New York. Nor were they prepared to secede from the Union in order to preserve slavery. After all, except for domestic staff, few of the mercantile class were slave owners. Granting, of course, that even non-slaveholders had an interest in preserving the plantation system, they still refused—as did President Lincoln—to see that objective as incompatible with the preservation of the Union. For this reason, many large slaveholders in the Garden District, men like Jacob Payne and Bradish Johnson, defended the institution of slavery and opposed secession. For this reason, too, Judah P. Benjamin, the Garden District's spokesman in the United States Senate and himself a slave owner, stood by the traditional Whig commitment to the Republic. Like James Robb, he knew that any talk of secession could only disrupt financial dealings; indeed, money was tightening as Benjamin cast his vote in favor of the Union.[7] Mercantile New Orleans knew it had much to lose if it seceded and nothing to gain. Even after Louisiana voted to withdraw from the Union in January,

1861, the *Daily Picayune* was still declaring "The Union—it must be preserved."[8]

Wealthy businessmen were not the only opponents of secession. The thousands of German immigrants living across Magazine Street near the river were divided in their sympathies. Although few owned slaves, outright abolitionism was unpopular among them. Most remained staunchly pro-Union and, with their leading paper, the *Deutsche Zeitung*, supported the Democratic candidate Stephen Douglas for president in 1860 in the hope that he would preserve the Republic intact. The other German newspaper, the *Louisiana Stuats-Zeitung*, went further by supporting the Free-Soil movement. After secession, many New Orleans Germans switched their allegiances to the Confederacy; their views on the federal Union had not necessarily changed, but they did not wish to arouse anti-German sentiment.[9] Others joined a Union Club that was formed after federal troops took control of New Orleans, and then elected one of their number, the anti-secessionist Michael Hahn, to represent Louisiana in the United States Congress and then to serve as governor of the state.

Americans are accustomed to viewing their Civil War as a tragedy in which region fought region. In the Garden District, however, neighbors fought neighbors. Virginia-born Charles Conrad passionately espoused secession in his drawing room on Prytania Street and took his campaign to Baton Rouge, eventually winning to his side a majority in the state legislature. Conrad was not alone. Canadian-born John A. Peel, a property owner on Prytania Street, was also outspoken in his new loyalty, as were many others.[10] With a few exceptions such as Peel, however, nearly all of the early partisans of secession were drawn from the Southern-born minority in the Garden District. They were men like Wirt Adams of Chestnut Street, the Mississippi planter who had practically no commercial ties with the North.

With the business establishment opposed, or at best cool, to secession, Charles Conrad and his faction had to look elsewhere for local leadership for the Southern cause. They found it in a most unlikely quarter, the Protestant clergy. Leonidas Polk, the first Episcopal bishop of Louisiana, served as rector of Trinity Church on Jackson Avenue. A graduate of the U.S. Military Academy, this North Carolina native had been a friend of Jefferson Davis since their days together at West Point. In the years immediately before the Civil War, Polk helped establish the University of the South in Tennessee, known as Sewanee. Working from his home on Magazine Street between Third and Fourth, he oversaw every aspect of the planning for the new school. In spite of the fact there were more practicing architects in the Crescent City than anywhere else in the South, Polk did not call on New Orleans designers to create the new campus. His outlook, apparently, was more southern than New Orleanian.

When secession loomed, he represented the Confederate cause to New Orleans, rather than vice versa. After secession, he joined the Confederate Army and was killed in action, having risen to the rank of general. For all Polk's heroism in war, various members of his New Orleans congregation, not to mention Episcopalians elsewhere, questioned whether the bishop's role on the battlefield was consistent with his vows to the Church. As late as 1893 this was so sore a point that Polk's son wrote a biography of the bishop-general to defend his name.[11]

Like Polk, the Reverend Benjamin Palmer was a southerner who settled in New Orleans. He lived a few blocks from Polk on Prytania Street. Before becoming pastor of the First Presbyterian Church of Lafayette Square in 1856, Reverend Palmer had burnished his oratorical skills at a church in Columbia, South Carolina.[12] He was a passionate defender of slavery, not as a system of labor but as a "providential trust." On Thanksgiving Day 1860 he delivered a rousing pro-slavery sermon that helped crystallize secessionist sentiment throughout the city.[13] Among those who sided with Palmer's highly moralistic defense of slavery was the builder-architect Samuel Jamison, president of the board of trustees of Palmer's church. Jamison's partner and fellow slaveholder, James McIntosh, also rallied to the cause, as did many other prominent Garden District residents.

No member of the economic or political elite of New Orleans doubted that a civil war would divide the city—even its neighborhoods—as much as the nation as a whole. Yet with the capture of Fort Sumter and the outbreak of hostilities, a remarkable semblance of unity was forged. Countless people who had opposed secession now cast their lot, however reluctantly, with their state and region. Senator Judah P. Benjamin served as Secretary of the Treasury (and

Designed in the prewar boom, Walter Robinson's palace at 1415 Third Street remained unfinished until 1867. Henry Howard, architect

eventually Secretary of State) of the Confederacy, and even such northern-born Garden District residents as A. W. Bosworth and Hiram Anderson flocked to the South's Stars and Bars. Charles Eager, though a native of Camden, Maine, was among those who fought gallantly in the Confederate Army.[14]

Builders and architects responded to the call to arms. Henry Howard and William Stehle enlisted in the Louisiana militia. Philadelphia-born Frederick Wing did so as well, and sold his newly built house in the depressed market of April 1862, probably to enable his family to survive.[15] For most, there was simply no alternative. As the practical-minded Henry Howard plainly stated in his published autobiography, the outbreak of war "upset my business prospects and caused me to go into the Confederacy...."[16]

But few anticipated the terrible speed with which the local economy began to crack. During the sixteen months between Louisiana's secession from the Union in January 1861 and the United States Navy's seizure of New Orleans in April 1862, the city's commercial life reeled under shock after shock. The Federal blockade of the mouth of the Mississippi effectively killed all cotton export, while even the lucrative western trade fell by more than half.[17] Unwilling to extend credit under such conditions, local banks saw their operations shrink to a standstill.

The shock to business caused rapid turnover in the property market. A typical house on Second Street was sold five times between 1861 and 1866; one on Camp saw three different owners between 1864 and 1865; and a property on Laurel changed hands three times between 1860 and 1864.[18] Although some houses declined in value, prices generally held up, probably because New Orleans remained a relatively secure place to live and because real estate, for all its uncertainties, still involved less risk than most alternative investments.

Following Louisiana's secession from the Union, few people dared undertake new building projects and so the construction business and its supporting industries were crippled. The Louisiana Sash Factory, for example, which employed forty workers in 1860, was down to half that number by the time Captain Farragut seized the city. Labor wages also went through a roller-coaster ride. As Army recruiting intensified, the cost of labor increased; after secession, it plummeted. In 1860 Sam Vosburgh received fifty-four dol-

lars a month for his job as foreman at the Louisiana Sash Factory; his paycheck rose to sixty-six dollars a month a year later. After the Federal capture of the city, Vosburgh's salary dropped to forty-four dollars.[19]

Conditions degenerated rapidly during 1861. Carnival was celebrated as usual, but looters attacked closed stores and arsonists started one or two conflagrations each night.[20] Confederate New Orleans was in a state of near anarchy. Slowly at first and then in a rapid stream, uptown business leaders began fleeing the city. Bradish Johnson, who always divided his time between the Crescent City and New York, locked up his New Orleans residence and, together with his New York-born wife, fled the city in order to sit out the war in Manhattan.[21] Florence A. Luling, a German-speaking immigrant from Alsace, had married into the wealthy Hermann family and settled in a comfortable Garden District home on Philip Street. At the outset of the war Luling sold his house and moved to New York. Thomas Smithfield Dugan, who had purchased the old Toby house in the late 1850s, also left New Orleans and seems to have spent the war years wandering between Paris, Dresden, Rome, Montreal, and the English spa town of Leamington.[22] The émigrés took many different paths. John McGinty went upriver to Cincinnati, married, and waited for the fighting to end. Henry H. Hansell chose to bide his time in Philadelphia, while William M. Perkins apparently left the country, to return only in 1869.[23]

Even native-born southerners joined the exodus. Walter G. Robinson, after considerable hesitation, concluded late in 1861 that he could not long survive in the collapsing economy of New Orleans. He might well have pondered what he would live on if he were to leave town. As a typical New Orleans entrepreneur, he enjoyed little liquidity. His assets were tied up in his business, his home, and his other properties locally. To remedy this problem, Robinson mortgaged his Third Street mansion in December 1861. The final deal, for $50,000, was notarized on 25 April 1862, the very day the Union Navy under Farragut took the city.[24] Scarcely was this arrangement concluded when Robinson, too, departed New Orleans for an unknown destination.

Many of those who were unable or unwilling to leave took the precaution of withdrawing their money from Confederate New

Orleans. Julius Weis had arrived in Louisiana from his native Alsace in 1845 with two dollars. By the time the state joined the Confederacy, he had amassed a large fortune, which he promptly withdrew from the Citizens Bank and deposited with Lazard Frères in Paris.[25]

The flight of capital from New Orleans to the North and abroad at the start of the Civil War attests clearly to the uptown business community's lack of confidence in the Confederacy. Small merchants shared this skepticism over the prospects of the Confederacy. They refused to accept Confederate currency even before Farragut's flotilla entered the Mississippi.[26] Indeed, whatever hostility they later expressed to the Yankees' occupation forces under General Benjamin "the Beast" Butler, New Orleans businessmen were prepared in 1862 to accept any regime that would assure the return of economic stability.

When the Navy approached New Orleans on April 25, 1862, workmen building the Campman house at 1328 Harmony Street followed its progress up the river from their perches on the roof.[27] The city surrendered peacefully. Federal commandant General Butler proceeded to establish himself and his officers in the expropriated houses of known Confederate supporters. The tale of Butler's eight-month reign in New Orleans has been retold many times. It is a story of tactlessness, venality, vengeance, and ruthlessness tempered by a practical concern for law, order, public health, and the promotion of trade. Even today, over a century later, the very mention of the walrus-faced leader of the occupation forces can evoke sneers in New Orleans. If for nothing else, Butler is despised for his infamous Order 28, which commanded New Orleans ladies to desist from insulting Federal officers and soldiers at the risk of being treated as women of the street.

The ladies' disdain reflects only part of the story. Fully 94 percent of New Orleans' adult white males took an oath of allegiance to the government of the United States soon after Butler's arrival.[28] To be sure, the alternative was to be declared hostile aliens and have their property confiscated. Perhaps they simply bowed to fate. Or perhaps, as seems most likely, the citizens of New Orleans had no strong commitment to the Confederate cause in the first place and were quite willing to give it up.

For those who refused to take the oath, the U.S. Congress in July 1862 passed a Confiscation Act.[29] According to this law, anyone remaining loyal to the Confederacy lost the legal rights to his property. This was beyond doubt the most feared piece of Federal legislation during the occupation. Far from pitting "the Beast" against the gentle residents of the Garden District, however, it divided the elite neighborhood against itself. The central figure in this dramatic episode was the gambler, horseman, and bon vivant of the Garden District, Cuthbert Bullitt.

Thanks to his marriage to the daughter of the prosperous plantation owner Maunsel White, Bullitt owned considerable property along St. Charles Avenue and Prytania Street. Indeed, he devoted most of his time to managing his spouse's considerable inheritance.[30] In 1854 he sold a parcel of land to Joseph H. Maddox's wife, and in 1856 he sold another parcel to the wife of Mandeville Marigny for their raised cottage.[31] Knowing Bullitt to be a trusted member of the community and knowledgeable in real estate matters, his neighbors called upon him to represent them in land transactions, as when Susan Hackett purchased her lots from the Conrad family in 1854.[32] Cuthbert Bullitt, in short, was a bulwark of the Garden District.

He was also an outspoken Unionist in his politics. No sooner did the Federal troops arrive in New Orleans than Bullitt presented himself to the commandant and offered his services to the Union. In return for this patriotic act, President Lincoln named him Marshal and Acting Collector of the Custom House. As General George Denison put it, these honors were conferred upon Bullitt "as an acknowledgment of [his] outspoken loyalty when it was dangerous to be loyal, and partly because it was most fitting that this particular office should be held by an old resident of the place."[33]

It helped that the United States Marshal be an "old resident of the place" because his role, bluntly, was to oversee the confiscation and resale of property belonging to his pro-Confederate neighbors. His job was to identify the residences of all rebels who refused to take the oath of allegiance. After confiscating their houses and furnishings, the Marshal would then either turn them over for use by Union officers or auction them off to the loyalist public. It was through such a process that Bullitt issued a writ for the sale of four

John Henry Campman house, 1328 Harmony Street, 1861–62. Perched on the roof, workmen building the house watched U.S. Navy ships approach New Orleans on April 25, 1862

Mrs. Nathaniel Banks hadn't the slightest difficulty adapting to the Garden District way of life: the double parlor of Robert Short's villa, occupied by the Gulf commandant and his wife during the Civil War. 1448 Fourth Street, by Henry Howard, 1859

lots belonging to his neighbor, the secessionist Charles Conrad.[34] Many other residents of the neighborhood experienced a similar fate. On the strength of Bullitt's zealous work, Federal control in the Garden District was reestablished by an insider.

How many Garden District residents sided with the rebellion? Once the Civil War was over, those whose property had been confiscated could petition Congress for its return. The rare published listing of such petitioners, issued in Washington in 1867 under the title *Property Seized in Louisiana*, provides a precise register of the political orientation of uptown New Orleanians during the Civil War.[35] It indicates that of the approximately forty largest property owners in the Garden District, only nine were considered rebels. Although there were more confiscations than these forty in the Garden District, the majority involved smaller property holders.

Confiscations were more numerous in the downtown Faubourg Ste. Marie, where the earlier wave of Anglo-Saxon immigrants to New Orleans had settled. Such people seem to have assimilated more completely to the southern political environment. Farther uptown, beyond the Garden District, lay the town of Jefferson. The

Anglo-Saxon population there was encased primarily in local trade, retail shops, and the like. Lacking any significant commercial links with the North, these people, too, found it easier to side with the Confederacy. The Garden District was thus an island of Unionist sentiment between two seas of southern sympathizers.

The process of confiscation of Garden District homes can be followed with great precision, thanks to careful records kept by the occupying forces. The fate of Robert Short's villa is typical. In the last days before New Orleans fell to Farragut's fleet, Short departed the city for his birthplace in Christian County, Kentucky. He was later to claim to Federal authorities that he merely intended to travel to Philadelphia for medical treatment and had no intentions of disloyalty to the Union.[36] Mrs. Short also left the city soon after under a pass from General Butler and joined her husband in Kentucky. Before departing, she packed the linens, stored them in a spare bedroom, and turned the house over to the care of her sister, a Mrs. Hammond. Short's medical excuses carried no weight with the Federal authorities, however, who confiscated the property. Mrs. Hammond was permitted to stay on in the house by paying seventy-five dollars a month in rent, a colossal sum at that time.[37] Lest she try to spirit family possessions out of the villa, the occupying forces prepared a detailed inventory of all the furnishings and household effects.

Thus matters stood until March 3, 1864. On that day Butler's successor, General Banks, ordered Mrs. Hammond out of the house and gave her two hours to pack her personal effects.[38] On the following morning Colonel Short's villa became the executive mansion for the newly elected Federal governor of Louisiana, Michael Hahn.[39] Until his election, the German-born Hahn had lived on Baronne Street near Clio, only a few minutes away from Short's house by horsecar. After the Civil War he settled permanently on Prytania Street in the Garden District. Hahn's inauguration was a splendid occasion and the newly designated executive mansion was decked out handsomely. Jacques' City Band serenaded the guests, and toasts were drunk to virtually everyone from Abraham Lincoln to "the Workingmen of Louisiana."[40]

Hahn's use of the Fourth Street villa lasted only two weeks, for the new commandant of the Department of the Gulf, General Nathaniel P. Banks, had his own ideas of how the Short mansion should be used. By the end of March he had installed his wife and family in the house. Banks was a self-made man from Waltham, Massachusetts, who had begun life working in a cloth mill and remained proud of his nickname, "the Bobbin Boy."[41] A ten-term veteran of Congress and former Speaker of the House, he was an adept, even wily, politician who had been among the national organizers of the Republican Party. His wife had not the slightest difficulty adapting to the Shorts' way of life. With little modesty but a fine proprietary sense, Mrs. Banks boasted to her husband on May 13, 1864 that her "reception was certainly very pleasant and brilliant....Rooms crowded with elegantly dressed people....Fine performers on the piano and many excellent singers....Our parlors are grand. We have them well lighted—plenty of beautiful flowers. Your dear wife, darling children, the beautiful flowers, elegant rooms—all together it was a picture for a painter."[42] Mrs. Banks concluded, "my house is excellent for entertaining. Nothing could be better."[43] Nor could it have been. During the spring of 1864, the Union and Confederate armies were locked in mortal combat at Spotsylvania, Virginia.

While the occupation government enforced the Confiscation Act, it was also imposing a number of stiff demands on the local economy. It will be recalled that New Orleans banks had made substantial "voluntary" contributions to the government of the Confederacy. The United States Treasury now required these banks to match their subvention of the Confederate with gifts to the federal government. It is no wonder that seven banks failed in 1863 alone. General Butler also imposed heavy taxes on wealthy secessionists to help finance his drainage and cleanup programs.[44] Coming at the very time that planters by the hundreds were defaulting on loans from their New Orleans creditors, these levies crippled the commodity factors. The uptown commercial elite—or what remained of it—was thrown into a state of chaos.

The situation was bleak, but it offered at least a few signs of hope. When the city government, installed by Federal troops, built a streetcar line up Levee Street as far as Toledano Street in the Garden District, it persuaded at least a few local residents that the mission of the occupying forces extended beyond milking the city financially. Strict policing put an end to pilfering, while the revival of a court system made it possible once more to enforce contracts, at least within New Orleans. As such measures multiplied in the autumn of 1863, the economy gradually revived.

The recovery eventually, and slowly, extended to the uptown building trades. In June 1863 the Louisiana Sash Factory had cut its payroll to only three persons; over the following year it rose to twenty, or two-thirds the 1860, prewar level.[45] With labor in short supply, craftsmen and skilled hands stood to profit handsomely. Allen Hill, a prominent dealer in building materials, prospered to the point that he could invest in a lot on Fourth Street during wartime.[46]

Even though labor was available, the New Orleans building trade faced high costs. The isolation from the hinterland meant the price of building materials, especially lumber, rose precipitously. This made the locally produced brick a far more attractive material than ever before. On the eve of the war the congregation of the Gates of Prayer Synagogue had decided to build a new temple on Jackson Avenue, between Annunciation and Chippewa streets. By the end of 1863 it had amassed 300,000 bricks on the site. The following spring it was able to commission architect Jacob Wilhelm

Wartime profits: cotton factor Julius Weis's grand residence was one of the finest Italianate styled houses in the Garden District, 1237 Jackson Avenue. Charles L. Hillger, architect; Peter Middlemiss, builder, 1876, now demolished (JOAN G. CALDWELL, "ITALIANATE DOMESTIC ARCHITECTURE...," HOWARD-TILTON LIBRARY, TULANE UNIVERSITY)

Thiel to design the temple. Construction was well advanced by the time peace was concluded at Appomattox.[47]

New Orleanians who had made their peace with the occupying forces were the individuals able to undertake the new construction during the war years. Itinerant carpetbaggers, however, also appear to have been operating successfully in the Garden District as early as 1862. In February of that year George W. Magee of Philadelphia purchased land on Prytania Street between Pleasant and Harmony. Another Philadelphian named Magee, possibly the brother of George W., joined with Napolean B. Kneass, also of Philadelphia, to invest in uptown real estate. Meanwhile, Garden District resident Henry H. Hansell fled to Philadelphia toward the end of the war and sold to another Philadelphian some fourteen Garden District lots he had bought in 1859. He had bought the lots for $12,500, and sold them five years later in 1864 at the handsome sum of $27,500.[48] Hansell returned to New Orleans in the late 1860s having recouped whatever southern losses he may have incurred.

Having recited this tale, the scale of northern involvement in the New Orleans real estate market should not he exaggerated. The best opportunities for carpetbaggers in New Orleans existed up to the economic revival of 1864. From then on, New Orleanians themselves moved swiftly back into the property market. By 1866 Messrs. Magee and Kneass found it advantageous to unload their uptown holdings, leaving the field to homegrown operators.[49]

The reason carpetbaggers had such difficulty operating in the Garden District is that many local residents could outbid them, utilizing the fruits of wartime profiteering. Such profit making took several forms. One method was to arrange deals with planters behind Confederate lines to market the planters' crops in New Orleans in violation of the Richmond government's ban on trade with Unionists.[50] This commerce happened also to violate a Federal law against trading with the enemy. Fortunately for the opportunists in New Orleans, Benjamin Butler's successor, General Banks, refrained from enforcing the rule in order to lure planters to the Union side. A second field for profiteering was to market such illegally obtained cotton or sugar in New York, while a third was to run northern-manufactured goods through the Confederate lines and sell them locally.

All three forms of trade flourished. A number of Garden District residents, capitalizing on their traditional ties with the North, made great fortunes by concentrating on the seaboard link. Julius Weis, for example, traded in baled cotton at the "back of the store" throughout the war, shipping it to New York in payment for dry goods. Because the price of cotton rose steadily, he made $30,000 on that side of the trade alone. At the end of the war his business had grown to the extent that he rented space in a building owned by a fellow Alsatian Jewish immigrant, Leon Godchaux, who operated a store on Canal Street. Within a few years Weis was to build one of the finest Italianate homes in the Garden District.[51]

Florence Luling, formerly of 1433 Philip Street, also exploited wartime dislocations in trade to line his own pockets.[52] For a short while after his arrival in New York in 1861, Luling lacked a clear business direction. Once the Union forces captured New Orleans, however, Luling entered at once into the lucrative North-South trade. It was risky business, but with a product such as turpentine costing only three dollars a barrel in New Orleans and bringing thirty-eight dollars in New York, it was worth it. The war was scarcely over when Luling returned to the Crescent City and commissioned architect James Gallier, Jr., to build for him the grandiose mansion that still stands on Leda Street, off Esplanade Avenue. Luling's choice of Gallier as architect and the design of his mansion, which recalls the refined classicism of Philadelphians John Notman and Samuel Sloan, suggest this ambitious merchant consciously tried to outdo James Robb's Washington Avenue palace.

Advertisements in the wartime newspaper *The Era* indicate a local demand for northern goods that rewarded entrepreneurs who could satisfy it in their stock trade. Typical was Poydras Street grocer P. Gallagher, who in 1863 offered up "New York sugar-cured shoulders," candles from Procter and Gamble in Cincinnati, and various other northern produce.[53] The same entrepreneurial climate that had earlier drawn young risk-takers to New Orleans before the Civil War now enabled a number of such men to survive and even to thrive during the nation's ordeal.

It cannot be denied that New Orleans and the business community suffered during the Civil War. Many sons and husbands died in the fighting. Hundreds of families lost their possessions. Wives of Confederate loyalists endured gross, personal indignities during the Federal occupation. Charles Conrad, Judah P. Benjamin, and others who had held high posts in the Confederate government were ostracized and lost the possibility of ever returning to their homes.

New Orleans proper, however, survived the war physically unscathed. Not only were the city's buildings spared bombardment, but also the policies of the Federal administrators actually strengthened the physical infrastructure as a center of trade and commerce. In contrast, visitors to Charleston in 1866 found a desolate city in ruins. Richmond, as Matthew Brady's photographs starkly reveal, lay smoldering. Atlanta, Vicksburg, and most of the South's other commercial hubs also suffered grievously. Even before secession New Orleans was four times larger than the next most populous southern city.[54] By 1865 it was virtually the only southern city still intact.

That New Orleans was fated to sit out the war in relative security was later the cause of embarrassment in some pro-Confederate circles. If the Civil War was not a heroic episode in the history of New Orleans, it nonetheless afforded the city benefits that were denied to other southern cities. It meant that New Orleans emerged after Appomatox in a unique position to prosper. Neither downtown business houses nor uptown residences had to be rebuilt. The ranks of the local elite had been thinned by war but the core was still relatively intact. Commerce could thus rebound rapidly. As that occurred, social and cultural life, including architecture and the building trades, resumed where they had left off.

Thanks to these fortuitous circumstances, the Garden District after 1865 enjoyed nearly a full decade of exuberant growth. The strangest irony of the early capture of New Orleans is that it enabled the city to flourish thereafter. The golden age of the Garden District, which had begun in the early 1850s, thus continued through the Civil War and on to the nationwide financial Panic of 1873. The postwar phase of the boom gave the District much of the character it retains to the present day.

CHAPTER TEN

Men and Mansions of the Postwar Bubble

I N ONE SENSE, the era of Reconstruction did not exist in New Orleans. No shelling had preceded the entry of Union forces into the city, and the Federal occupation had improved rather than destroyed the port facilities. Hence there was nothing to reconstruct. To many contemporaries, however, it seemed the war had caused the normal order of life to collapse. The Reverend Benjamin Morgan Palmer surveyed the situation after the conclusion of the peace accord and wrote, "Just now the earth is very dark...."[1] J. W. Labouisse, a commission merchant of Thalia Street, reached a similar conclusion in 1868. "Everything," he said, "is going to the devil here in a hard gallop."[2] More than a few New Orleanians would have concurred with the judgment of later historians that the years following the Civil War were a "dreadful decade," a "tragic era."[3]

Certainly New Orleans was not lacking in personal tragedies. When forced loans to the Confederacy and then to the Federal government drove local banks to ruin, many private fortunes collapsed with them. Henry Lonsdale, for example, watched helplessly as his second fortune evaporated. In a desperate attempt to recoup, he sold his house at 2521–23 Prytania Street at auction in 1868.[4] The proceeds scarcely left a mark on Lonsdale's huge debts, and within the year he died in poverty.

[FACING PAGE] *Railroad wealth: Scotsman Archibald Montgomery, president of the Crescent City Railroad Company, hired Henry Howard to design his cottage at 1213 Third Street, 1867–70*

Two blocks away, at 2618 Coliseum Street, the widow Amenaide Fortin, also emerged from the Civil War impoverished. For nearly a decade she struggled vainly to make ends meet, but even her best efforts were insufficient to provide for herself and her two daughters. The one exploitable resource she had was the land adjacent to her house. She mortgaged her residence to finance the construction of speculative housing there, to be developed by Daniel Kelly. The project was never built. Now desperate, the hapless Madame Fortin eventually sold her remaining eleven lots, yet even the profits of this sale did not prevent her house from falling into the hands of a local insurance company. Thus, from the day of Appomattox to her final eviction in 1887, Amenaide Fortin's life was a story of progressive ruin.[5]

No group was more devastated by the war than the planters. Few Garden District residents had built their fortunes on land and slaves, but those who had now paid dearly. At the start of the war, after Walter G. Robinson mortgaged his unfinished palace on Third Street, he left town in 1862. Returning to New Orleans in 1866, Robinson managed to regain the presidency of the Merchants and Traders Bank, but only at the cost of his health. He was soon incapacitated by "nervous prostration" and alcoholism. His old partner, David C. McCan, stepped in to help by buying Robinson's mansion. At the closing, Robinson was in so pitiful a state that he had to sign his name with an X.[6] Soon afterward he died of cirrhosis of the liver, leaving behind a paltry estate. A brother in Missouri, who had probably hoped to retire on his legacy, had to go to court to claim so much as one horse.[7]

The collapse of the planters was due to several causes, only one of which was the loss of their slaves. Fighting in the countryside had left the levee system in a shambles, exposing cotton land to devastating floods. The dreaded boll weevil blighted cotton crops in both 1866 and 1867. Most of the expensive machinery on sugar plantations had fallen into ruin as well.[8] Such conditions, no less than Emancipation, drove former slaves from the land and plunged New Orleans-based planters into poverty.

The Confiscation Act of 1863 nationalized the property of Confederate supporters. It ruined the few Garden District residents who had sided with the secessionists and, ironically, some who did not. Jacob Payne, for example, had been an outspoken opponent of secession. Once Louisiana withdrew from the Union, however, Payne was drawn into the Lost Cause and saw all his property vanish. Thanks to the personal intervention of President Lincoln in 1865, Payne regained his civil rights, but he still had to devote the rest of his life paying off the staggering debts he had accumulated.[9]

The case of Robert Short typifies the arduous road back that many Garden District property owners trod. Like Payne, Short had opposed secession. Ambivalent in his politics, he nonetheless fled to his native Hopkinsville, Kentucky, while the fighting raged. This move saved him from designation as a "registered enemy," but did not prevent his valuable Fourth Street mansion, used by Unionists Governor Hahn and General Banks, from being seized as abandoned property. In an act of conciliation that was hailed by the New Orleans press, the government restored Short's property to him in October 1865.[10] Short regained his home, but was unable to reestablish himself as a cotton factor. He was luckier than many of his neighbors, however, for his brother-in-law from Kentucky knew the fine art of distilling. Mortgaging himself to the hilt, Robert Short finally managed to establish a distillery on the corner of Clio and Locust Streets and thereby keep his debtors at bay.[11]

The deck appeared to be stacked against the old leadership. The city emerged from the Civil War with a huge debt, which mounted rapidly in the late 1860s. The only means of reducing the debt was to increase property taxes. Since members of the prewar leadership still held the most valuable property, such taxes fell most heavily on them.[12] By the early 1870s the tax burden became so onerous that, in the opinion of one contemporary observer, "it would not pay to purchase...."[13]

No less important, the Republican regime installed by the Federal forces was militantly hostile to the city's old commercial leadership. Even before the Civil War, the labor faction had claimed a more dominant position in local affairs; the last two prewar mayors had been a printer and a stevedore, respectively.[14] Under the Radical Republicans, labor's hold on the city government tightened, with predictable results for business. Labor consolidated its power the more easily because so many members of the former leadership were disenfranchised. Until its demise in 1869, the Bureau of Refugees, Freedman and Abandoned Lands (commonly known as the Freedmen's Bureau) exercised sweeping powers from its downtown office on Julia Street. When the Radicals installed black representation on the City Council in 1866–68, the confrontation took a nasty racial turn. Later, when white Democrats managed to regain control of the city government, they struck back in 1874 by establishing a White League, with headquarters at Prytania and Felicity Streets.[15] Michel Musson, the pioneer Creole settler in the Garden District, took a prominent role in the League's agitation. The very existence of this extrapolitical band attests to the fact that radical Reconstruction had turned yesterday's insiders into outsiders.[16]

The extent of this social, economic, and political turnabout would appear to reinforce historian C. Van Woodward's observation that southern history is dominated by sharp breaks and discontinuities.[17] Yet on the whole New Orleans presents a picture of continuity at war's end. Undeniably, many suffered gravely as a consequence of the Confederate defeat. But even a cursory glance at the postwar architecture of uptown New Orleans shows that the prewar building boom promptly revived and gained new momentum. Whereas earlier the architecture had exhibited at least a modicum of restraint, now conspicuous consumption and a devil-may-care quest for all the trappings of worldly comfort prevailed. The completed form of the Garden District owes as much to the postwar phase of the boom, which lasted until 1873, as to its prewar phase.

Contemporaries attested to the prosperity of postwar New Orleans. The *Daily Picayune* boomed that "the merchants and bankers of New Orleans…are in a thoroughly healthy condition.…"[18] James D. B. DeBow, one of the keenest observers of the economy, wrote in 1866, "The young men of the army who have survived are here, and all at work with vigor and energy.…The levee is crowded with steamers and ships and merchandise and busy men, and the shops are filled with goods."[19] Still another contemporary, Edward King, toured the Garden District in the early 1870s and concluded that the well-to-do Americans "have been able to keep about them some appearance of comfort since the war."[20] As if to celebrate their recovery, wealthy New Orleanians contributed bountifully to aid victims of the great Chicago fire of 1871 and proudly banded together to mount the first modern Mardi Gras when the Russian Grand Duke Alexei visited the Crescent City in 1872.[21]

So great was the impact of the postwar boom on architecture that it is necessary to pause to consider its cause. Paramount was the physical survival of the city. New money could go into new building, rather than into reconstruction. Scarcely less important was the speed with which New Orleans restored communications with the outside world. No sooner had Vicksburg and Port Hudson fallen to the Yankees in 1863 than the upper Mississippi basin was reopened to shipping.[22] Railroad lines, devastated by flooding caused by breaches in the levees, were also quickly rebuilt.

Such work created new fortunes. Thomas Pickles had been a pharmacist before the Civil War. A few years after the fighting ceased, he had amassed sufficient wealth through a fleet of ten ferryboats plying the Mississippi River to build the handsome columned house at 3303 Coliseum Street.[23] Meanwhile, the Belfast-born Archibald Montgomery concentrated his energies on railroads, which he dreamed of pushing from New Orleans to the Pacific. He never realized his vision, but his grandly scaled "cottage" at 1213 Third Street, designed by Henry Howard and recalling equally immodest antebellum "cottages" built along Summit Street in Philadelphia's Chestnut Hill, is testimony to the profits Montgomery reaped as president of the Crescent City Railroad.

The cotton market did not bounce back so quickly. Even the reduced crops had to be marketed, though, and many of the old pillars of that field had left town or retired. This left room for younger men such as John F. Randolph, a cotton weighter at the Pelican Cotton Press, who built a sturdy house for himself at 1205 Seventh Street during 1867–70.[24] Armant St. Amant, a cotton classer whose trade was immortalized by Edgar Degas in his painting, *The Cotton Market at New Orleans*, built an unusually fine five-bay Italianate house at 1427 St. Mary Street with the rewards from his specialized profession.[25]

Even the limited revival of the cotton market would have been impossible without the support of banks. Several local banks had collapsed by 1864, their assets depleted by two avaricious governments. New banks were swiftly created with funds advanced by New York capitalists eager to reopen the cotton trade. By 1866 ten banks operated in New Orleans, among them James Robb's newly established Louisiana National Bank. Thus, in a repeat of the process that had first brought American capital to the Crescent

[LEFT] *The residence of pharmacist-turned-ferry fleet owner Thomas Pickles, 3303 Coliseum Street, 1868–69*

[FACING PAGE] *The elegant setting of the Fortin family's decline, 2618 Coliseum Street. Built by London-born Louis de Saulles, circa 1845*

City half a century earlier, more money was available for lending in New Orleans than anywhere else in the South.[26]

Cotton factors were the traditional link between capitalist and plantation, and their businesses, too, had to be rebuilt from the ground up. Henry S. Buckner was among those factors that returned to town with New York money, even before Appomattox. He soon found that the labor situation upriver was so confused as to make any loans to planters a grave risk. To protect themselves, Buckner and his partners, like other factors of the postwar period, required planters to put up their land as well as their crops as security for loans, and they charged high rates of interest reflecting the level of risk involved.[27] Another firm of cotton factors, that of Meyer Deutsch and Julius Weis, demanded that the owner of Woodland Plantation mortgage his entire holdings before they would extend a loan of only $2,700.[28] It is no wonder that Weis had the fortune to build a lavish Garden District home during Reconstruction. Through interest rates on residential mortgages and commercial loan rates of up to 25 percent, factors passed the risk along to the struggling planters. In other words, the rural economy of the lower Mississippi Valley was bled not by Yankee loan sharks directly but by New Orleans bankers and factors domiciled in the Garden District.

A bitter irony of this battle between city and countryside was that the inevitable foreclosures on mortgages left the urban factors as owners of many large plantations. David McCan, for example, a Cincinnati-born former blacksmith who lived in a raised cottage that once stood on Coliseum Street, established himself as a major sugar planter in this way. This process eventually transformed Garden District society, making it far more rural in orientation, less closely linked with the Northeast, and withal, more "southern." This paved the way for New Orleanians, for the first time, to romanticize their southernness.

Changed conditions pushed new people to the fore, diversifying Garden District society in the process. Julius Weis, Samuel Newman, Meyer Deutsch, and Jamaica-born Isaac Delgado were just a few of the Jewish traders who emerged suddenly in society, first as factors and then as planters. Formerly, brokers, factors, commission merchants, and insurance men dominated the neighborhood. Now Joseph C. Morris, a mere cordage dealer, had taken residence at 1331

First Street, and George Soulè, a schoolmaster, lived at 1620 Eighth Street.[29] At 1749 Coliseum Street below Jackson in the Lower Garden District lived John Henry, a shoe merchant with enough money to add crystal chandeliers, stained-glass windows, and frescoes to the old Rodewald house.[30] A. Walter Merriam at 2336 St. Charles Avenue had bought into the exclusive enclave with the profits of his Crescent Billiard Hall on Canal Street, claimed by Merriam to be the largest such gaming establishment in the entire United States.[31] Former Confederate General John B. Holed moved into a Second Empire house at 1206 Third Street. Whatever their differences, John Henry, A. Walter Merriam, and the hero of Round Top had all settled in New Orleans in the hope of building—or rebuilding—their fortunes. All three succeeded.

The arrival of such men, coupled with the wartime slump in construction activity, caused real estate values in the Garden District to soar. Henry Lonsdale's Prytania Street mansion had been built in 1856 for $30,000; by 1868 it was worth $43,000.[32] Walter C. Robinson's residence increased in value from $30,000 to $40,000 between 1864 and 1867.[33] Rents, too, rose precipitously, doubling in 1865 alone.[34]

The consequent building boom changed the face of New Orleans. Magazine Street adjacent to the Garden District became a major shopping center overnight. Block-long commercial buildings sprang up on both sides of the thoroughfare all the way from St. Mary Street to Jackson Avenue. In these blocks the eighteenth-century notion of an architecturally unified ensemble of independent shops flourished in New Orleans. With apartments above for the shopkeepers' families and galleries to protect the sidewalks from rain, they were an instant success, selling at more than $8,000 per unit.[35] Complementing these were carefully planned open-air markets established at several points farther out along Magazine Street. Meanwhile, dozens of great houses rose on the remaining vacant lots in the Garden District.

The building trades had to adapt rapidly to meet the new conditions. Those few firms that had maintained their own crews of slaves had either to adjust to the rigors of a free labor system or go out of business. Jamison and McIntosh dissolved their construction partnership, and Samuel Jamison reemerged as an architect-entrepreneur. Robert Huyghe, in contrast, plunged into the new market, hiring craftsmen on hourly wages in order to build most of the Magazine Street shopping complex. Changed circumstances forced the pace of specialization. True, Charles Hillger continued to straddle the fence between architecture and building, as did Frederick Wing and William Fitzner. Such mixed practices concentrated increasingly on the less expensive side of the residential and commercial markets, however, leaving the major jobs to design specialists. In New Orleans the modern building professions date from the post-Civil War boom.

ARCHITECTURE FOR A NEW AGE

The Garden District society that emerged after the Civil War was a study in contradictions. Many old families lived on, while others returned from self-imposed exile in the North or abroad. Even more numerous were the newcomers, who hailed from throughout the country and owed their wealth to the most diverse undertakings. Once a homogeneous enclave, the District was transformed into a medley of people with different origins and accents, professions, religions, and ideals. Probably their only common bonds were the pursuit of money, hostility to the Federal occupation and its neighborhood symbol, the Freedman's Bureau quartered on Euterpe Street, and loyalty to the Democratic Party, which became the main champion of local white interests after the collapse of the old Whigs. These new sources of coherence emerged very slowly, however. For at least a decade after 1865 the Garden District was a social and political hodgepodge.

Inevitably, this patchwork came to be reflected in the architectural styles that emerged in the houses patrons built for themselves. Earlier, the perceived unity of the District's society caused the reigning eclecticism of the age to be moderated and the various styles softened. Now everyone went his own way. With no accepted norms around which local life could turn, conformity vanished.

Except for the Gothic, all styles that were evident in embryo in the 1850s came to fruition after the war. As part of this trend,

even the prewar strain of conservatism made itself felt once more, albeit as a more muted element. When William Wright, a cotton factor, built his three-bay columnar house on Sixth Street in 1866–68, he reverted to the standard prototype of the 1840s and 1850s.[36] Similarly, James E. Reade's three-bay residence at 3313 Prytania Street harkens back to the early 1850s, even though it was constructed in 1871–72.[37] The same retrospective mood is to be discerned in such five-bay houses as that of tobacco merchant Watson Van Benthuysen at 3209 St. Charles Avenue.[38]

Some houses preserved traditional forms but were updated with Italianate details. The jigsaw ornaments that were hung on Armant St. Amant's house seemed to turn the columns into Tuscan arches, and the paired columns at the Edward Ivy house at 2113–15 Prytania Street were dressed with a similar Italianate touch.[39] Another modification in traditional plans was to stretch the scale upward, as at the residence of Captain Thomas Pickles. Yet neither the updated ornaments nor altered scale obscures the fact that all these designs were throwbacks to a generation earlier.

The most striking manifestation of the conservative strain in postwar life is the appearance of many raised cottages. The postwar decade marked the apogee of this regional style. Whether one speaks of the Louis D'Homergue house at 3211 Prytania Street or of the residences of Louis Gabb or Eugene Schmitt at 1224 and 1424 Louisiana Avenue, respectively, one is dealing with buildings that differ from earlier prototypes only in superficial details.[40] Indeed, the ability to absorb new impulses with a minimum of change is the surest proof of the vitality of old forms. Frederick Wing's raised cottage at 1329 Seventh Street and William C. Murtagh's cottage at 1208 Eighth Street display the picturesque and painterly qualities of the reigning Italianate style. At the same time, the floor plan in each case remains true to the earliest cottage prototypes.[41]

By far the richest elaboration of the raised cottage was the house Shepherd Brown built on St. Charles Avenue in 1872.[42] Long known as the Chaiffraix house (after Desiré A. Chaiffraix) and now demolished, this exceptional building featured an imposing portico of eight Corinthian columns and lush Italianate moldings over all major portals. One of the finest buildings in the Garden District, the Brown residence, revealed the extent to which dramatic new

[ABOVE] *The ultimate raised villa, Shepherd Brown's house, 2833 St. Charles Avenue, 1872, now demolished*

[RIGHT] *Loyalty to an old prototype: a postwar, three-bay Greek Revival raised villa at 2703 Camp Street*

[FACING PAGE] *Chalet of Garden District maverick and bon vivant Cuthert Bullitt, moved to 3627 Carondolet Street. German-born architect Edward Gottheil designed the Swiss folly, circa 1868*

contents could be expressed through the medium of half-century-old forms.

However strong the forces of continuity, they were outweighed by the forces of change. To a large extent, these were fostered by changes in social life. Early Garden District residents designed their homes for family life and for formal receptions. Now public partying on a lavish scale placed its mark on design. At the Montgomery and the James Eustis houses, the single long salon, or ballroom, replaced the traditional double parlor. When Alfred Moulton took over the old Maddox house on Prytania Street in 1867, he engaged a Viennese artist to turn the double parlor into an opulent ballroom, complete with a niche for the orchestra. At the old Brevard house the new owner, Emory Clapp, in 1869 added a large hexagonal library, in reality a smoking room. Hexagonal bays were used to enlarge dining rooms as well, while at the Robinson house James Gallier, Jr., remodeled the original dining room to create a banquet hall of heroic proportions.

The founders of the Garden District had been self-made and independent men, yet the conflict between Creoles and Anglo-Saxons led the latter to band together in a common enterprise. Those who reestablished Garden District society after the Civil War lacked this collective impulse. Their individualism asserted itself in architecture, as one can see by the appearance of several houses in a picturesque and self-consciously folksy style. The ever-independent Cuthbert Bullitt blazed the trail with his flamboyant Swiss chalet, now moved to 3627 Carondolet Street. Never mind that the architect, German-born Edward Gottheil, took pains to assure that the interior conformed to canons of the raised cottage. The curving roofline, deep overhanging eaves, and the non-functional *Fachwerk* on the facade all declared that Bullitt remained the Garden District's leading individualist and dandy. Whether or not Gottheil borrowed the concept from the designs of several Swiss chalets at the 1867 International Exhibition in Paris (at which he was a Louisiana commissioner), he succeeded in broadening the architectural vocabulary of New Orleans.

By comparison with Bullitt's extravaganza, Thomas Flanner's country Victorian house at 2045 Coliseum Street and Austin Roundtree's jigsaw Gothic cottage at 1421 Josephine Street seem tame indeed.[43] But they, too, stand out boldly in their neighborhood and flaunt the fact that their owners felt no need to conform to some uptown stereotype.

Aside from Bullitt's Swiss folly, the most assertively picturesque home in the Garden District was that designed by Willian Freret for James Eustis in 1876. Eustis, it will be recalled, had married a daughter of Henry S. Buckner and was thus linked with one of the city's leading architectural patrons. A surviving drawing that Freret prepared for Eustis's brother-in-law, John Buckner, suggests that the house at Coliseum and Fourth is a variant of an earlier Buckner residence that had been designed but never built.[44] For the Coliseum Street house Freret appears to have taken inspiration from the plates in *Holly's Country Seats* (1863), or a similar pattern-book.[45] The steeply pitched Germanic roofing, the asymmetrical massing, and the heavy quoining on corners all have their antecedents in Holly's designs. In the interior Freret goes beyond this basic reference, however. The rustic, jigsaw-cut shadow moldings and the chunky plaster ceiling medallions seem a deliberate caricature of the highbrow classicism still so much in vogue.

Those New Orleanians who were enriched by the city's unexpected postwar boom sought an architecture that expressed their triumphs. Most prewar styles bored them, for they carried no sense of a fresh beginning. Most picturesque styles were too bland. However, one of them—the Italianate mode taken to its ornate extreme—possessed all the qualities they sought: exuberance, originality of plan, grandeur of scale, and the possibility of unabashed ostentation.

The fact that Italianisms had made only slow progress in antebellum New Orleans added to their appeal. More than one northern writer had declared that the so-called bracketed style had peaked before the Civil War.[46] Not so in New Orleans, where it was still a novelty. Between 1865 and 1873 the new commercial leaders of New Orleans went on an Italianate binge. Borrowing from everywhere, their architects indulged in the style at its most florid.

The Italianate style became the lingua franca of New Orleans builders almost overnight. By the late 1860s it had become the standard idiom at all the local building supply houses. When new mantles were installed at an antebellum house on Fourth Street, they were standardized Italianate.[47] When the cotton broker James Coyle built his double house at 2103–05 Baronne Street in 1866, he

*Another villa commissioned by Henry S. Buckner, this one for son-in-law James
Eustis at 2627 Coliseum Street, designed by William Freret, 1876. Perhaps a
variant of an earlier residence Freret had designed for Buckner, but never built*

James Eustis reception parlor

too used standardized Italianate brackets, cornices, door frames, and fittings. The ironmonger John Armstrong built a spacious three-bay residence that still stands at 2085 Carondelet Street; in addition to the standardized segmental arches and interior fittings, his firm cast an elaborate gallery for the facade and a sculptural gate. About the same time similar ironwork appeared on a host of other houses, both new and old. John McGinty's house at 1322 Felicity Street, Joseph Carroll's and J. C. Morris's houses at 1315 and 1331 First Street, and J. M. Lewis's house at 2405 Prytania Street, now demolished, are among the most imposing of several dozen structures that paralleled Armstrong's masterpiece.

These houses were unabashedly extravagant. The fate of three houses that avoided such extreme ostentation is instructive. In 1869 Charles Hillger designed a restrained adaptation of the typical Italianate home for John A. Blaffer. Notwithstanding the practicality of its plan and its exceptional detailing, the house was simply too restrained to attract imitators.

Immediately after the Civil War Samuel P. Griffin, a commission merchant, built for himself an impressive three-story palazzo at 2702 St. Charles Avenue.[48] The unknown architect designed a

[LEFT] *Folksy cut-out shadow moldings in James Eustis's house*

[RIGHT] *Gates from John Armstong's foundry, in front of the ironmonger Armstrong's residence, 2805 Carondolet Street, 1869. Design attributed to Frederick Wing*

Lacey cast iron on an otherwise plain double house, 1235–37 St. Andrew Street

second residence in the same style for Charles Gallagher, who lived next door. With fourteen rooms "finished in the very best style, with black walnut stairs, large and elegant arched parlors, library, etc.," the two houses met the highest standards of elegance and comfort.[49] Both, now demolished, were among the most imposing ever built on St. Charles Avenue. Yet like the Blaffer residence, their exteriors were too severe for new tastes locally. They, too, remained unique, with no progeny.

The two Italianate residences that became the standard-bearers for the style were Lewis Reynold's Folger mansion on St. Charles Avenue, discussed earlier, and Charles Hillger's Jackson Avenue residence for Julius Weis. The Folger house in particular achieved its imposing effect by virtue of its sheer mass, rather than through the addition of any galleries, arcades, and porticoes. The McLellan house at 1006 Washington Avenue and the Syer house at 2302 St. Charles Avenue, in contrast, relied on peripheral galleries for their visual definition.[50] While galleries were more appropriate to the climate, both houses pale by comparison to the sheer mass of the Folger residence.

Julius Weis's now demolished mansion owed much to the Folger house. To be sure, Hillger surrounded it with a narrow one-story gallery, but this did not obscure the ranks of segmentally arched long windows, the rusticated pilasters, bold quoining, and the deep overhang with ornamented brackets. Crowning the Weis house was a four-story tower with mansarded cupola, topped by a striking round dormer that repeated the main façade's capping motif. Here, finally, the Italianate style reached its zenith in New Orleans.

It has been suggested that the appeal of late-Italianate architecture to postbellum New Orleanians lay in its ostentation. This quality was vigorously displayed in the interiors. Lafayette Folger was said to have imported a team of Parisian carpenters to carry out his immodest designs, and when John Piffet purchased the Syer house at 2302 St. Charles Avenue, he commissioned elaborate interior frescoes. Yet the Italianate style could go only so far in this direction. After all, it had first been introduced in Scotland and America as an honest antidote to the formal pomposities of high classicism. Beyond a certain point, the Italianate style could not bear the load of vanity.

Commission merchant Samuel P. Griffin's postwar palazzo, 2702 St. Charles Avenue, 1866, now demolished (STUART LYNN, PHOTOGRAPHER; THE HISTORIC NEW ORLEANS COLLECTION)

[RIGHT] *The marriage of Tuscan motifs and galleries: ship merchant William H. McLellan's house, 1006 Washington Avenue, 1868–69*

[FACING PAGE] *London plan house transformed into a postwar palazzo. William Syer's widow, Virginia Peebles, built this house at 2302 St. Charles Avenue, 1871–72*

The Second Empire reaches Eighth Street: Daniel C. Byerly house, 1437 Eighth Street, 1871–73

The Second Empire style, freshly imported from the Napoleon III's Paris via New York City, filled the breach. Based on Visconti and Lefuel's 1852–57 additions to the Louvre, the Second Empire style was in fact a return to classical symmetry, but on a gigantic scale and enriched with extravagant baroque ornamentation on both the interior and exterior, as well as the ever-present mansard roofs. In contrast to the picturesque style, and even to the Victorian Gothic, which reigned everywhere but in New Orleans, the Second Empire style was militantly urban. Had its ascent not been thwarted by the recession that followed the financial Panic of 1873, it would have given a thoroughly metropolitan air to the Garden District. Even the few residences built in this style before the panic lent a new flavor of urbanity to the neighborhood.

By far the most distinguished Second Empire residence in uptown New Orleans is Bradish Johnson's mansion at 2343 Prytania Street, apparently the work of Lewis E. Reynolds. In this brick and plaster edifice are present all the signature traits of the style except for multicolored patterned slating, polychrome masonry, and

terra-cotta work. Doubtless, these too would have been present had the requisite materials been more readily available.

New Orleanians were ingenious in adapting the Second Empire style to brick, and even to wood. The William Henderson house at 2126 Prytania Street of 1886–87, now demolished, and the Richard Flower house at 3005 St. Charles Avenue, built in 1874, are admirable translations into wood.[51] Like the Italianate style, the Second Empire baroque could be applied to many building forms. Daniel C. Byerly's house at 1437 Eighth Street, built 1871–73, is distinguished by the concave mansard roof and the unusual rounded molding over the door and windows. Yet it remains essentially a raised cottage with Corinthian columns. The same can be said of the Daily house at 3120 Coliseum Street and the now destroyed Alexander Hill mansion at 903 St. Charles Avenue, but these were built on a larger scale.[52]

For sheer opulence, no Second Empire mansion in the Garden District ever rivaled the Charles Whitney residence at 2233 St. Charles Avenue, built 1870–71. Long since demolished, this palatial house once occupied half of the lakeside block between Jackson and Philip Streets. With formal gardens and stables larger than most New Orleans houses, it was the perfect monument to the recovery of New Orleans banking.

It is uncertain whether Mrs. Charles A. Whitney retained any parts of William Haneman's brick raised cottage that had stood on the site since 1853.[53] It seems more likely that she simply swept the site clean to build her three-storied mansion with mansard roof. The unusual bays on the facade so closely resemble those on Bernard Kock's house on Third Street as to suggest that the same architect was involved, namely the active Edward Gottheil. The interior was sumptuous and featured the first appearance of the fashionable Japanese decor in New Orleans. As much as any other building, the Whitney house helped transform St. Charles Avenue from a common transportation artery into the grand boulevard it eventually became.

Scarcely was it completed than the Whitney mansion became one of the chief sights of the city. Wide-eyed tourists would peer through the iron gate as their local hosts explained to them the wonders of this fashionable pile and of its occupants. *Jewell's Crescent City*, the last word in guides to New Orleans, devoted a whole page to the mansion. To contemporaries, it epitomized the new New Orleans.

And so it did. Through its vast grounds, it isolated itself from its neighbors, creating its own environment. Only James Robb had heretofore dared to do this, and most Garden District residents concluded from his demise that such theatrical ostentation entailed at least as much risk as gratification. During the Reconstruction boom, however, many New Orleanians aspired to Robb's status, his independence as much as his wealth. The proliferation of exotic styles attests to this urge, so different from what went before. At the same time, the forces of continuity were also in evidence. The raised cottages interspersed with Italianate villas, the ranks of three- and five-bay columned houses punctuated by Second Empire

Mr. and Mrs. Charles A. Whitney's showcase at 2233 St. Charles Avenue, 1870–71, now demolished. The 1853 William Haneman house on the site may have been incorporated into this later mansion, or destroyed when the Whitneys built their home. Mrs. Whitney's vast collection of Oriental and European art filled two wings. (THE HISTORIC NEW ORLEANS COLLECTION)

extravaganzas or by the overblown efforts at the picturesque—this very disharmony embodied the essence of the era.

The old forces of community had broken down. New ones had yet to appear. Had the local economy been depressed, this anarchic phase might have passed, leaving few traces. Instead, the burst of prosperity between 1865 and 1873 permitted these peculiar social conditions to place their permanent stamp on the architecture of the Garden District. Henceforth, this pioneer garden suburb would embody two diametrically opposite ideals: community, harmony, and conformity, on the one hand, and individualism and eccentricity on the other. During its last great epoch down to the end of the century, a new synthesis finally emerged in Garden District society. That renewed sense of community, however, never eradicated the cachet of flamboyant individuality introduced by those who were enriched by Reconstruction.

CHAPTER ELEVEN

End of An Era

THROUGHOUT THE DOZEN years following the Civil War, New Orleans hovered on the edge of anarchy. Radical Republicans clung to power with the help of the army but were unable to beat back the formation of home rule movements. At length, the contending parties, each pretending to exercise the full powers of legitimate governments, sent armed troops into pitched battles against one another, bloodying the streets of New Orleans on two occasions. Political power began to pass from a corrupt carpetbag government to equally corrupt local forces in 1872.[1]

The reestablishment of self-rule after fifteen years of Federal occupation should have released the pent-up civic energies of New Orleanians. It did not, however, for the simple reason that such energies did not exist. They had certainly been present in the early postwar years, but that had been a prosperous era. By the time Reconstruction ended in 1877, New Orleans had already spent four years in the depths of an economic depression far more damaging than any the city had known.

The national economy crashed suddenly in September 1873, triggered by the failure of key New York banking houses. Several New Orleans banks closed their doors, commodity prices plummeted, and interest rates soared. The heretofore prosperous city and its inhabitants were plunged into

[FACING PAGE] *An eclectic original: wine merchant George Jurgens' house at 1517 Eighth Street near Prytania, late 1880s*

poverty almost overnight. Thousands of families were pushed to the brink of starvation, and suicide became commonplace.[2] Merchants suffered along with everyone else. A third of a million bales of cotton piled up in warehouses but traders could not borrow against it, nor could they sell the crop abroad, since the British had also been hard hit. While markets and families suffered nationally, "Probably no city in the nation fared worse than New Orleans," as one recent authority on the Panic of 1873 put it.[3]

Property values in the Garden District registered the collapse of prices with clinical precision. The great Robinson house fell in value from $40,000 in 1872 to $22,000 by 1875.[4] Of course, recessions were nothing new. On the basis of past experience, people expected the economy to rebound after a year or two and for real estate prices to pick up shortly thereafter. This time, however, the recovery did not come and real estate values did not bounce back. After diving to $10,000 in 1876, the value of the luxurious Shepherd Brown house hovered around that low figure until well into the 1880s. Not until 1890 did real estate values attain their pre-panic levels. Clearly, this was no temporary cyclical crisis. Structural changes in New Orleans' economy were at work.

The twin pillars on which New Orleans prosperity had rested since the start of the American era began to totter. For the first time, King Cotton faced withering overseas competition as the British in Egypt and then the Russians in their newly conquered Central Asian territories opened new lands to cotton. The encouragement it inadvertently gave to the development of these sources of competition is the price the South paid for secession. Simultaneously, New Orleans lost its preeminence as a wholesaling center. The wartime interruption of agriculture drove impoverished planters into country towns, where they established general stores. New telegraph lines enabled these rural storekeepers to place orders directly in the North, thus cutting out the middlemen in New Orleans. The extension of railway lines hurt the Crescent City in the same way, since it permitted northern manufacturers to ship directly to their customers in the South.

New Orleans' position as an important center for international trade also eroded rapidly. Whereas in 1858 the city accounted for six percent of all U.S. imports, its share twenty years later had shrunk to three percent.[5] Exports, too, shifted back to the East Coast, and especially to New York. In the years immediately before the Civil War, New Orleans had vied with New York as the nation's leading export center. During 1894–98, however, New York gained 44 percent of the export trade, while New Orleans' share shrunk to a paltry eight percent.[6]

Had they been able to shift their capital into manufacturing, members of the New Orleans business elite might have weathered these blows. This formula had given Boston and other established ports on the eastern seaboard a new lease on life in the late nineteenth century. The Crescent City's renowned economist, James D. B. DeBow, understood this and declared categorically that "we have got to go to manufacturing to save ourselves."[7]

A handful of New Orleanians acted on DeBow's advice. John H. Maginnis made a fortune manufacturing soap, cottonseed oil, and fertilizers. With his new riches he bought Alexander Harris's old house at 2127 Prytania Street and settled into the life of a factory baron.

Unfortunately, Maginnis's success was exceptional. Capital was scarce, and those who had "old money," that is, money earned a generation earlier, stuck with such tried and true products as cotton and sugar. The ironmongers who produced machinery for the sugar and cotton industries remained the largest element of New Orleans manufacturing.

THE MYTH OF OLD NEW ORLEANS

The uptown establishment was in a state of crisis. The Panic of 1873 ravaged old fortunes, and there existed neither the entrepreneurial skills nor fresh capital needed to form new ones. The moneymaking machine that Anglo-Saxon immigrants had built in the 1840s ground to a halt. A class that had known little but victory suddenly confronted defeat.

It was under these conditions that uptown New Orleanians discovered their southern identity. In a feast of sour grapes, people rationalized their commercial failures by taking refuge in the notion that they were too refined and civilized to compete successfully against the vulgar moneygrubbers of the North. Much the same shift in mentality had occurred earlier in the nineteenth century in Charleston, South Carolina, and had hastened that city's decline.[8] Genteel pretensions now threatened to inhibit the changes that were necessary in New Orleans.

In this mood of defensive self-pity, members of the New Orleans elite even idealized the Confederate government toward which they had been so conspicuously cool at the outset of the rebellion. The dedication of a monument to General Robert E. Lee at the former Tivoli (now Lee) Circle on February 22, 1884 was the occasion for special self-romanticization.[9] The general's posture on the monument, dignified but expressing as much resignation as repose, reflected the uptown plight. There was no way out. When former Confederate President Jefferson Davis died at Jacob Payne's house on First Street, 150,000 New Orleanians paid their respects at City Hall, where he lay in state. They mourned the dashing of their own hopes in recent years as much as the death of the great Mississippian.[10]

Those who were once winners now became losers. As this switch in identity occurred, the Anglo-Saxon uptown establishment for the first time began sympathizing with the Creoles against whom they had earlier contended. Charles Gayarré, the aging Creole historian of old New Orleans, became the darling of ladies of the Garden District, nearly all of them Anglo-Saxons. As the psychological distance between Creoles and Anglo-Saxons shrank, marriages between the two groups became more commonplace. A new local identity emerged. Its hallmark was the notion of New Orleans as a community steeped in charm and too refined to succeed in the modern world. The main locus of this view was the old Yankee suburb, the Garden District.

George Washington Cable, a dour Connecticut-born Presbyterian from Annunciation Square, became the bard of this new mentality. After a frustrating career as a would-be civic reformer in New Orleans, Cable became enamored of many of the very qualities of the old city that he had been unable to change. He built himself a traditional raised cottage at 1313 Eighth Street in the Garden District and hoped to settle into a pleasant life as a local-color writer. However, members of the Creole aristocracy took violent

The end of uptown New Orleanians' ambiguity over their southernness: uptown monument to Robert E. Lee, Lee Circle

exception to his portrayal of their forebears in his novel *The Grandissimes* and in his collection of dialect stories, *Old Creole Days.* Eventually he left town.

Self-romanticization was a balm to economic and political defeat. At times this took the form of good-natured escapism, as in the fresh burst of Mardi Gras pageantry among Anglo-Saxon new Orleanians after 1872–73. At other times this new romanticism led members of the New Orleans elite to ascribe noble qualities to one another. Published obituaries of the day reflect the manner in which ordinary mortals were transformed into Homeric heroes.

Bradish Johnson, for example, was in life a New Yorker and foe of secession who left the South during the war and made no contribution to the southern cause. In death he was acclaimed as a "Louisiana planter of wealth, and a gentleman...."[11] Lafayette Folger had been an avaricious importer of coffee who burned himself out by his forty-eighth year. In death he turned into "a man of Herculean and stately form and physique."[12] Thomas Leathers, the self-made steamboat magnate, was similarly hailed in death as a man of "magnificent physique, tall, commanding form and a fine, aristocratic face...." Though he had preferred to have his steamboats constructed in the North, Leathers in death was hailed as "the typical old Southern gentleman."[13] Similarly, James P. Freret, the former sheriff, traced his ancestry to England. In death, however, he was miraculously reborn as the scion of "a noble race of Creole gentlemen."[14]

[LEFT] *The raised villa of the gingerbread man, Robert Roberts, owner of the Louisiana Steam Sash, Blind, and Door Factory. Thomas Sully designed 2821 St. Charles Avenue, circa 1889, now demolished. Similar house at 3120 Coliseum Street* (HERMANN-GRIMA/GALLIER HISTORIC HOUSES)

[RIGHT] *Prefabricated elegance: Roberts's catalogue of wooden steam-sawn brackets* (HERMANN-GRIMA/GALLIER HISTORIC HOUSES)

[FACING PAGE] *Novelist George Washington Cable's raised cottage, 1313 Eighth Street, 1876. Hoping to keep alive the old spirit of the District's integrated architectural environment, Cable ordered architect Frederick Wing to paint his house like one at St. Charles Avenue and Seventh Street.*

THE FAILURE OF MYTHIC ARCHITECTURE

The myth of old New Orleans that arose in the 1870s was potentially rich with implications for architecture. It could have generated a new appreciation of French colonial prototypes from the era described in Cable's stories. Or it could have seized on elements from the most advanced styles of the day and adapted them to local conditions. The impetus for the creation of an authentic regional style was definitely present. Yet the new style was stillborn.

Double houses, where people of all backgrounds were neighbors, 2900 block of Camp at Sixth Street

Instead, Garden District patrons stuck with the familiar. Robert Roberts, the owner of the Louisiana Steam Sash, Blind, and Door Factory, could have produced for himself virtually any kind of new building. Instead, he chose for his house a tame mansarded version of the traditional raised cottage at the corner of St. Charles Avenue and Conery Street, now demolished.[15] When Thomas McDermott built his residence at 2926 St. Charles Avenue, another opportunity to declare a new regionalism presented itself. Instead, McDermott's architect chose the familiar Italianate style. With its brackets, single-floor gallery, Corinthian columns, and heavy rustication, the McDermott house could have been built fifteen years earlier.[16]

However conservative they seem today, the Roberts and McDermott houses were strikingly liberated by comparison with most other houses built in the years following the Panic of 1873, such as the once identical frame structures at 1230–32 and 1238–40 Harmony Street, also from the 1870s. In spite of their deep over-hangs, heavy entablature, brackets, and segmental arched windows, they are in essence double three-bay dwellings of the 1850s, only slightly modified. No less a throwback is the huge double house at 1329 St. Andrew Street, built in 1883 by the second-generation Irish grocer, Edward Conery, Jr. The broad cornices and generous overhang were the clichés of the immediate post-Civil War years. The cast-iron galleries are impressive, but the structure differs from numerous earlier prototypes only in its vast scale. Still more retarded in style was the three-bay galleried house that Nova Scotia-born furniture storeowner James McCracken built at 2604 Coliseum Street in 1878.[17]

Only two houses of the period embody any clear attempt to create a distinctively local idiom. The first, the 1891 remodeling of an earlier three-bay house at 1604 Fourth Street, abandons the tra-ditional London plan in favor of a collection of separate rooms. On the outside, the traditional three bays are maintained, but the cor-nices and gable are heavily ornamented with whimsical plaster-work. The result is a pleasingly romantic adaptation of a traditional New Orleans building type.[18]

The second house that provided at least the embryo of a new local idiom was built for George Jurgens in the 1880s. The unknown architect of the unusual Italianate dwelling at 1517 Eighth Street near Prytania borrowed freely from virtually every era and type of

Garden District mansion. The final product was highly original. The heavy segmental arches on the first floor combine with the ceremoniously formal entrance stairs flanking the center three bays to create a wonderfully theatrical effect. To the modern observer, this house presents all the elements for a romanticized yet essentially traditional Garden District dwelling. The fact that no later housed copied this intriguing experiment indicates how little inspiration the mythology of New Orleans provided for architects.[19]

The romantic currents of the 1870s found their best expression in the written word. They gave rise to novels and stories, poems and pamphlets, most of them "polemical and forensic," as W. S. Cash put it in his study, *The Mind of the South.*[20] In architecture, so poorly suited to polemics, the new romanticism spawned little more than a lame flight into the past.

COMMON PEOPLE AND THE GARDEN DISTRICT

The impact of the great Panic of 1873 was not confined to large brokers and commission merchants. Middle- and lower-income New Orleanians felt the shock equally, although with different consequences. Had they been in most other large American cities, they quite likely would long since have been drawn into the gray world of the factory laborer. With few new industries to attract them, however, the middling people of New Orleans remained artisans, shopkeepers, and the employees of small or middle-sized firms.

They also remained part of a relatively stable community. The inability or disinclination of the commercial elite to establish modern manufacturing made New Orleans an unappealing place for new immigrants. Tens of thousands of fresh arrivals to the United States poured through New Orleans each year, but few stayed. Newcomers who settled down included some 25,000 Sicilians who arrived from the villages around Palermo. But for the most part the population remained nearly static. Over the entire decade of the 1870s the population rose a paltry 13 percent, which fell to a more anemic population gain of 12 percent in the 1880s.[21]

This social stagnation brought subtle but immensely important benefits. With fewer poverty-stricken immigrants to house, New Orleans had little need for tenements. In the North, such large blocks of multiple apartments gave masses of the urban poor a bleak, barracks-like existence.[22] In New Orleans the very term *tenement* was rarely used. There were large buildings composed of rental units, to be sure, but these structures differed little from middle-class housing in outward appearance. The spread of cultural amenities accessible to the poorer parts of the population reinforced the social stability of the uptown area. By 1890 some thirteen streetcar lines crisscrossed the Garden District and the Irish Channel.[23] After 1880 the Rex Theater offered vaudeville and potboilers for a few cents.[24] A roller-skating rink at Washington Avenue and Prytania Street gave thousands access to that fad for a few years after 1884, and the gymnasium built across the street staged prize fights at low admission fees. All this, it should he stressed, was within the bounds of the elite Garden District.

The slumping economy of New Orleans had little room for a true middle class. Illiteracy, the mark of lower-class life, was three times more common in the Crescent City than in Chicago or St. Louis.[25] Nor did education provide a sure path to success. With channels for mobility otherwise blocked, New Orleans laborers advanced fastest not by attending school but by buying a house. Property ownership imposed habits of thrift and discipline on the entire family. Those able to carry a mortgage—they were mostly white, but included some blacks as well—were on the surest path to nonmanual employment.[26]

This unusual situation provides the key for understanding New Orleans' ubiquitous single-family "shotgun" houses. Whatever their architectural charms, these structures were above all a ticket into the lower-middle class. An intriguing article that appeared in the New Orleans press, "Homes for the People," stated it plainly: "The most of the small cottages are occupied by the owners. The German element predominates on the outskirts of the city [e.g. around the Garden District], where these houses are built. The most thrifty and industrious of the colored population are also creating homes for themselves instead of continuing to pay monthly tribute to landlords."[27]

Jigsaw fantasy: exotic Moorish ornament on a camelback shotgun house, 2731 Chestnut Street, 1890. Built for Elizabeth Ruth, widow of grocer John Nutter.

❧ CRESCENT CITY VERNACULAR

Single- and double-unit shotgun houses literally surround the Garden District. Dating from the late nineteenth century, they are one of the most distinctive and pervasive features of the city's architectural legacy. Prevailing economic and social conditions greatly favored their construction, just as these same factors discouraged alternative styles that were more common elsewhere in America.

Yet general conditions do not directly dictate architectural form and style. Visitors encountering these florid shotgun houses might ask, "Where did they come from?" A satisfactory response accounts for three aspects of these buildings: their plan, their construction materials, and their often profuse ornamentation. Each feature leads in a different direction, yet all have one thing in common: the heavy reliance on local sources. Built in response to peculiar conditions not prevailing elsewhere, and in a period during which New Orleans was more isolated than any time since the

American takeover, these small houses constitute a true local vernacular. As such, they are perhaps more genuinely distinctive than any other building types in uptown New Orleans.

Shotgun houses take their name from the fact that a shotgun blast fired through the front door could reach the back wall unimpeded. Notwithstanding claims regarding their supposed rural or even West Indian origin, shotgun houses trace their immediate ancestry to Greek Revival examples in New Orleans and the surrounding region.[28] Residences at 937 St. Andrew Street and 1121–27 Eighth Street clearly reveal this genealogy.[29] Whether plain or ornamented with columns, such houses are in reality three-bay London plan dwellings in which the typical hallway is replaced with an outdoor gallery. Not only does this unusual elongated plan fit the long narrow parcels of land common in New Orleans, but also it permits maximum circulation of air in each room. The shape of available plots of land also determined that the basic shotgun house would be extended upward rather than outward. The two-story version—the so-called camelback—is as distinctive as the one-story model. The high cost of land in the Garden District, rather than building codes, dictated that the second-story bedroom be added only above the low kitchen in the rear, rather than at the front of the house.

Shotgun houses were built exclusively of materials available locally. The development of commercial lumbering in the vast Atchafalaya Basin assured that insect-proof cypress boards would be cheaply available for lap siding. Cypress is not suited for weight-bearing structural members, however, so the traditional yellow pine continued to be used for the basic frame. To prevent rotting and to discourage vermin, local builders raised shotgun houses up on low brick footings.

A further requirement was that shotgun houses be easily constructed. Builders like Louis Wilkins, William Arms, and William Braun all made their profits on speculative development and therefore strove to produce base models without upgrade options as inexpensively as possible.[30] Plans called for balloon frames, which were universal, and mass-produced sashes, moldings, and window frames. Several firms specialized in the manufacturing of these elements. One of the most active was Robert Roberts's Louisiana Steam Sash, Blind and Door Factory, which employed a hundred

Camelback double residences by German-born architect William Fitzner, 1223–29 and 1233–41 Harmony Street. Built for investor-owner John Ohmstede, 1872

workers at its sprawling plant on Gravier Street. In the late 1860s the firm had shown a fully prefabricated "Louisiana Cottage" at the Universal Exposition in Paris.[31] Thereafter Roberts and other local manufacturers offered virtually every component of the shotgun house in knocked-down form. The designs for such crafted items were borrowed from carpenters, especially those who had made wooden patterns for the local cast-iron works. Robert Roberts himself had been a pattern maker at the Bienville Iron Works.

The 1880 catalog of Roberts's Louisiana Steam Sash firm shows a sample of wooden ornament available from this one supplier. Elaborate brackets with inverted tendons, ornamental columns, scrollwork, roof ornaments, and door frames are but a few of the items offered for sale. Double shotgun houses on Josephine Street and Harmony Street stand as good examples of what extrav-

agant fantasy could be achieved by anonymous builders using catalogs.[32] It is significant that Roberts's 1891 catalogue also contains several pages of model facades, all of which are far less inventive and probably in the end more expensive than those neighborhood builders created on their own.[33]

With plan, materials, and construction type dictated by practical circumstances, the shotgun house held little attraction for major architects eager to display their design skills. True, James Gallier, Sr., in the 1840s had produced at least one early plan for the old city of Lafayette.[34] Moreover, the German-born architect and builder William Fitzner (1845–1914) showed his skill at designing elaborate doubles, most notably four camelbacks at 1223–29 and 1233–41 Harmony Street.[35] These were rare exceptions for Fitzner, however. Given the scale of his practice, it is unlikely that the architect would have been attracted to the Harmony Street commissions had they not constituted part of a single large project.

The one instance of a major architect producing a significant work in the shotgun genre is "Hall's Row" at 2305–29 Coliseum Street, designed by Henry Howard. John Hall, a native of Martinsburg, West Virginia, had purchased a plot of land on Coliseum Street in 1824. Only in 1868 did he develop the property with eight units, all of which still survive.[36] For some mysterious reason these virtually identical houses are known locally as the "Seven Sisters." To impart some diversity to what otherwise would have been a monotonous row, Howard varied the facades, alternating between Greek Revival and Italianate galleries. The effect is charming yet no less dignified than the great mansions that stand nearby.

While it might be tempting to trace the Italianate design of the Seven Sisters to some published source, such as Plate XXI of Samuel Sloan's *The Model Architect* (1851), this is not necessary. Every element in both versions of Howard's cottages had been used repeatedly in the Garden District over several decades. Indeed, the Greek Revival variant is simply the lower story of the typical square-columned London plan house. Similar local sources can be found for other shotgun fantasies of the era. The exotic Moorish ornaments on a camelback shotgun house at 2731 Chestnut Street might have been borrowed from the "oriental villa" in Sloan's *The Model Architect* or from the "Saracenic style" model in the exhibition hall at Philadelphia's Fairmont Park in 1876.[37] But the same motifs were part of the regional vernacular and had long since figured in earlier Louisiana architecture and could be seen, for example, in Howard's Mount Airey Plantation in St. James Parish (destroyed) or his Nottaway Plantation in Whitecastle, Louisiana. The essence of the shotgun style was that it brought together tried and true florid motifs copied from the great mansions of the city and region and combined them in startling, exotic, and cost-effective combinations.

SHOTGUN CULTURE

Vernacular architecture drew on the legacy of highbrow architecture but reworked that legacy in fanciful ways. Homebuilders for the lower- and middle-income residents who lived in these vernacular dwellings borrowed elements more readily from the great houses, simply because of the proximity of one with the other. There was a far smaller middle class standing between themselves and the wealthy. The worlds of rich and poor thus interacted at many levels in the Garden District, which facilitated a similar process of adaptation and innovation in other cultural areas besides architecture. One might inquire whether the same processes that turned shotgun houses into playful reworkings of elite housing nearby might also have occurred in fields as diverse as dress, language, and cuisine. Emulating the rich, the working-class inhabitants of the small wooden dwellings dressed with far greater formality than did their counterparts in the North. New Orleans workingmen—whether white native Americans, immigrants, or blacks—were slow to adopt the national costume of industrial labor. Moreover, they sprinkled their speech with colorfully misapplied fragments of highbrow English. On their side, the rich Anglo-Saxons adopted the cuisine of their black servants.

Following this hypothesis, one might find fruits of such interaction to have been especially notable in the area of music. Joseph Oliver, for example, was the son of a black plantation cook from Abend, Louisiana, who moved to the city in the 1880s. Raised entirely in the Garden District, Oliver lived in a succession of shotgun houses that his family rented from lower-middle class white families. Typical was the house at 2710–12 Dryades Street where Oliver lived for many years: German immigrant Frederick Pohlmann, who lived next door, owned the house and was unavoidably in daily contact with his tenant. During the days Oliver did yard work for a First Street family and odd jobs for others. In the evenings he played cornet in local bands, both in the infamous red-light district downtown and later for parties organized by wealthy Garden District youths. Legendary "King" Oliver was among the pioneers of jazz.

Other pioneer jazz musicians who lived in or immediately adjoining the Garden District were Edward "Kid" Ory, Chris Kelly,

Shotgun chic: Henry Howard's design for "Hall's Row" at 2305–09 Coliseum Street, 1868. West Virginian John Hall developed these eight housing units

Clarence Williams, Frank Dusen, Sam Dutrey, and the brothers John and Warren "Baby" Dodds.[38] Between the Irish Channel on one side and the area around Baronne Street on the other, the uptown suburbs produced a significant percentage of the founders of America's most distinctive art form.

Jazz music has many sources. Among them was the popularized salon music favored by Garden District residents for their parties and dances. Without straining the point, let us merely suggest that the new vernacular music had much the same relationship to the so-called legitimate music of the Garden District as the vernacular architecture had to the formal architecture of the great houses. In both cases, the exuberant and improvisatory native art gave it a vitality and creative originality greater than the immediate sources from which it drew. Patrons of the vernacular architecture were patrons of the vernacular music: the people and their respective cultural preferences are the connection here.

PRIVATE WEALTH AND PUBLIC SHOW

However rich its vernacular architecture, New Orleans by the 1880s had become a backward city of ill-paved streets, muddy municipal drinking water, a nonexistent sewage system, and irregular garbage collection. In these ways it had fallen behind cities that it had once scorned. Suffice it to say that municipal expenditures per capita were one half those of Louisville and one third those of Philadelphia.[39]

A new factor was thrust into this situation during the 1880s with the appearance of a reformist ideology that sought salvation through the creation of a "New South." Adherents to this view, originally proclaimed by New Orleanian J. D. B. DeBow, held that the South must soften its old belligerence and embrace the cause of progress as it was understood in the North.[40] Believers in the New South program candidly acknowledged their respect for Yankee dynamism. This was easier because in inland cities like Atlanta and Nashville where the sentiment became most firmly planted, the new

leaders who emerged in the 1880s were young men of humble origins who had had no stake in the antebellum establishment.[41]

When Mark Twain returned to New Orleans in 1882 after a long absence, he visited his friend George Washington Cable in the Garden District. There he heard the frustrated reformer sing Creole songs to his own guitar accompaniment. One may suppose the Missourian reveled in Cable's version of Old New Orleans. However, Twain chose to spend most of his time not at Cable's raised cottage but in the central business district. There he discovered that "the city is well outfitted with progressive men—thinking, sagacious, long headed men. The contrast between the spirit of the city and the city's architecture is like the contrast between waking and sleep. Apparently there is a 'boom' in everything but that one dead feature."[42]

Twain's "long headed men" scored a number of successes in their efforts to bring New Orleans in step with the New South. Eight new banks with over $26 million dollars in deposits were founded between 1880 and 1895. The value of local manufacturing increased nearly four-fold in the same years. A formal board of liquidation attacked the city's huge debt, and a reform party took power in 1888 after two unsuccessful bids. There was grandeur in the vision that impelled these new leaders to sally forth each morning from their homes in the Garden District. They were men whose fresh ideas had more in common with those of the suburb's founders in the 1840s and 1850s than with members of the generation that made its peace with backwardness after the Panic of 1873. Their worldly success gave rise to the last great epoch of new construction in the Garden District.

To understand the architecture of this last era, we should picture a city and a suburb divided against itself. With a solid majority content to carry on traditional enterprises and a romantically southern way of life, and a modernizing faction equally dedicated to pulling the city back into the national mainstream, Garden District society looked simultaneously forward and backward.

In Atlanta and Nashville, those intent on building a New South were earnest men who abjured vanity and hedonism in all areas, including their domestic life.[43] In New Orleans a love of show manifested itself early among this group, with the result that the business leaders of the 1880s embraced architecture as a fitting sphere in which to demonstrate their worldly success. Their most enduring achievement in architecture and city planning was St. Charles Avenue. For half a century it had been unpaved and often a muddy rut fittingly named Nayades Street, after the mythological Greek naiads, who dwelt in brooks and streams. Although a number of fine residences had been built along it by the 1870s, the street's role was primarily functional, namely to carry traffic along the route of the old steamcar line to Carrollton. During the 1880s it was transformed into a model French boulevard, comparable to Commonwealth Avenue in Boston, Euclid Avenue in Cleveland, Prospect Avenue in Milwaukee, or Summit Avenue in St. Paul.

Every step of the transformation was accompanied by scandal. There were threats on all sides and at least one city councilman was charged with the embezzlement of funds. Each contending party hired private detectives to spy on the opposition.[44] In the end, though, the New South faction created a grand boulevard that boasted the first asphalt paving in New Orleans. The real purpose of St. Charles Avenue, like that of the new Parisian-style avenues created elsewhere in America at the time, was to provide a kind of a parade ground for the rich.[45]

By its very existence, the pompous new avenue was a challenge to the ideal of semi-rural withdrawal upon which the garden suburb had been founded. The clash of ideals is readily apparent as a comparison of privacy in the two eras. In the antebellum decades those who moved to the suburb sought withdrawal from the teeming city, yet their suburban retreat was fully accessible to all: low iron fences and low or nonexistent hedges invited visitors to stroll the streets and gaze at the life visible beyond the sidewalks. By the last two decades of the century this visual openness had given way to a mood of arrogant exclusion. The new rich welcomed the emergence of St. Charles Avenue as a boulevard for the display of wealth, but by no means all of those who could afford to live there chose to do so. Instead, private streets and private places made their debut.

The notion of closing entire streets to the "vulgar" masses had been introduce first in Fenton Place in St. Louis in 1869. Within the next few years that city acquired a number of private streets, the most famous of which was Vandeventer Place, laid out in 1870. This baneful practice was impossible in the densely settled environment of the Garden District, so those wishing to adopt it in New Orleans had to develop new land farther out on St. Charles Avenue. The first private streets in New Orleans were Audubon Place and Rosa Park of 1895. Dunleith Court followed these projects in 1913. In each case the goal was the same: to isolate the rich by making public thoroughfares private. By comparison, the antebellum Garden District had been relatively accessible, sociable, and tolerant.

THOMAS SULLY: ARCHITECT OF THE GILDED AGE

Even before the Cotton Centennial Exposition in 1884, suburbanization had reached far beyond the old Garden District. With the paving of St. Charles Avenue and the electrification of the horsecar line, this process accelerated. A number of architects jumped in to claim the business that resulted. James Freret achieved great popularity through his early command of the Queen Anne style, which had been introduced nationally at the 1876 Centennial Exposition in Philadelphia. His design for Charles Adams' house at 1206 Second Street was widely admired when it was built in 1886. As the *Daily Picayune* observed, the Adams residence was designed "after the present rage in buildings, the relaxed and comfortable Queen Anne style, and is very ornamental."[46] The firm of Stafford, Muir, and Fromherz was even busier than Freret. As architect-builders they adhered to the old nonspecialized system and achieved economies for their patrons in the process.

Ornament was the key to the architecture of the 1880s, and the Queen Anne style was the perfect vehicle for it. With its picturesque turrets, arresting colors and textures, and rich decorative motifs, it carried the day, especially for those who felt no loyalty to the dominant historical styles of the Garden District. There were other styles, to be sure. A ponderous French chateau arose uptown at 5931 St. Charles Avenue at the same time that a house in the Georgian Revival style was built across the street. On the whole, though, New Orleanians shied away from manor houses, marble palazzi, Jacobean fantasies, and even the Romanesque shingle style developed by Louisiana-born Henry Hobson Richardson. They

Colonel Joseph A. Walker's house, 2503 St. Charles Avenue, by Thomas Sully, 1885–86

were content with the eclectic Queen Anne style, which permitted ample borrowings from many sources. Only with the rise of the movement for honesty in architectural design spearheaded by Charles Eastlake at century's end did the Queen Anne style meet a real challenge in uptown New Orleans.

The fact that the Queen Anne style lacked all local referents may have recommended it to those eager to break with the past. Never mind that the Queen Anne house at 3203 Prytania had exact counterparts all over the country, or that the Fornaris house farther uptown on Palmer Avenue was borrowed wholesale from "Residence Design No. 216" of *Shoppell's Modern Houses* of 1888.[47] What counted was that the Queen Anne style was "in." To live in such a house showed that one was in touch with the latest trends nationally and had moved beyond the carefully conforming society that for half a century had revolved about the conventional classical and Italianate mansions of the Garden District. Besides, the Queen Anne style, in its absence of restrictive symmetry and axial plans, meant comfort and ease, the presence of a relaxed family atmosphere in the entire home.

The absolute master of the Queen Anne style in New Orleans—and of virtually every other style employed there in the late nineteenth century—was Thomas Sully (1855–1939).[48] Sully was prodigiously productive. Between 1882 and his retirement in 1905, he designed hundreds of buildings of every description. He created office blocks, warehouses, hospitals, orphanages, schools, banks, and factories. He built such major edifices in the central business district as the Maritime Building on Carondelet and Common Streets, long the highest building in New Orleans, and he also designed modest shotgun dwellings for the suburbs.

Sully's office in the Morris Building at Camp and Canal Streets covered an entire floor. In some respects an eccentric—in his office he kept a pet alligator given him by a friend—Sully was above all intensely practical, even to the point of publishing advertising brochures on his firm. His fame soon spread throughout the South, leading to commissions for the Lookout Mountain Inn in Chattanooga, the Great Southern Hotel in Gulfport, Mississippi, and other hotels in Vicksburg and Hattiesburg. It is doubtful that any architect in the history of New Orleans ever produced more than Sully.

In his day, Sully completely dominated the field. Naturally, it fell to him to design most of the new mansions along St. Charles Avenue, not only within the Garden District but all the way to Carrollton. Indeed, the avenue as a whole became a monument to Sully's industriousness. He personally built and occupied three different houses there and on Carrollton Avenue, none of them in the historic Garden District.[49] All three houses still stand, as does the large carriage house behind Sully's first Carrollton Avenue home, where the architect kept a snappy surrey with a fringe on the top and bells on its roof. Driving in his surrey from Carrollton to Lee (formerly Tivoli) Circle in 1900, the architect could have admired over five dozen examples of his own work.

Thomas Sully was the great nephew of Thomas Sully (1783–1872), the English-born portraitist who immortalized every prominent American from the time of Jefferson to the Civil War, and the son of George Washington Sully, a cotton broker who settled in the Garden District on Prytania at Ninth Street before 1845. George Sully was also a competent amateur painter, as several surviving canvases reveal. The 1857 tax rolls indicate that the senior Sully owned no slaves, which may account for the family's decision to wait out the Civil War in nearby Covington, Louisiana. It was presumably during the war years that George Sully had time to encourage his son's love for drawing.

Between the war's end and the Panic of 1873, Thomas Sully studied at a private school in New Orleans run by a Dr. Sanders. With the collapse of business in New Orleans, the eighteen-year-old Sully left for Austin, Texas, apparently to sell sewing machines.[50] Sully's professional interest in architecture dates to his stay in Austin. He later claimed to have been associated with the firm of Larmour and Wheelock there, but his role could not have been more than draftsman, for he as yet had no training.

Sensing the need for formal study, Sully traveled to New York, where he apprenticed in the office of George Slade and Henry Rutgers Marshall. These were the years when wealthy merchants in the Northeast were building commodious summer houses at Long Branch and adjacent Elberton, New Jersey, and later in Newport, Rhode Island. Requiring little or no heating, such houses could be generous in scale. They could be inventive in form because of summertime's freer social patterns, not to mention the desire of

their wealthy patrons to show themselves as creative and forward-looking. The firm of Slade and Marshall mostly designed office buildings for the Soho district of New York City than innovative villas. Nonetheless, we can be sure that Sully became acquainted with these sprawling houses during his years in New York. The designs for summer houses attracted much attention within the profession and the architectural press, and the social new resorts and their architecture roused so much interest in the popular press.

Returning to the Crescent City in 1877 at the age of twenty-two, the young architect took employment as a surveyor. Sully's name appears frequently on notarial surveys of the period. With the building industry still in a slump, however, there was no position for him in an established firm. He therefore simply presented himself at construction sites, and within a few years gained sufficient practical experience to set himself up as a builder and to be listed as such in city directories.

Thomas Sully went into business on his own in 1883, the year after Henry Howard designed his last building. Reynolds was dead, and only James Freret posed any major competition. Sully's recent ties with New York made him the obvious candidate to serve as court architect to those "long-headed men" whom Mark Twain encountered in New Orleans.

Who were Thomas Sully's patrons? Sully had literally hundreds of clients throughout New Orleans and the South. If one speaks of just the eight who built the major houses in the Garden District or lower reaches of St. Charles Avenue, they emerge as a highly diverse group. Together they were typical of the "long-headed men"—builders of the New South. Among Sully's first clients in the uptown area was Simon Hernsheim, whose house at 3811 St. Charles Avenue just beyond the Garden District is well known today as the Columns Hotel. The firm of S. Hernsheim Brothers & Company was the largest manufacturer of cigars in the United States. Its factory employed a thousand workers in the 1890s and produced nearly forty million La Belle Creole cigars annually.[51]

Hernsheim, a Louisiana native, was the son of Jewish immigrants from Alsace. Isidore Newman, another Sully client who lived just outside the Garden District, was also Jewish, born in Kaiserlautern just across the Rhine from Alsace. After the collapse

of an early business venture in Catahoula Parish during the Civil War, Newman came to New Orleans in 1865 and took a position as a bookkeeper. Three years later he started his own banking and brokerage business and grew rich lending money at high interest rates to struggling planters. On the strength of this lucrative trade, Newman became one of the few bankers with liquidity at the time of the 1873 panic. He parlayed this so as to make himself a leading power in Southern finances. As a leader of the modernizing movement locally, Isidore Newman played a prominent role in settling the city's staggering bond indebtedness, in constructing the street railway system, and in establishing a pioneer school for industrial education.[52]

No less notable than the presence of numerous Jewish residents among the modernizing elite was the prominence achieved by Catholics. Thanks to the involvement of such men as Durant Da Ponte in the upbuilding of the 1880s, the Protestant monopoly over uptown business and social life was broken. Da Ponte, a native New Yorker and the grandson of Mozart's librettist, Lorenzo Da Ponte, lived just outside the Garden District on St. Charles Avenue. A journalist for many years, Da Ponte served as the first editor of the *Daily Picayune* and the *Daily Delta*, respectively. After serving with the Confederate Army, he plunged into the postwar boom. The

Panic of 1873 set him back temporarily, but by the early 1880s he had amassed a fresh fortune through stock trading.[53]

The 1873 panic had bred extreme financial caution among those members of the old Garden District elite who survived it. In contrast, the modernizers of the 1880s and 1890s were swashbuckling capitalists, even outright gamblers. Joseph A. Walker, for example, for whom Sully designed the mansion that still stands at 2503 St. Charles Avenue, entered New Orleans business by buying into Colonel Walter Merriam's fabled Crescent Billiard Hall. A native of Montreal who had been in New Orleans since 1860, Walker quickly amassed enough money in the gambling business to open his own bank in 1869. Even during the 1873 panic the billiard hall continued to turn a good profit, which made it possible for Walker's bank to give change in specie to all customers who wished it. In the laconic phrase of his obituary, "this improvement vastly increased the popularity of Colonel Walker."[54] Like Newman, Walker's innovative and multiple enterprise enabled him to prosper in hard times.

Still more of a gambler was John Morris, a native of Jersey City, New Jersey, for whom Sully designed a massive residence at 2525 St. Charles Avenue. After graduating summa cum laude from Harvard College in 1856, Morris married the daughter of a New

Orleans family and thereafter spent part of each year in the Crescent City. Morris, a fanatical horseman, maintained first-class stables in Louisiana, and at a ranch north of San Antonio and his estate in Westchester County, New York. In 1889 he built the Morris Park racetrack outside New York City and organized the New York Jockey Club.

Even though he was born to wealth, Morris had little need after his first investments were made to rely on inherited money for these projects. In New Orleans he amassed a fortune by developing downtown real estate. It was through this activity that he first met Sully. Far more important, Morris invested so heavily in the shares of the infamous Louisiana State Lottery that he quickly became its driving spirit. This monster spread its tentacles of venality and corruption nationwide, creating some of the largest fortunes in the Crescent City. With droll irony reminiscent of Joseph Walker's obituary, Morris's biographer declared that "had he consulted selfish or timid convenience, [Morris] might well have preferred to retire from this connection, when the issues involving so much fanaticism, bitterness and defamation arose. But his was not a nature to withdraw weakly under such stress from a trust undertaken in circumstances of complete public approbation . . . and to whose continued exercise he deemed himself bound by considerations of loyalty to his associates and the state of Louisiana."[55] Morris, in other words, was a high roller and proud of it.

These sketches suffice to draw the profile of the new men upon whose fortune Thomas Sully's career was built. To be sure, not all of them were as ingenious as Hernsheim or Newman, as adaptable as Da Ponte, or as colorful as Walker or Morris. They were resourceful nonetheless, as the cases of three of Sully's Garden District patrons attest. Albert Ranlett of 2362 Camp Street pursued the old New Orleans-New York link as a member of the cotton exchanges of both cities.[56] The career of John Rainey of 2631 Prytania Street followed the antebellum pattern that led from the insurance business to other local investments.[57] Similarly, Samuel Adams Trufant, descended from French Canadian settlers from Maine, developed a grain export firm much like the great cotton brokerages of antebellum days.[58] Yet the balance had shifted decisively toward men who made their money in new ways.

Unlike the founding fathers of the Garden District, Sully's patrons had little in common with one another beyond the desire to see the community as a whole prosper in a manner beneficial to themselves. That most possessed genuine civic spirit is beyond question. But they shared no common background, they followed no line of common professions, and they faced no common enemy, as did the old Garden District Whigs. Centrifugal social forces exerted strong pressures on their lives. As believers in the reintegration of New Orleans into the national economy, they established far-flung business ties that isolated them still further from one another.

These were the new men who settled in the Garden District and built the mansions that stretched for five miles along St. Charles Avenue to Carrollton. In due course they were fully absorbed into New Orleans life and society. Initially, however, they constituted a powerful force for change in the uptown suburbs. The nature of that change can still be seen today by viewing the residences Thomas Sully designed for them.

Sully's major houses are massive. He introduced third floors into the Garden District and surmounted them with steep-pitched roofs and chimneys or towers that reached still higher. Lest a viewer's eyes might underestimate a house's sheer scale, Sully frequently amplified the design by piercing the main gables with dormers and chimneys and dramatic porches. The porches are invariably one story and never obscure the looming mass of the building itself. Sully's finest houses dwarf even the largest residences by Howard and Reynolds. Sully's designs incorporate no servants' wing, the staff being relegated to separate buildings that can stand unto themselves as some of the more imposing structures in the neighborhood, as with the Newman residence.

In keeping with his more illustrious contemporaries in the Northeast—Richard Morris Hunt, Dudley Newton, and the firm of McKim, Mead and White—Sully adhered to no one formula for his designs. The large Morris house, for example, scarcely differs in plan from the traditional five-bay Garden District mansion of the 1850s. The residence for Francis Johnson at St. Charles and Washington Avenues, by contrast, has a notably free plan.[59] The one common feature of dozens of Sully floor plans is that they are not organized around linear halls. Rather, the hallway is transformed into a reception room or "living hall," in Sully's phrase,

Newspaper editor Durant Da Ponte's seraglio, 3512 St. Charles Avenue, just outside the Garden District. Designed by Thomas Sully, 1894, now demolished (THE HISTORIC NEW ORLEANS COLLECTION)

Cigar maker Simon Hernsheim's residence was one of the first houses Thomas Sully designed in the uptown area, 3811 St. Charles Avenue, 1898 (COLLECTION OF CLAIR CROPPEL)

Parlor in the Hernsheim house (TAWNEY HARDING)

which is wide open to all the major parlors. At the Trufant residence at 1239 Philip Street, one of Sully's most subtle works, the reception hall dominates the house, serving both as reception room and as a huge central ventilating shaft that enables air to circulate to three floors. Such open planning, so appropriate to New Orleans, is a direct borrowing from contemporary seashore residences in New Jersey, Rhode Island, and Massachusetts. Sully's houses are also notable for their three-dimensionality. Instead of the traditional single grand entrance, he opened up two or even three facades with doorways, one of them often being a covered carriage entrance, or porte cochère.

The fact that the Sully mansions are ultimately derived from summer houses rather than adapted from town houses makes them starkly individualistic. We can better appreciate the communal character of the older galleried houses of the Garden District when their relative uniformity is contrasted to the diversity of Sully's designs. The former naturally group together to form ensembles; the latter appear as so many soloists. The same, of course, can be said of the patrons themselves.

Such individualization was deliberate. When earlier Garden District architects modified the interior spaces of standard three- or five-bay houses, they took pains to disguise the fact on the exteriors. Sully, in contrast, used the exterior elevations to accentuate and even exaggerate his innovations within. Virtually every exterior surface is broken up with protruding or inset porches and balconies. The Johnson house on St. Charles Avenue at Washington had no fewer than five porches. Sometimes these were added purely for visual effect, not really for sitting. Always they are set off with contrasting Tuscan or Ionic columns, or with curved railings that appear to have been draped between the posts.

In their geometric flare and dramatic scale the major Sully houses seem flamboyant and extroverted. These qualities had been present in such postwar Italianate residences as the Weis house on Jackson Avenue. Even the boldest postwar architects and builders, however, shied away from the use of towers and turrets that were the stock in trade of Italianate mansions in the Northeast. Such reticence was not for Sully and his clients. At the Hernsheim house on St. Charles Avenue he attached an enormous four-story octagonal tower at the very front, dwarfing even the fine Tuscan gallery that

has now been replaced with vulgarly inappropriate columns. The heavy rustication, the ornamented moldings at each floor level, and the enormous viewing gallery rising above like a band shell makes the Hernsheim tower all but shout out for the passerby's attention. By comparison with the flamboyant onion-shaped dome on the Da Ponte house, however, the Hernsheim tower was positively understated. Since this piece of exotica has no rival in the entire corpus of Sully's work, one is tempted to think that Da Ponte himself ordered the feature so as to give his house the appearance of a stage set from an opera buffa by his grandfather.

Such unrestrained devices exceed even the fanciful vocabulary of the Queen Anne style. In practice, Sully exploited whatever stylistic vocabulary served his ends. Whereas his own two uptown houses on Carrollton Avenue are safely within the Queen Anne tradition, his overall portfolio of works for clients showcase virtually every contemporary trend in architecture. Norman elements predominate at the Newman house, his only stone mansion, while Elizabethan oriel windows are called for in the plans of the modest J. D. Bloom house.[60] For all this diversity, however, the Queen Anne style sets the tone for most of Sully's exteriors. Shingles in contrasting colors, patterned brick, and stick-style traceries appear repeatedly. At the Morris house and elsewhere he even employed shingle lap siding.

The historical record strongly suggests that Sully tailored the interiors of his houses to fit the personalities of his clients. Isidore Newman was among Sully's most sober and earnest patrons. The architect paneled the reception hall and several rooms of Newman's St. Charles Avenue home with a fittingly dark oak that framed deep golden silk wall panels. Durant Da Ponte, by contrast, was a high-living extrovert; appropriately, the interiors of the now-demolished Da Ponte residence on St. Charles Avenue are said to have featured panels of gaudy painted silk and a bewildering variety of rich details. The interiors of the Morris house, like the arrangement of rooms there, adhered closely to older Garden District prototypes, probably reflecting Mrs. Morris's established, New Orleans origins, having grown up in the more subdued environment of the Garden District in an earlier day. This could scarcely be said of Simon Hernsheim. Although a New Orleanian by birth, Hernsheim was a self-made man burning to proclaim his worldly success. The

Central hall in the Hernsheim house (TAWNEY HARDING)

Samuel Trufant's house, 1339–41 Philip Street. Thomas Sully's practical and direct Eastlakian design, 1890

interiors of his residence, which are still partially preserved, attain a level of gaudiness rarely equaled in the entire South except elsewhere on the New Orleans showcase of wealth, St. Charles Avenue. Even the fountain John Morris installed in front of his house and the twelve-by-four stained glass window depicting *L'Aurore* that Joseph Walker imported from Chicago paled by comparison.[61]

While Sully obviously relished these uninhibited projects, he was fully capable of some degree of modesty. Samuel Trufant was known as an austere man who inherited some of his father's New England reserve. For Trufant's house at 1339–41 Philip Street, Sully adopted the "honest" approach to architectural design espoused by Charles Eastlake. In his *Hints on Household Taste in Furniture, Upholstery, and Other Details* (1872), Eastlake defended "constructive purpose" in interior design. All showiness repelled him, and even curved lines he took to be marks of extravagance. In the Trufant house of 1890, Sully applied Eastlake's philosophy with admirable results. Granted that Eastlake would have objected to the bulbous columns that Sully employed, the Trufant residence as a whole is notable for its practicality and directness. The typical Sully house was enormous and profusely ornamented, reflecting the expansive temper of the age. In the antebellum Garden District a degree of modesty had been a la mode; the spendthrift habits of a Henry Lonsdale or James Robb had shocked the old suburb. By 1890 such flamboyance had become the rule rather than the exception, and it is the restrained Trufant house that stands out in contrast.

The irony of the situation was that the new wealth of the 1880s and 90s was not as great as the architecture suggests and those who held it were not particularly numerous. The "New South" of which the new business leaders dreamed did not come into being in New Orleans as elsewhere. Between 1880 and 1890 the number of manufacturing firms in the city more than doubled, but in comparison with several dozen other American cities, New Orleans' pace of development was modest. Worse, it became evident well before the turn of the century that the spurt that had occurred in the 1880s had fizzled out. Between 1890 and 1900 the number of local industries fell by a quarter. Not only did the pace of economic development flag but political reform collapsed. After only four years of reform government, the electorate threw out the partisans

of local renewal in 1892. The Cotton Centennial Exposition they had mounted in 1884 had been a financial disaster, and many of their cultural and educational institutions failed to develop as they had expected. By 1900, the Sully mansions along St. Charles Avenue had become monuments to a dream that was no more.

From the perspective of the boosters of the 1880s, the decline that set in during the 1890s was a misfortune. Nonetheless, it brought unexpected benefits to the social and architectural fabric of the Garden District. It forced the "new men" to integrate themselves into the life of a suburb that they had earlier set out to transcend. It thwarted their tendency to encapsulate themselves in a ghetto for the affluent and stopped the further spread of private streets. Economic backwardness in effect sustained the unique social and cultural environment of the Garden District into the twentieth century.

It also thwarted for half a century the process of galloping urban growth that had given rise to the Garden District in the first place. The commercial center continued to develop, but at a modest pace. Suburbanization continued as well, but the further expansion uptown and the in-building in older areas did not upset housing patterns to the extent that the original garden suburb was abandoned for outer pastures. It is impossible to know what uptown society might have done had vast new sources of wealth been opened to it in the early twentieth century. Because this did not occur, residents of the Garden District stayed there. The fortunate consequence of the failure of progress in New Orleans was to slow the process of flight and, happily, to preserve the architecture of one of America's greatest residential suburbs.

Only with the creation of new wealth from oil and natural gas in the 1970s did this situation change. Prosperity accomplished the work of destruction that poverty had thwarted. During the decade of the seventies, when New Orleanians attained greater wealth than they had known for a century, scores of the finest suburban mansions from the previous century were destroyed, both within the Garden District and in the city generally. There have recently been a few signs that further demolition in the Garden District may finally have been checked. In the absence of definitive evidence, one can only hope that this book will contribute to that much-desired end.

INTRODUCTION

1. Sam Bass Warner, Jr., *Streetcar Suburbs: The Process of Growth in Boston, 1871–1900* (Cambridge, 1978), viii.

2. Quoted in Michael H. Ebner, *Creating Chicago's North Shore: A Suburban History* (Chicago, 1988), 6.

3. Kenneth T. Jackson, *Crabgrass Frontier: The Suburbanization of the United States* (New York and Oxford, 1985), 3–11.

4. United States Census, 1840, Louisiana, New Orleans Public Library; also Edwin Adams Davis, *The Story of Louisiana*, 4 vols. (New Orleans, 1960), 1:165.

5. Robert A. M. Stern, "La Ville Bourgeoise," *AD (Architectural Design)*, 51 (October–November 1981): 14. For a cogent and sustained attack on the American suburb, see Robert Fishman, *Bourgeois Utopias: The Rise and Fall of Suburbia* (New York, 1987).

6. Mark Twain, *Life on the Mississippi* (New York, 1977), 250–51.

7. Thomas Kelah Wharton diary, MS, New York Public Library, May 27, 1858.

8. John P. Coleman, "The Buckner-Eustis Residence," *States*, April 8, 1923. The mansion at 1410 Jackson Avenue was erected in 1856 for Henry Sullivan Buckner by architect Lewis E. Reynolds at a cost of $30,000. Notarial Archives, H.B. Cenas, 1856, vol. 64, 603.

9. A rare exception is Talbot Hamlin, who touches on several Garden District residences in *Greek Revival Architecture in America* (London, 1944).

10. Friends of the Cabildo, *New Orleans Architecture*, 6 vols. (New Orleans, 1971–80).

11. Martha Ann Brett Samuel and Ray Samuel, *The Great Days of the Garden District* (New Orleans, 1961).

12. The works by these scholars are cited in relevant chapters below.

13. A good example of such a doorway is to be found at 1302–04 Jackson Avenue, built in 1850–51 for Joseph Fernandez. Notarial Archives, Amedee Ducatel, 1851, vol. 49, 53. Other examples include 1121–27 Eighth Street and 937 St. Andrew Street.

14. *Daily Crescent*, August 7, 1858, 3; see also *Lafayette City Advertiser*, January 1, 1842, 2; July 1842, p. 2; *Deutsche Zeitung*, March 19, 1850, 2.

15. Civil District Court 503-568, Succession of Ada Belle Skardon, 2423 Magazine Street.

16. 1625–27, 1629–33 Josephine Street. Probably built in 1878–79 for Charles Campbell. Notarial Archives, P. C. Cuvellier, 1873, vol. 32, no. 292; Octave Morel, 1866, vol. 2, no. 12; Succession of T. B. Poindexter, Conveyance Office Book 86, folio 361.

17. 1129 Jackson Avenue was apparently built for John Phelps, a commission merchant and cotton factor, in 1869–70. Notarial Archives, Theodore Guyol, 1869, vol. 53, no. 276; William J. Castell, 1869, vol. 22, no. 3983. 3005 St. Charles Avenue was built in 1874 for a commission merchant, Richard Flower; Notarial Archives, P. C. Cuvellier, 1872, vol. 29, no. 36; William J. Castell, 1872, vol. 33, no. 6078. Among major buildings that have been destroyed are the houses of Julius Weis, 1237 Jackson Avenue; A. Luzenberg, 2103 Chestnut Street; James Pagaud, 1302 Philip Street; Charles Gallagher, 1236 Fourth Street; Hunt Henderson, 2126 Prytania Street; Charles Conrad, 2343 Prytania Street; Lafayette Folger, 2508 St. Charles Avenue; Shepherd Brown, 2833 St. Charles Avenue; and Robert Roberts, 2821 St. Charles Avenue.

CHAPTER ONE

1. Carlos Trudeau, "Plan of the Ville Gravier," May 14, 1796. Notarial Archives, Plan Book 4, folio 461. See also Francis P. Burns, "The Graviers and Faubourg Ste. Marie," *Louisiana Historical Quarterly* 22 (April 1939): 395–97.

2. Benjamin Moore Norman, *Norman's New Orleans and Environs* (New Orleans, 1845), 73–74.

3. *Louisiana Courier*, April 14, 1824; Norman, 68.

4. A. E. Fossier, "A Funeral Ceremony of Napoleon in New Orleans, December 19, 1821," *Louisiana Historical Quarterly* 13 (April 1930): 246–52.

5. Eliza Ripley, *Social Life in Old New Orleans* (New York and London, 1912), 167.

6. John Smith Kendall, *History of New Orleans*, 3 vols. (Chicago and New York, 1927), 1:85.

7. Benjamin Henry Boneval Latrobe, *Impressions Respecting New Orleans*, edited by Samuel Wilson, Jr. (New York, 1951), 35.

8. Ibid, 106.

9. Cf. Montgomery Schuyler, "The Small City House in New York," *Architectural Record* 8 (April–June 1899): 857 ff.

10. See William J. Murtagh, "The Philadelphia Row House," *Journal of the Society of Architectural Historians* 16 (December 1957): 8–13.

11. Latrobe, 42.

12. Samuel Wilson, Jr., "Early History of the Lower Garden District," *New Orleans Architecture: The Lower Garden District*, vol. 1, edited by Samuel Wilson, Jr., and Bernard Lemann (Gretna, LA, 1971), 6–30; also Meloncy C. Soniat, "The Faubourgs Forming the Upper Section of the City of New Orleans," *Louisiana Historical Quarterly* 20 (January 1937): 192–99.

13. Wilson, 10–12.

14. Christopher Tunnard and Henry Hope Reed, *American Skyline: The Growth and Form of Our Cities and Towns* (Boston, 1955), 50 ff.

15. Harriet P. Bos, "Barthelemy Lafon" (M.A. thesis, Tulane University, 1977), 5.

16. Wharton diary, February 28, 1856.

17. Wilson, 15.

18. 928 Euterpe Street, *New Orleans Architecture: The Lower Garden District*, 94, 125.

19. A. Oakey Hall, *The Manhattaner in New Orleans* (New York, 1851), 35.

20. "The Anglo-American Suburb," *AD (Architectural Design)* 51 (October–November 1981): 19.

21. Catherine E. Beecher, *Treatise on Domestic Economy for the Use of Young Ladies at Home and at School* (New York, 1864).

22. Rev. Theodore Clapp, *Autobiographical Sketches and Recollections, During a Thirty-Five Years' Residence in New Orleans* (Boston, 1857), 69.

23. Kathryn C. Briecle, "A History of the City of Lafayette," *Louisiana Historical Quarterly* 20 (October 1937): 904–8. For the plan see Notarial Archives, Louis T. Caire, 1832, Vol. 18, no. 174.

24. Jefferson Parish Notarial Records, J. M. Harang, May 24, 1825; December 30, 1829.

25. Notarial Archives, Louis T. Caire, 1832, vol. 18, no. 174. These transactions are reviewed in detail by Briede, 908–16.

26. Rita Katherine Carey, "Samuel Jarvis Peters," *Louisiana Historical Quarterly*, 30 (April 1947): 441 ff.

27. For an appealing sketch of Marigny, see Grace King, "Bernard de Marigny," *Grace King of New Orleans: A Selection of Her Writings*, edited by Robert Bush (Baton Rouge, 1973), 352–76.

28. Kendall, *History of New Orleans*, 1: 125.

29. Ibid.

30. On Peirce see *Daily Southern Star*, April 6, 1866, 1.

31. The plan for Cosmopolite City appears on Springbett and Pilie's 1839 map of New Orleans. This project was likely conceived on the eve of the panic of 1837 and failed amidst the subsequent real estate depression. See Betsy Swanson, *Historic Jefferson Parish* (Gretna, La., 1975), 122.

32. Notarial Archives, Christoval de Armas, 1824, vol. 10, no. 188.

33. 2830 Coliseum Street. Notarial Archives, C. Pollock, 1837, vol. 57, no. 45.

34. Kathryn T. Abney, "The Land Ventures of General Lafayette in the Territory of New Orleans and the State of Louisiana," *Louisiana Historical Quarterly* 16 (July 1933): 359 ff; also Francis P. Burns, "Lafayette Visits New Orleans," *Louisiana Historical Quarterly* 29 (April 1946): 296 ff; cf. building contract by Louis St. Amant, Notarial Archives, Christoval de Armas, vol. 10, no. 188, 1824.

35. James A. Renshaw, "The Lost City of Lafayette," *Louisiana Historical Quarterly* 2 (January 1919): 47–55. See also Colin B. Hamer, Jr., "Records of the City of Lafayette (1833–1852) in the City Archives Department of the New Orleans Public Library," *Louisiana History* 13 (Fall 1972): 413–31.

36. United States Tax Records, 1840, New Orleans Public Library; see entries for Manuel Garcia, Thomas Pipkin, Emile Trudeau.

37. Ibid, 1850.

38. *Arrivals and Port Register*, 1834, City of Lafayette, Tulane University Archives.

39. 1208 Philip Street. Constructed by Abram Howell, builder, for the wholesale grocer Luther Wilson Stewart, for $6,000; Notarial Archives, T. J. Beck, vol. 5, no.

40. United States Census, City of Lafayette, 1850.

41. Sylvia J. Pinner, "A History of the Irish Channel, 1840–1860" (M.A. thesis, Tulane University, 1954), 16 ff.

42. United States Census, City of Lafayette, 1850.

43. 719 Fourth Street. Probably built for Owen Reilly after 1848. Notarial Archives, L. R. Kenny, 1848, vol. 7, no. 45.

44. 2342 Rousseau Street. Built circa 1850 for a medical doctor, Moses M. Dowler. Notarial Archives, L. R. Kenny, 1847, vol. 6, no. 426; L.R. Kenny, 1848, vol. 7, no. 262.

45. 436 Seventh Street. Built for Mary Ann Grigson, apparently in 1838. Notarial Archives, Octave de Armas, 1834, vol. 22, no. 211.

46. Lynn Adams, "Research Reveals One of Oldest Shotguns," The Historic New Orleans Collection Newsletter, vol. III, no. 2 (Spring 1985), 5.

47. 2709 Camp Street, built in 1845–49 for Matthew Crooks. Notarial Archives, L. R. Kenny, 1845, vol. 3, 312.

48. 730–32 and 734–36 Washington Avenue; built before 1866 for Gerd Heinrich Wilhelm Lehde; Notarial Archives, Joseph Cohn, 1866, vol. 19, no. 177; Joseph Cohn, 1866, vol. 19, no. 176. 2308 Chippewa Street, built after 1846 for the blacksmith John Freidenstein; Notarial Archives, L. R. Kenny, 1949, vol. 9, no. 138.

49. 1020 Fourth Street. Designed by George Purves and constructed 1849–50 by builders Frederick H. Robertson and Charles H. Shaw for Isaac Bogart at a cost

of $2,000. Notarial Archives, L. R. Kenny, 1849, vol. 11, no. 72.

50. 3232 Laurel Street, built in 1856–58. Notarial Archives, Theodore Guyol, 1856, vol. 34, no. 127; Plan Book 24, folio 23.

51. Notarial Archives, Plan Book 51, folio 24.

52. Jefferson Parish Notarial Records, F. J. E. Dugue Livaudais, 1834–35, vol. 1, 143; also Notarial Archives, Charles de Armas, 1835, vol. 3, no. 81.

53. Notarial Archives, Livaudais, 1836, vol. 4, 594–97.

54. Lafayette Tax Rolls, 1850.

55. H. Didimus, *New Orleans As I Found It* (New York, 1845), 20.

56. William L. Robinson, *The Diary of a Samaritan* (New York, 1860), 81.

57. City Council of New Orleans, *Report of the Sanitary Commission of New Orleans on the Epidemic of Yellow Fever of 1853* (New Orleans, 1854), 402.

58. Clapp, 249.

59. Wharton diary, September 8, 1854.

CHAPTER TWO

1. *Louisiana Courier*, July 20, 1818, 2.

2. 1302–1304 Jackson Avenue, built 1850–51. Notarial Archives, Amedè Ducatel, 1851, vol. 49, 53.

3. 3116 Prytania Street; Notarial Archives, L. R. Kenny, 1815, vol. 3, no. 256. 1229 Second Street; Notarial Archives, Daniel Israel Ricardo, 1844, vol. 1, no. 16.

4. Michel Musson built the house at 1331 Third Street after 1850. The cast-iron gallery was added by Charles M. Whitney after 1884. Samuel Wilson, Jr., papers, Southeastern Architectural Archive, Tulane University.

5. Daniel Browne, "Burnside's Grave," *Times Democrat*, August 24, 1890, 3.

6. On the 1837 panic in Louisiana see Joseph George Tregle, Jr., "Louisiana and the Tariff 1817–1846," *Louisiana Historical Quarterly* 25 (January 1942): 33–121.

7. *States*, March 12, 1900, 4. Jacob Payne built the house at 1134 First Street in 1849. Notarial Archives, Felix Puig, 1935, vol. 108, no. 65; C.D.C. 230–794, Succession of Hedwig Penzel Forsyth.

8. See Alfred H. Stone, "The Cottage Factorage System of the Southern States," *American Historical Review*, 20 (1915): 516; also Harriet E. Amos, *Cotton City: Urban Development in Antebellum Mobile* (University of Alabama, Mobile, 1985), 28 ff.

9. Vincent Nolte, *Fifty Years in Both Hemispheres; or, Reminiscences of the Life of a Former Merchant* (New York, 1854), 308.

10. Isaac Thayer built the house at 2520 Prytania Street for Thomas C. Gilmour in 1853 at a cost of $9,500. The first plan specified a portico with columns but the surviving cast-iron gallery was substituted prior to the signing of the contract. Notarial Archives, J. Claiborne, 1853, vol. 5, no. 5.

11. 1415 Third Street, built in 1859 for Walter G. Robinson. Wharton diary, January 15 and March 7, 1859. David McCan purchased the house from Robinson in 1873. Notarial Archives, P. C. Cuvellier, 1873, vol. 32, no. 290.

12. Among other cotton factors or brokers who built major Garden District houses were Charles Gallagher, 1236 Fourth Street (demolished); Henry Short, 1448 Forth Street; Alexander Harris, 2127 Prytania Street; E. K. Bryant, 2220–22 Prytania Street; Thomas Toby, 2340 Prytania Street; Edward Davis, 2504 Prytania Street; Louis de Saulles, 2618 Coliseum Street; Samuel H. Kennedy, formerly 641 Camp Street, now 1201 First Street (demolished); Manuel Goldsmith, 1122 Jackson Avenue; and Henry S. Buckner, 1410 Jackson Avenue.

13. Cf. obituary, *Daily States*, April 16, 1900, 8. Adams's house at 2423 Prytania Street was built in 1860–61. Ferdinand Reusch, Jr., purchased the house from Adams in 1896. Samuel Wilson, Jr., papers, Southeastern Architectural Archive, Tulane University.

14. J. K. Collins & Co. built the house at 2521–23 Prytania Street in 1856 for Henry T. Lonsdale at a cost of $30,000. *Daily Crescent*, October 21, 1856, 2. Notarial Archives, Theodore Guyol, 1868, vol. 52, no. 104.

15. See Cohen's *New Orleans City Directory for 1855* (New Orleans, 1855), n.p.

16. Harry A. Mitchell, "The Development of New Orleans as a Wholesale Trading Center," *Louisiana Historical Quarterly* 27 (October 1944): 944–57.

17. See *Jewell's Crescent City Illlustrated*, edited and compiled by Edwin L. Jewell (New Orleans, 1873), 50–52.

18. Thomas Austin Adams built a house at 2624 Prytania Street in 1848–49. Notarial Archives, J. B. Marks, 1848, vol. 44, no. 77. The Adams house burned shortly before World War II.

19. Henry H. Hansell residence at 3000 Prytania Street was built in 1859–61. Notarial Archives, Richard Brenan, 1859, vol. 15, no. 162. The house at 2507 Prytania Street was erected in 1852 for Joseph H. Maddox by John Barnett, architect, John R. Eichelberger, builder, and Edward Gotthiel, superintending architect. Samuel Wilson, Jr., papers.

20. Charles Conrad's house was built in 1841 on the present site of the Bradish Johnson house, now the Louise M. McGehee School for Girls. Notarial Archives, Adolphe Mazureau, 1841, vol. 24, p. 35. The Levi Peirce house stood at 147 (old) St. Charles Avenue.

21. Henry Howard and Henry Thiberge designed the house at 2027 Carondelet Street in 1859 for Captain Thomas P. Leathers. Builder William K. Day erected the house for $24,590. Orleans Parish court records, J. Baumiller vs. T. P. Leathers; Edward Lynch vs. T. P. Leathers, testimony, November 26, 1860. A transcript of these records is in Samuel Wilson, Jr., papers.

22. Thomas K. Wharton built the A. W. Bosworth house at 1126 Washington Avenue in 1859. Wharton diary, May–June 1859.

23. The house at 1410 Second Street was built for Lewis Elkins in 1858–59 by Frederick Wing and Bro. for $12,000. Notarial Archives, William L. Poole, 1858, vol. 6, no. 524; "Building Improvements," *Daily Crescent*, September 12, 1859, p. 2. Hunt Henderson housed his large art collection there after he built the house in 1907. John P. Coleman, "The Hunt Henderson Residence," *States*, December 23, 1923. The house of Samuel E. Moore at 2925 Coliseum Street was built in 1853–58. Notarial Archives, James Graham, 1853, vol. 3, no. 618.

24. The house of Mrs. Mandeville Marigny at 2524 St. Charles Avenue was built in 1856–57; "City Improvements," *Daily Crescent*, October 21, 1856, 3; Notarial Archives, William L. Poole, 1857, vol. 5, no. 358. The house at 1220 Philip Street was built in 1857 for Aurore Mather Tureaud, widow of Augustin Marius Tureaud. Samuel Wilson, Jr., papers.

25. Amos, 58.

26. James De Bow, "Natives and Inhabitants of the Leading Cities," *De Bow's Review* 19 (September 1855): 262; see also William W. Chenault and Robert C. Reinders, "The Northern-born Community of New Orleans in the 1850s," *Journal of American History* 51 (September 1964): 232–47.

27. *Daily Crescent*, June 7, 1851, quoted by Chenault and Reinders, 232. In this respect New Orleans surpassed even Mobile, the second most "northern" city in the South, where 37 percent of the urban leadership was northern-born in the antebellum era. Harriet C. Amos, "'Birds of Passage' in a Cotton Port: Northerners and Foreigners Among the Urban Leaders of Mobile," in *Class, Conflict, and Consensus*, edited by Orville V. Burton and Robert C. McMath, Jr. (Westport, CT, 1982), 232–61.

28. On Samuel H. Kennedy, see Jewell, 104.

29. Chenault and Reinders, 237.

30. Norman, 74–75; Chenault and Reinders, 242.

31. Roger G. Kennedy, *Architecture, Men, Women and Money in America, 1600–1860*, (New York, Random House, 1985), 402.

32. Manuel Goldsmith house at 1122 Jackson Avenue was designed by the firm of Howard and Diettel and built in 1859 at a cost of $8,500. Notarial Archives, Joseph Cohn, 1859, vol. 6, no. 275.

33. Robert Grinnan's house at 2221 Prytania Street was designed by Henry Howard in 1850 and built by John Sewell for $19,800. Notarial Archives, H. P. Caire, 1850, vol. 1, no. 137.

34. Louis de Saulles built his house at 2618 Coliseum Street in the 1840s. Edith Long, *The Story of 2618 Coliseum* (New Orleans, 1967).

35. Peter Conrey's house at 2039–41 Prytania Street was designed by Henry Howard shortly after the Civil War; Wilson and Lemann, *New Orleans Architecture: The Lower Garden District*, 142. James Coyle's house at 2103–05 Baronne Street was built in 1866; Historic District Landmarks Commission record. John McGinty built the house at 1322 Felicity Street in 1872–73; Notarial Archives, W. J. Castell, 1870, vol. 25, no. 4617; M. Carmen, 1872, vol. 16, no. 519.

36. Cohen's *New Orleans Directory*, 1855, n.p.

37. Wharton diary, October 21, 1857.

38. *Daily Picayune*, December 20, 1883, 4.

39. *Times Democrat*, April 16, 1900, 7.

40. A. Oakley Hall, *The Manhattaner in New Orleans*, 23.

41. Henry Bertram Hill and Larry Gara, "A French Traveler's View of Ante-Bellum New Orleans," *Louisiana History* 1 (Autumn 1960): 337.

42. Dale A. Somers, "The Rise of Sports in New Orleans, 1850–1900" (Ph.D. dissertation, Tulane University, 1966), 58.

43. Eleanor K. Kayman, "Leisure-Time Activities in New Orleans, 1855–1863" (M.A. thesis, Tulane University, 1966), 93–94.

44. Ibid, 16.

45. A. Oakley Hall, *The Manhattaner in New Orleans*, 23.

46. Ibid. These persons resided at 1236 Jackson Avenue (Sweet); 2427 Camp Street (Anderson); 1531 Jackson Avenue (Warren); 1236 First Street (Godwin); 2507 Prytania Street (Maddox); and 3000 Prytania Street (Hansell).

47. New Orleans Tax Rolls, 1857, New Orleans Public Library, n.p. 2221 Prytania Street (Grinnan); Notarial Archives, Henry P. Caire, 1850, vol. 1, no. 137. 1134 First Street (Payne); New Orleans Tax Rolls, 1857. 1448 Fourth Street (Short); Notarial Archives, John F. Coffee, 1859, vol. 7, no. 131.

48. Wharton diary, May 16, 1857.

49. Notably H. M. Wright, whose house at 1205 Esplanade Avenue cost $50,000; Dr. Charles Campbell's house at St. Charles Avenue and Julia cost $40,000; and Cyprien DuPour's house on Esplanade Avenue cost $30.000. "Building Improvements in New Orleans for the Year Ending Aug. 31, 1859," *Daily Crescent*, September 12, 1859.

50. Martha Eshleman, "Toby-Westfeldt House, 2340 Prytania Street: Approach II," MS, May 1967, 1, 6, 10, 14; Samuel Wilson, Jr., papers. On Toby's support of Texas see his *A Vindication of the Conduct of the Agency of Texas in New Orleans* (New Orleans, 1836).

51. Notarial Archives, Philippe Lacoste, 1850, vol. 17, no. 114.

52. 2507 Prytania Street. Second District Court no. 7371, Deed Book H. p. 262.

53. The house at 2265 St. Charles Avenue was sold by Lavinia Dabney to Robert W.

Boyd on January 28, 1859. Notarial Archives, Joseph Lisbony, 1859, vol. 21, no. 39. James Gallier, Jr., designed this house, which cost $8,500 in 1856. Notarial Archives, Theodore Guyol, 1856, vol. 36, no. 684; ibid, no. 709. Samuel Wilson, Jr., "Episcopal Diocese Preserving One of Last Gallier-Designed Homes," States 13 (June 1953).

54. Wharton diary, January 17, 1855.

55. David P. Handlin, *The American House, Architecture and Society* 1815–1915 (Boston and Toronto, 1979), 238–39.

56. William K. Day, builder, erected the house at 1506 Seventh Street for John M. Chilton in 1859. Notarial Archives, James Graham, 1859, vol. 18, no. 4141; *Daily Picayune*, 24 November 1859.

57. Orleans Parish court records, J. Baumiller vs. T. P. Leathers; Edward Lynch vs. T. P. Leathrs, testimony of November 26, 1860.

58. Victor McGee and Robert S. Brantley, "Greek Revival to Greek Tragedy, Henry Howard, Architect, (1818–1884)," unpublished MS. 158–59.

59. Notarial Archives, Adolphe Mazureau, 1841, vol. 24, no. 35.

60. Henry Howard designed Simon Forcheimer's Magazine Street house. It cost $7,650 in 1859. Notarial Archives, Joseph Cohn, 1859, vol. 5, no. 139.

61. 2265 St. Charles Avenue. Notarial Archives, Theodore Guyol, 1856, vol. 36, no. 709.

62. Notarial Archives, E. G. Gottschalk, 1869, vol. 23, no. 41.

63. Cf. Samuel Sloan, *The Model Architect*, 2 vols. (Philadelphia, 1851), 2: plate XCIII, prototypes of plaster medallions, far more detailed that those in most Garden District houses.

64. Jewell, 52.

65. Cohen's *New Orleans Directory*, 1855, n. p.

66. *Dictionary of American Biography*, "Conrad, Charles Magill"; edited by Walter Lynwood Fleming, *The South in the Building of a Nation*, 12 vols. (Richmond, VA., 1909), 11:224.

67. *New Orleans Democrat*, August 3, 1881, 2.

68. Tregle, 100–21, for analysis of Whig financial doctrines, especially on the tariff in Louisiana. On Clay's overall program, see Holman Hamilton, *Prologue to Conflict: The Crisis and Compromise of 1850* (New York, 1966), Ch. 3.

69. Leon Cyprian Soule, *The Know Nothing Party in New Orleans: A Reappraisal* (Baton Rouge, 1961), 21–28.

70. City Council of New Orleans, *Report of the Sanitary Commission*, 402–34.

71. Cited in Kendall, *History of New Orleans*, 1: 165–66, 213.

72. John Archer, "Country and City in the American Romantic Suburb," *Journal of the Society of Architectural Historians* 42 (May 1983): 139–56.

73. *Daily Delta*, August 12, 1855, 4.

74. See George Rogers Taylor, *The Transportation Revolution, 1814–1860* (New York, 1951).

75. Christopher Thacker, *The History of Gardens* (Berkeley and Los Angeles, 1979), 230–33.

76. John Archer, "Ideology and Aspiration: Individualism, the Middle Class, and the Genesis of the Anglo-American Suburb," *Journal of Urban History* 14:2 (February 1988): 218 ff

77. Cited by Tunnard and Reed, 62.

78. Andrew Jackson Downing, *A Treatise on the Theory and Practice of Landscape Gardening* (New York, 1859), i–ix; *The Horticulturalist* began publication in 1845.

79. Alan Gowans, *Images of American Living* (New York, 1976), 319.

80. Gervase Wheeler, *Homes for the People, in Suburb and Country* (New York, 1855), 438–43.

81. Calvert Vaux, *Villas and Cottages* (New York, 1857), 40.

CHAPTER THREE

1. On the history of architectural taste, see Frank Jenkins, *Architect and Patron* (London, 1961).

2. Hamlin, 48.

3. Mrs. Frances Trollope, *Domestic Manners of the Americans* (London, 1832), cited in Hamlin, 48.

4. Andrew Jackson Downing, *The Architecture of Country Houses* (New York, 1850) iv.

5. For 2221 Prytania Street, *Daily Picayune*, September 19, 1850, 2.

6. For 2521 Prytania Street, Wharton diary, Mary 16, 1857.

7. *Autobiography of James Gallier, Architect* (New York, 1973), 18.

8. Notarial Archives, Daniel Clark, Jr., 1848, vol.3, no. 69.

9. George Washington Cable built his raised cottage at 1313 Eighth Street for $3,000 in 1876. Notarial Archives, Algeron S. Beck, 1876, vol. 3, no. 33.

10. Notarial Archives, Theodore Guyol, 1853, vol. 26, no. 318.

11. William A. Freret designed Edward Davis's 2504 Prytania Street house at a cost of $10,000 in 1858. "Building Improvements," *Daily Crescent*, September 12, 1859.

12. Notarial Archives, Louis T. Caire, 1841, vol. 81, no. 490. Now demolished.

13. Henry S. Buckner built his house at 1923 Coliseum Street (now 1401 St. Andrew Street) in 1849 and gave it to his sister-in-law, Mrs. Archie Allan Brand, in

1857. Notarial Archives, Hilary B. Cenas, 1857, vol. 68, no. 436.

14. Notarial Archives, Hilary B. Cenas, 1857, vol. 68, no. 436.

15. The house at 2607 Coliseum Street was built in 1850 for Edward Briggs, and later enlarged by architect William Freret for Newton Buckner, who purchased the property in 1869. Notarial Archives, Henry P. Caire, 1850, vol. 2, 135; John P. Coleman, "First Home of English Lawyer," *States*, May 13, 1924; now demolished. The house at 2627 Coliseum Street was built shortly after 1876 for Mrs. Ellen Buckner Eustis, wife of James B. Eustis. Notarial Archives, A. J. Armstrong, 1876, vol. 1, no. 55.

16. Morris house at 1331 First Street, *Daily Picayune*, November 30, 1869, 1.

17. Twain, 251.

18. Clapp, 246–7.

19. The house at 2340 Prytania Street was built in the late 1830s for Thomas Toby and his wife. J. H. Behan, carpenter and builder, made extensive alterations to the house in 1855. Notarial Archives, Edward Barnett, 1855, vol. 58, no. 385. Thomas Smithfield Dugan purchased the house in 1858–59. Eshleman, "Toby West-feldt House," 3–4.

20. 3008 Camp Street, probably built in 1853 for Christopher Neal Pasteur. Notarial Archives, Richard Brenan, 1853, vol. 4, no. 296.

21. Notarial Archives, Octave de Armas, 1824, vol. 10, no. 188.

22. Notarial Archives, Adolphe Mazureau, 1841, vol. 24, no. 35. Now demolished.

23. 1527 Washington Avenue was built in 1853–54. Notarial Archives, H. B. Cenas, 1853, vol. 55, 717.

24. 2233 St. Charles Avenue was built at a cost of $3,000. Notarial Archives, P. C. Cuvellier, 1853, vol. 3, no. 38. Now demolished.

25. 2120 Carondelet Street. Wilson and Lemann, *The Lower Garden District*, 121.

26. 840 Fourth Street. Probably built by wine merchant James R. Borgstede after 1847. It was described in 1857 as a one-story building with a two-story stable and chicken house. Sixty District Court No. 3610, James R. Borgstede vs. creditors; Notarial Archives, Plan Book 38, folio 3, 1854.

27. Lawrence P. Maxwell, an accountant, built the house at 1431 Josephine Street in 1852. Notarial Archives, W. L. Poole, 1856, vol. 4, 584.

28. Jewell, 143.

29. 1525 Louisiana Avenue was built in 1858–59 for James Freret. Notarial Archives, R. Brenan, 1854, vol. 6, no. 252; Theodore Guyol, 1856, vol. 36, no. 634.

30. 2127 Prytania Street was erected for Alexander Harris in 1857–58 by builders Day and Calrow. Notarial Archives, James W. Breedlove, 1857, vol. 2, no. 225; Wharton diary, February 10, 1858.

31. 1314 St. Mary Street was built in 1858 for commission merchant Jethro Bailey. Notarial Archives, William Shannon, 1858, vol. 9, no. 75, no. 86.

32. Quoted in John Maass, *The Gingerbread Age* (New York, 1957), 34–35.

33. Calvert Vaux, 45.

34. Hamlin, 194–95.

35. Built at 1420 First Street in 1844 for Jane Amelia Fawcett, wife of James D'Arcy, at a cost of $3,250, by architect Henry Howard, and builders John Holland Behen and George McConnell. Notarial Archives, E. Duplessis, 1844, vol. 2, no. 237. Originally built as a two-story, three-bay house, it was enlarged in the late 1850s to five bays and moved to 1427 Second Street. McGee and Brantley, 27–28.

36. Notarial Archives, 1856, Plan Book 64, folio 30.

37. Notarial Archives, Plan Book 86, folio 36.

38. Notarial Archives, 1854. Plan Book 97, folio 26.

39. 2120 Philip Street was built by builder Abram Howell for Luther Wilson Stewart in 1858 at a cost of $6,600. Notarial Archives, T. J. Beck, 1858, vol. 5, no. 150.

40. Architect James H. Calrow designed the house at 1239 First Street, built in 1857 by Charles Pride for Albert Brevard at a cost of $13,500. Notarial Archives, W. H. Peters, 1857, vol. 4, no. 2. Emory Clapp bought the house in 1869 and added the library on the Chestnut Street side; Samuel Wilson, Jr., papers. 1506 Jackson Avenue was built in 1856 by W. K. Day, builder, for Lewis W. Lyons, a clothier, at a cost of $12,000; now demolished. Notarial Archives, Joseph Lisbony, 1856, vol. 17, no. 64; *Daily Crescent*, October 21, 1856.

41. The house at 2103 Chestnut Street was built 1859 by Mrs. Charles A. Luzenberg, who sold it in 1860 to Wirt Adams; now demolished. Notarial Archives, A. Commandeur, 1860, vol. 2, no. 205.

42. James Gallier designed John J. Warren's 1531 Jackson Avenue home in 1859–61. Notarial Archives, Richard Brenan, 1859, vol. 15, no. 189.

43. John H. Rodenberg built the house at 1238 Philip Street in 1853–54 and sold it to Patrick Gallagher in 1867 for $21,350. Notarial Archives, Andrew Hero, 1867, vol. 7, no. 1048.

44. Robert Huyghe built the house at 1448 Fourth Street in 1859 at a cost of $23,750 for Henry Short, using plans by architect Henry Howard. Notarial Archives, John F. Coffee, 1859, vol. 7, no. 131. The firm of Wood and Miltenberger manufactured the cornstalk-patterned cast-iron fence.

45. 2427 Camp Street. A careful examination of the twice rebuilt Anderson house reveals traces of the original form, 1852–55. Notarial Archives, Theodore Guyol, 1852, vol. 24, no. 546.

46. 2220 St. Charles Avenue. Notarial Archives, Theodore Guyol, 1851, vol. 19, no. 615.

47. 1205 Louisiana Avenue. Notarial Archives, William L. Poole, 1859, vol. 7, no. 920.

48. Wharton diary, May 1, 1857.

49. Arthur Scully, Jr., *James Akin, Architect* (Baton Rouge, 1973), 116–18.

50. Groceryman Michael Hans built the house at 2928 Prytania Street in 1866–70. Notarial Archives, T. J. Beck, 1866, vol. 9, no. 193.

51. The original drawings are in the Louisiana State Museum. See John Ferguson, "Decay, Vandals Seal Plantation's Fate," *Times Picayune/States-Item*, February 6, 1982.

52. Theodore Dwight, *Things as They Are* (New York, 1834), 36.

53. Quoted in Scully, 149.

54. *Daily Picayune*, August 5, 1906, 7.

55. 2423 Prytania Street. Andrew Jackson Downing, *Cottage Residences* (New York, 1844), Design 11, figs. 9 and 10.

56. 2624 Prytania Street, Brunswig house. Historic New Orleans Collection, photograph archives, accession no. 1982.32.8; New Orleans Public Library, New Orleans and Louisiana picture file, no. 79–134.

57. John P. Coleman, "One of the Most Attractive Here," *States*. A copy is in the Louisiana Collection, Tulane University.

58. Edward Gottheil built the house at 3627 Carondelet Street in 1864. It originally stood at 3811 St. Charles Avenue. *Times Picayune/States-Item*, December 18, 1982.

59. 1236 Fourth Street house, built in 1859–61 by Charles Gallagher, a cotton factor, may have been in the picturesque style, judging by the eccentric plan; now demolished. Cf. Elisha Robinson, *Atlas of the City of New Orleans, Louisiana* (New York, 1883).

60. See Joan G. Caldwell's definitive study, "Italianate Domestic Architecture in New

Orleans, 1850–1880" (Ph.D. dissertation, Tulane University, 1975).

61. Caldwell, 25 ff.

62. 805 St. Charles Street, demolished in 1965. Only the carriage house remains.

63. Cf. Charles Lockwood, "The Italianate Dwelling House in New York City," *Journal of the Society of Architectural Historians* 31 (May 1972): 145–51.

64. 2520 Prytania Street. Notarial Archives, J. Claiborne, 1853, vol. 5, no. 5.

65. Caldwell, 66.

66. 1746–48 Jackson Avenue. Notarial Archives, Plan Book 49, folio 22; Plan Book 87, folio 38; now demolished.

67. The two-story frame house stood on Second Street opposite Clay Square, built 1868 for Hanna Hersheim, widow of Charles Oury; Lewis E. Reynolds, architect, and Louis Shorman, builder; cost of $6,000. Notarial Archives, Joseph Cohn, 1868, vol. 25, no. 296; now demolished.

68. "Notes on Democratic Architecture," *The Atlantic Monthly* 1 (January 1858): 361, quoted in Caldwell, 105.

69. Vaux, 37.

70. McGee and Brantley, 184.

71. John Cude, builder, erected the house at 3031 Coliseum Street, at a cost of $6,330. Notarial Archives, W. L. Poole, 1859, vol. 7, no. 832.

72. Notarial Archives, 1850, Plan Book 16, folio 34; 1848, Plan Book 27, folio 25.

CHAPTER FOUR

1. Wharton diary, November 12, 1854. The author is indebted to Caldwell, who first drew the parallel with the Philadelphia Atheneaum, 72–75, and to Patricia Brady Schmit, "Robb Papers Discovered," *The Historic New Orleans Collection Newsletter* IV no. 1 (Winter 1986): 3–4.

2. *Cincinnati Commercial*, 1881, reprinted in Democrat, August 3, 1881, 3.

3. New Orleans Tax Rolls, 1857, n.p.

4. *Democrat*, August 3, 1881; August 7, 1881.

5. On Robb's relation to Clay see George E. Jordan, "Robb and Clay: Politicians and Scholars," *New Orleans Art Review* 3 (January–February 1984): 6–7.

6. James Robb to Mary Robb, January 9, 1827, Robb Papers.

7. *Democrat*, August 3, 1881. On all aspects of Robb's career see Harry Howard Evans, "James Robb, Banker and Pioneer Railroad Builder of Antebellum Louisiana," *Louisiana Historical Quarterly* 23 (January 1940): 170–258.

8. Caldwell to Stephen Caldwell, November 18, 1834, Robb Papers.

9. Thomas P. Ray to James Robb, December 12, 1834, Robb Papers.

10. Marcus Wilson to James Robb, January 23, 1835, Robb Papers.

11. J. Clark to James Robb, January 23, 1836; John Fawcett to James Robb, February 2, 1836, Robb Papers.

12. S. Brody to James Robb, June 29, 1837; anon. to James Robb, November 15, 1837, Robb Papers.

13. John Fawcett to James Robb, February 16, 1836; May 31, 1838, Robb Papers.

14. George C. McCall to Henry McCall, December 7, 1837, Robb Papers.

15. *Democrat*, August 7, 1881.

16. John Bayard to James Robb, May 31, 1838; August 30, 1838, Robb Papers.

17. Ibid., August 3, 1881, August 7, 1881; Evans, 175.

18. On Robb's feud with Powers, see Miner K. Kellogg, *Justice to Hiram Powers, Addressed to the Citizens of New Orleans*

(Cincinnati, 1848); also Nancy Clow Farrell, "Hiram Powers: His Life and His Art" (ALA thesis, Michigan State University, 1959), 62–66.

19. *Democrat*, August 3, 1881.

20. Anon. to Robb, n.d., Robb Papers.

21. Norman, 169–71; also Prescott N. Dunbar, *History of the New Orleans Museum of Art*, MS, 1–7.

22. Dunbar, 6–7.

23. Hiram Powers to Sampson Powers, January 17, 1849, Powers Collection, Cincinnati Historical Society.

24. Ibid.

25. Sidney D. Maxwell, *The Suburbs of Cincinnati* (New York, 1974), 51.

26. *Democrat*, August 3, 1881.

27. Anon., *History of Cheviot*, undated typescript, provided by Ann Buchanan, Office of the Mayor, Cheviot, Ohio.

28. James Robb to William P. Converse, letters, April 15–27, 1851, Robb Papers.

29. Evans, 187–89; *Laws of Louisiana*, 1852, no. 71, 42–45; no. 72, 55–57, as cited by Evans, 188.

30. *Democrat*, August 3, 1881.

31. Quoted by George E. Jordan, "Robb and Clay: Politicians and Scholars," *New Orleans Arts Review*, January–February 1984, 6–7.

32. Report reprinted *De Bow's Review* 11 (July 1851): 74–80.

33. Evans, 211–27.

34. Lease of April 12, 1851, Robb Papers.

35. Gallier Papers, Labrot Collection, Southeastern Architectural Archive, Tulane University.

36. Constance M. Greiff, *John Notman, Architect: 1810–1865* (Philadelphia, 1979),

23, 71–102. Caldwell was the first historian to note the relationship of Robb's house to Barry and Notman, 72.

37. Robb contributed paintings to an exhibition in Philadelphia in 1847. He visited Philadelphia in 1851 and again in 1854. C. Macalaster to James Robb, March 12, 1847, Robb Papers.

38. Arthur Scully, Jr., *James Dakin, Architect* (Baton Rouge, 1973), 169–70.

39. Harold N. Cooledge, *Samuel Sloan, Architect of Philadelphia 1815–1884* (Philadelphia, 1986), illustration, 58. Also, Samuel Sloan, *The Model Architect* (Philadelphia, 1852).

40. William H. Jordy and Christopher P. Monkhouse, *Buildings on Paper: Rhode Island Architectural Drawings 1825–1945* (Providence, 1982), 150–52.

41. Cf. R. Morris Smith, *The Burlington Smiths: A Family History* (Philadelphia, 1877), 156–57.

42. Gallier Papers, Labrot Collection.

43. Specifications for Smith's variant, in the Robb Papers, provide information by analogy on Gallier's later rendition of the design.

44. This legend is recorded by John Coleman, "The Robb-Burnside Palace; Once Locus of Newcomb," *States*, 1923.

45. Historic New Orleans Collection, archives, document 1951.16.5, i–iii. For 1136 and 1237 Washington Avenue, see also Notarial Archives, Plan Book 64, folios 44 and 45, January 16, 1860. The relationship of Robb's daughters to these houses was accurately presented by Patricia Brady Schmit and Lynn D. Adams, "New Evidence: Robb's Twin Houses," *The Historic New Orleans Collection Newsletter* IV no. 1 (Winter 1986): 7.

46. A. L. McCrea to James Robb, July 25, 1850, Robb Papers.

47. A. L. McCrea to James Robb, January 15 and March 11, 1853, Robb Papers.

48. Anon. Correspondent, Galveston, to James Robb, April 10, 1853; R. C. Brinkley to James Robb, April 15, 1853, Robb Papers.

49. William Hoge to agent of Hoge and Robb, Havana, February 23, 1855, Robb Papers.

50. Correspondence of May–June 1855; A. C. M. Cram (?) to James Robb, November 12, 1855, Robb Papers.

51. *Daily Crescent*, October 21, 1856; also Gallier Papers, Labrot Collection.

52. Jan Cigliano, "The Architectural Profession in America, 1830–1930," MS, 10–11.

53. Caldwell, 121.

54. On Canova in New Orleans see Caldwell, 207–19.

55. Wharton diary, March 8, 1859.

56. Quoted in Schmit and Adams, 4.

57. *Daily Crescent*, July 2, 1858; September 1, 1858; Democrat, August 7, 1881.

58. The origins and global impact of the financial crisis are analyzed by Hans Rosenberg, *Die Weltwirtschaftskrisis van 1857–1859* (Berlin and Stuttgart, 1934).

59. *Daily Picayune*, August 4, 1881.

60. Gito Angelini to James Robb, 1857, Robb Papers.

61. The house in 1859 and for a mere $55,000, after the recession had passed. Notarial Archives, Walter H. Peters, 1859, vol. 6, no. 159. On the art sale, see Jordan, 6–7, and Dunbar, 7 ff.

62. Wharton diary, March 8, 1859.

63. James Robb to anon., February 7, 1859; Elizabeth Church Craig to James Robb, September 1858, Robb Papers.

64. Polk, a New Jersey native, invited Robb to deliver an oration at the dedication of the University of the South in

Sewanee, Tennessee. Leonidas Polk to James Robb, September 25, 1860; also Polk to Robb, April 25, 1861 on "the madness of a bloody conflict between brothers," Robb Papers.

65. On Robb as slaveholder, see letter from anon. (S. Robert?) in Grand Gulf, Louisiana, cautioning Robb on the need to supervise the morals of his household more closely, lest further pregnancies among female slaves occur. June 17, 1844; on Robb and the Anti-Slavery Female Society, see John Hayard to James Robb, May 31, 1838; on an appeal to Robb regarding the settlement of ex-slaves in Liberia see William Sain, March 29, 1855, Robb Papers.

66. James Robb to anon. in Chicago, August 9, 1860, Robb Papers.

67. James Robb to Alonzo W. Church, November 30, 1860, Robb Papers.

68. James Robb to anon., New York, September 7, 1861, Robb Papers.

69. On June 3, 1862 eighteen Union supporters petitioned Lincoln to appoint Robb military governor of Louisiana. The Chicago press opposed Robb's candidacy. Elizabeth C. C. Robb to James Robb, June 4, 1862, Robb Papers.

70. Brandt V. B. Dixon, *A Brief History of the Sophie Newcomb Memorial College 1887–1919* (New Orleans, 1928).

CHAPTER FIVE

1. Wharton diary, May 15, 1857.

2. Gallier, 27.

3. Henry Hudson Holly, *Modern Dwellings in Town and Country* (New York, 1878), 83.

4. Ibid, 82.

5. Charles Gardner, *Garner & Wharton's New Orleans Directory for the Year 1858* (New Orleans, 1858), 332.

6. Gallier, 25–26.

7. Notarial Archives, W. J. Castell, 1853, vol. 2, no. 119a.

8. Mortgage Book, vol. 63, 388.

9. Jenkins, 93 ff.

10. Gallier, 2. Gallier stresses that his family name had originally been French and he is merely resuming the correct form.

11. Ibid, 21.

12. 2319 Magazine Street.

13. Notarial Archives, P. C. Cuvellier, 1853, vol. 3, no. 38.

14. Information from Reverend Spencer E. Thiel, New Island, Illinois. Samuel Wilson, Jr., papers.

15. William A. Freret's house stands at 1524 Third Street, which he built in 1859 for $6,000; "Building Improvements in New Orleans for the Year Ending Aug. 31, 1859," *Daily Crescent*, September 12, 1859. 2504 Prytania Street (Davis house). Freret also lived at 1715 Second Street for several years, one of the five once identical detached houses at 1703, 1707, 1711, 1715, and 1719 Second Street, which he built circa 1859 on speculation. Historic District Landmarks Commission Nomination, 1715 Second Street; "Building Improvements," *Daily Crescent*, September 12, 1859. The row of five once-identical houses at 2700, 2708, 2714, 2720, and 2726 Coliseum Street was built by Freret in 1861 on speculation; Robert J. Cangelosi, Jr., notes for National Trust tour, 1989.

16. The following buildings were attributed to Frederick Wing by Wing's sister-in-law, according to his granddaughter, Mrs. Jessie Wing Sinnott, interview with author, New Orleans: 1329 Seventh Street; 1412 Seventh Street; 1429 Seventh Street; 2927 Prytania Street; 2504 Prytania Street; 2912 Prytania Street; and 1212 Eighth Street.

17. Samuel Jamison built the five-bay house at 1315 First Street in 1869 for cotton broker Joseph W. Carroll; Notarial

Archives, T. O. Stark, 1870, vol. 25, no. 28. Samuel Jamison built the house at 1331 First Street in 1869 for Joseph C. Morris; the cast-iron galleries, identical to those on the Carroll house, are from the firm of Jacob Baumiller; *Daily Picayune*, November 30, 1869.

18. Lewis E. Reynolds, *A Treatise on Handrailing, Comprising Three Original Systems of Applying the Trammel . . .* (New Orleans, 1849).

19. Gallier, 46; Second District Court 26420, Succession of Mrs. Lewis E. Reynolds; Jewell, "L. E. Reynolds, Esq.," 152.

20. McGee and Brantley, 198.

21. Notarial Archives, Octave de Armas, 1849, vol. 44, no. 34; Notarial Archives, Richard Brenan, 1854, vol. 6, no. 299.

22. 1703, 1707, 1711, 1715, and 1719 Second Street.

23. 2700, 2708, 2714, 2720, and 2726 Coliseum Street.

24. Originally built on St. Charles Avenue at First Street, this house now stands at 1633 First Street. By 1857 the Howard family lived at the corner of First and St. Charles; the Howards occupied this site until 1865. McGee and Brantley, 150.

25. Gardner, *New Orleans Directory for 1859*, n. 293

26. The house at 1429 Seventh Street was built between 1853 and 1860 for Frederick Wing, architect; Notarial Archives, G. Rareshide, 1853, vol. 3, no. 431. Other residences included 1633 First Street (Howard); 1715 Second Street (Freret); 1205 Louisiana Avenue (Wilson): First and Rousseau Streets (Huyghe); Prytania near Urania Street (Day); Jackson Avenue near Coliseum Street (Purves); St. Mary Avenue near Carondelet Street (Thief).

27. From the minutes of the congregation, Samuel Wilson, Jr., papers.

28. McGee and Brantley, 146.

29. Notarial Archives, Walter H. Peters, 1857, vol. 4, no. 2.

30. Notarial Archives, T. J. Beck, 1858, vol. 5, no. 150.

31. The house at 1237 Jackson Avenue was designed by architect Charles L. Hillger in 1876 for Julius Weis and built by Peter Middlemiss for $23,400. Notarial Archives, Joseph Cohn, 1876, vol. 39, no. 43; now demolished.

32. Sloan, 1–7; Wheeler.

33. Wharton diary, April 21, 1855.

34. Notarial Archives, Henry P. Caire, 1850, vol. 1, no. 137.

35. Notarial Archives, J. Claiborne, 1853, vol. 5, no. 5.

36. Orleans Parish court records, J. Baumiller vs. T. P. Leathers; Edward Lynch vs. T. P. Leathers, testimony of November 26, 1860.

37. Wharton diary, August 11, 1860.

38. Notarial Archives, Adolphe Mazureau, 1841, vol. 24, p. 379.

39. Howard and Thiberge designed the grocery store and home at 2139 St. Charles Avenue in 1860 for Philip T. Philips. Builder Peter Middlemiss constructed it for $12,300. Notarial Archives, William L. Poole, 1860, vol. 7, no. 787.

40. Karl J. R. Arndt, editor, "A Bavarian's Journey to New Orleans and Nacogdoches in 1853–1854," *Louisiana Historical Quarterly* 23 (April 1940): 493.

41. Notarial Archives, Adolphe Mazureau, 1841, vol. 24, 35.

42. Cook and Moorhouse ledger, Southeastern Architectural Archive, Tulane University.

43. United States Census, 1860, Slave Inhabitants of Louisiana, 11: see also Jerrye Louise Martin, "New Orleans Slavery, 1840–1860: Testing the Wade Theory" (M.A. thesis, Tulane University, 1972).

44. Marcus Bruce Christian, *Negro Iron-workers in Louisiana, 1718–1900* (Gretna, LA, 1972), 112; Conveyance Office Book 28, Folio 121, 1840, May 7.

45. McGee and Brantley, 40.

46. Joseph Karl Menn, *The Large Slave-holders of Louisiana—1860* (New Orleans, 1964), 303.

47. Cook and Moorhouse ledger.

48. Frederick L. Olmsted, *A Journey in the Seaboard Slave States, with Remarks on Their Economy* (New York, 1856), 590.

49. United States Census, New Orleans, 1860.

50. Henry Howard designed the house at 1617 Fourth Street in 1849 for John H. Norton; builder Cornelius Collins constructed it for $1,260. Notarial Archives, A. E. Bienvenu, 1849, vol. 2, no. 85.

51. Notarial Archives, L. T. Caire, 1832, vol. 21, no. 645. Tchoupitoulas Street, address unknown.

52. The house at 1328 Felicity Street was designed by Charles Hillger and constructed by Ferdinand Reusch in 1869 for John Auguste Blaffer, a building supplier, at a cost of $11,000. Notarial Archives, E. G. Gottschalk, 1869, vol. 23, no. 41.

53. Henry Hudson Holly, *Modern Dwellings in Town and Country* (New York, 1878), 56.

54. Notarial Archives, Edward Barnett, 1847, vol. 37, no. 520.

55. Notarial Archives, Adolphe Mazureau, 1841, vol. 24, p. 35.

56. Edward Gotthiel was both architect and builder of the Bernard Kock house, 1206 Third Street, at a cost of $6,750. Notarial Archives, P. C. Cuvellier, 1852, vol. 2, no. 93. It was built as a typical gallery-framed house. Confederate General John B. Hood purchased the house 1871, adding a side bay and an elaborate mansard roof, the latter having been replaced by a simpler version which survives. Notarial Archives, J. Eustis, 1873,

vol. 2, no. 82; Notarial Archives, J. Eustis, 1875, vol. 3, no. 33.

57. Rachael Edna Norgress, "History of the Cypress Lumber Industry in Louisiana," *Louisiana Historical Quarterly* 30 (July 1947): 986–98.

58. Notarial Archives, Joseph Cohn, 1859, vol. 6, no. 275.

59. Notarial Archives, Edward G. Gottschalk, 1869, vol. 23, no. 41.

60. Notarial Archives, Joseph Cohn, 1859, vol. 5, no. 139.

61. Catalogues and other materials on the Hinckle firm are archived in Cincinnati Historical Society.

62. *Cohen's New Orleans Directory* (New Orleans, 1854), n.p.

63. Louisiana Sash Factory, Time Book and Payroll, Special Collections, Tulane University.

64. Daily Sales Record Book, 1854–1857.

65. Gallier, 26.

66. Ibid.

67. Notarial Archives, T. J. Beck, vol. 5, no. 150.

68. Notarial Archives, Joseph Cohn, 1868, vol. 25, no. 296. Architect John Barnett and builder Thomas O'Brien created William McLaughlin's bar, built for $1,500. Notarial Archives, William J. Castell, 1853, vol. 2, no. 119a; probably demolished.

69. Wharton diary, March 7, 1859.

70. On Richards see Huber et al., T*he Cemeteries*, 30.

71. Notarial Archives, T. J. Beck, 1858, vol. 5, no. 150; W. J. Castell, 1853, vol. 2, no. 119a.

72. See Ann Masson, *Cast Iron and the Crescent City* (New Orleans, 1975).

73. Daily Picayune, advertisement, March 1, 1858.

74. Masson, 35.

75. For a survey of work by the C. C. Shiteman, Leeds, Shakespeare, and Lurges foundries see Mary Louise Christovich, "Cemetery Ironwork," in Leonard V. Huber, *New Orleans Architecture: The Cemeteries*, vol. 3, Peggy McDowell and Mary Louise Christovich (Gretna, LA, 1974), 139–88.

76. *Daily Picayune*, November 30, 1869. An advertisement in *Republic*, April 26, 1873, attributes the house to architect Frederick Wing, as cited by Robert L. Pratt, "John Armstrong Residence, 2805 Carondolet Street," MS., May 1982, 3.

CHAPTER SIX

1. Samuel Wilson, Jr., "Ignace François Broutin," in *Frenchmen and French Ways in the Mississippi Valley*, edited by John Francis McDermott (Chicago, 1969), 231–94.

2. Minter Wood, "Life in New Orleans in the Spanish Period," *Louisiana Historical Quarterly* 22 (July 1939): 642–709.

3. Almonester's work in New Orleans is revived by Samuel Wilson, Jr., and Leonard W. Huber in *The Cabildo on Jackson Square* (New Orleans, 1970).

4. "Death of a Great Architect," *Times-Democrat*, November 26, 1884.

5. Hamlin, plate LXI.

6. In the absence of firm documentary evidence regarding the architect of the Johnson house, the case for Reynolds as architect is made convincingly on stylistic grounds, in McGee and Brantley, Appendix D.

7. Jewell, 96, 149, 152.

8. McGee and Brantley, 89.

9. On Sewell, see Mary Louise Christovich, et al., *New Orleans Architecture: The American Sector*, vol. 2 (Gretna, LA, 1978), 231.

10. Jewell, 96.

11. Scully, 173–75; see also Stanley C. Arthur, *A History of the United States Custom House* (New Orleans, 1940), 38–39.

12. McGee and Brantley, 26; also Jewell, 96.

13. Notarial Archives, D. I. Ricardo, 1845, vol. 4, no. 675; demolished.

14. During the years 1845–47 Reynolds served as draftsman for builders James Rand and George Spooner; Notarial Archives, D. I. Ricardo, 1845, vol. 4, no. 675; demolished. Notarial Archives, William Christy, 1846, vol. 54, 651 (Frances Dean Gott); Notarial Archives, Theodore Guyol, 1846, vol. 4, no. 233A (Joseph L. Sater).

15. 1783 Coliseum Street; demolished. This large residence was designed by Henry Howard in 1858 for Shepherd Brown and built at a cost of $30,000; McGee and Brantley, 157.

16. 1228 Race Street. Built for John T. Moore in 1867 by Henry Howard, architect, and Frederick Wing, builder. The cost of construction was $24,697; Wilson and Lemann, *The Lower Garden District*, 99. The Lafayette Folger residence at 2508 St. Charles Avenue was built in 1867–69; Notarial Archives, Edward Barnett, 1867, vol. 87, no. 222; demolished.

17. Architects Howard and Thiberge designed the two double houses at 2331–33 Magazine Street for Louis Meyer in 1860. Elizah Cox built them for $15,000. Notarial Archives, J. Cohn, 1860, vol. 7, no. 124. One of the houses has been demolished.

18. Ship chandler Austin Eager built the house at 1406 Seventh Street, between 1860 and 1868; it originally faced Coliseum Street; Notarial Archives, James Graham, 1860, vol. 19, no. 4381. Henry Howard, architect, and Frederick Wing, contractor, built the residence at 1236

Jackson Avenue in 1874 for George Sweet, proprietor of the St. Charles Hotel; McGee and Brantley, 263.

19. James Gallier, *The American Builder's General Price Book and Estimator* (New York, 1833).

20. Philips Grocery, 2139 St. Charles Avenue; Notarial Archives, William L. Poole, 1860, vol. 7, no. 317.

21. The house at 1213 Third Street was built in 1867–70 for Archibald Montgomery; Notarial Archives, N. P. Trist, 1867, vol. 1, no. 114.

22. Jewell, "L. E. Reynolds, Esq.," 149.

23. Notarial Archives, G. R. Stringer, 1848, vol. 11, no. 69.

24. Notarial Archives, Thomas Beck, 1851, vol. 2, no. 118.

25. Notarial Archives, H. B. Cenas, 1856, vol. 64, p. 603; Mortgage Book, vol. 76, p. 65, August 15, 1860.

26. Notarial Archives, Adolphe Mazureau, 1859, vol. 53, no. 90, demolished.

27. Lewis Reynolds, *The Mysteries of Masonry* (Philadelphia, 1870), iii.

28. McGee and Brantley, 269.

29. *Daily Picayune*, April 23, 1874.

30. Second District Court 26420, Succession of Mrs. Lewis E. Reynolds.

31. "Death of a Great Architect."

32. Death Certificate of Lewis E. Reynolds, August 9, 1879, New Orleans Public Library.

33. C.D.C. 19460, Succession of Lewis E. Reynolds.

34. Ibid; on the funeral, see *Times-Picayune*, August 9, 1879, 4.

CHAPTER SEVEN

1. Jackson, 60.

2. Wharton diary, May 27, 1858.

3. Notarial Archives, Plan Book 64, folio 27. Notarial Archives, Theodore Guyol, 1856, vol. 24, folio 23. Notarial Archives, Plan Book 51, folio 24.

4. Frank J. Scott, *The Art of Beautifying the House Grounds* (New York, 1870); Jacob Weidemann, *Beautifying Country Homes: Handbook of Landscape Gardening* (New York, 1870).

5. On G. W. Cable as a champion of gardening, see Handlin, *The American House*, 190 ff.

6. J. B. Jackson refers to the "lawn culture" of the era; cited by Fishman, *Bourgeois Utopia*, 147.

7. The Historic New Orleans Collection.

8. At the Blaffer house, 1328 Felicity Street, the base of the cistern stood eight feet tall. Notarial Archives, E. G. Gottschalk, 1869, vol. 23. no. 41.

9. Wharton diary, September 9, 1858.

10. Notarial Archives, J. Cohn, 1868, vol. 25, no. 296.

11. William L. Hodge to James Robb, May 24, 1855, Robb Papers.

12. Notarial Archives, H. P. Caire, 1850, vol. 1, no. 137; John P. Coleman, "A Palatial Prytania House," *States*, November 4, 1923.

13. 1240 Sixth Street was built in 1866–68 for William Wright; Samuel Wilson, Jr., Papers.

14. Information provided by contemporary owner of 2423 Prytania Street, Prescott N. Dunbar, who discovered the subterranean icehouse during a 1982 renovation.

15. Wharton diary, November 25, 1858.

16. See Sloan.

17. Jacqueline S. Wilkie, "Submerged Sensuality: Technology and Perceptions of Bathing," *Journal of Social History* 19 no. 2 (Summer 1986): 649–64.

18. Notarial Archives, H. P. Caire, 1850, vol. 1, no. 137; Notarial Archives, J. Claiborne, 1853, vol. 5, no. 5.

19. John P. Coleman, "In Heart of Garden District," *States*, May 13, 1924.

20. Notarial Archives, Adolphe Mazureau, 1841, vol. 24, p. 35.

21. Grocer John Tiner built the 1452–56 Jackson Avenue house in the late 1840s. In 1866, it was sold at auction, described as a "splendid three-story brick house and wing (No. 244 Jackson Street) with iron verandah in front, containing on the ground floor one large store and laboratory, now occupied as a drug store, eight rooms, two privies, vestibules, two cisterns and two sheds in the rear, flagged yard, garden, etc." Notarial Archives, Selim Magner, 1866, vol. 19, no. 123.

22. Catherine E. Beecher and Harriet Beecher Stowe, *The American Woman's Home* (New York, 1869), Ch. 35.

23. George E. Waring, "Out of Sight, Out of Mind: Methods of Sewage Disposal," *Century Magazine* 47 (1894): 439 ff; cited in Handlin, *The American House*, 470.

24. Notarial Archives, H. P. Caire, 1850, vol. 1, no. 137.

25. Notarial Archives, E. G. Gottschalk, 1869, vol. 23, no. 41.

26. Notarial Archives, Theodore Guyol, 1856, vol. 36, no. 684.

27. The residence at 1241 Fourth Street was built for Edward Ogden circa 1851; Notarial Archives, H. P. Caire, 1852, vol. 4, no. 19.

28. "Louise Dugan Diaries (1868–1879)" (MS, Tulane University), May 4, 1876.

29. Ibid, March 16, 1872.

30. Ibid, April 16, 1872.

31. Information provided by the late Muriel Bultmann Francis, owner of the Freret home, 1983. On the male domination of main floors of nineteenth-century European dwellings, see Donald J. Olsen, *The City as a Work of Art* (New Haven and London, 1986), 108.

32. Grace King, "The Evening Party," in *Grace King of New Orleans: A Selection of Her Writings*, edited by Robert Bush (Baton Rouge, 1973), 165.

33. The house at 2328 Coliseum Street was built for Hannah Killingley Walford, widow of Edmund Briggs, in 1858–60; Notarial Archives, Hilary B. Cenas, 1858, vol. 71, 1162. Edwin F. Briggs purchased the property in 1867 and sold it to the Prytania Street Presbyterian Church in 1871.

34. Dugan diaries, June 20, 1878.

35. United States Census, 1860, 1870.

36. Mr. and Mrs. Samuel Palmer Griffin built their residence at 2702 St. Charles Avenue in 1866. Notarial Archives, J. W. Breedlove, 1866, vol. 9, 202; demolished. In 1867, the house was advertised for sale at auction and described as a "splendid brick mansion…containing fourteen rooms, finished in the very best style," in *Daily Picayune*, April 6, 1867.

37. The residence of Mr. and Mrs. Charles A. Whitney at 2233 St. Charles Avenue was built circa 1870; demolished. Notarial Archives, G. W. Christy, 1870, vol. 4, no. 499. An earlier house on this site was built for William Haneman in 1853; Notarial Archives, P. C. Cuvellier, 1853, vol. 3, no. 38. Among the many other properties bought by women are those described in Conveyance Office Book 92, folio 584, 29 July 1867; N. B. Trist, 1866, vol. 1, no. 70.

38. Winnefred Hubbard bought the property at 3116 Prytania Street in 1845 and built a house there, now demolished and replaced. Notarial Archives, L. R. Kenny, 1845, vol. 3, no. 256.

39. Jessie Poesch, *Newcomb Pottery: An Enterprise for Southern Women*, 1895–1940 (Exton, PA, 1984); D. Clive Hardy, The

World's Industrial and Cotton Centennial Exposition (New Orleans, 1978), n.p.

40. *The Era*, 1863.

41. Twain, 343.

42. John Benson Company ledger, Gallier House Museum, Tulane University.

43. United States Congress, House of Representatives, *Property Seized in Louisiana*, Executive Document 102, 40th Congress, 2d session, 1867.

44. Vaux, 27–28.

45. George L. Hersey, "Godoy's Choice," *Journal of the Society of Architectural Historians* 18 (October 1959): 104–11, as cited in Caldwell, 41.

46. Maude O'Bryan Ronstrom, "Seignouret and Mallard, Cabinetmakers," *Antiques* 46 (August 1944): 79–81.

47. Gowans, *Images of American Living*, 85 ff.

48. John N. Pearce, Lorraine W. Pearce, and Robert C. Smith, "The Meeks Family of Cabinetmakers," *Antiques* 85 (April 1964): 417.

49. Ronstrom; advertisement for Howell & Bourke, Inc., *New Orleans Republican*, April 10, 1867.

50. Oscar P. Fitzgerald, *Three Centuries of American Furniture* (Englewood Cliffs, NJ, 1982), 243–44.

51. C.D.C. 17209, Succession of Walter G. Robinson.

52. *New Orleans States*, December 8, 1940.

53. List provided by the staff of the Historic New Orleans Collection; cf. index of paintings by Paul Poincy, The Historic New Orleans Collection; *Louisiana State Museum Biennial Report for 1932–33* (January 1934), 57.

54. C.D.C. 10217, Succession of H.S. and Catherine Buckner.

CHAPTER EIGHT

1. Ripley, 37.

2. John S. Kendall, "New Orleans' 'Peculiar Institution'," *Louisiana Historical Quarterly* 23 (July 1940): 870.

3. United States Census, Louisiana, 1860, Slave Inhabitants, II.

4. New Orleans Tax Rolls, 1857. The house at 1332 First Street was built 1852–54 for John Holmes and occupied by Samuel B. Newman after 1854; now demolished. Notarial Archives, L. K. Kenny, 1852, vol. 19, no. 45. Mrs. S. Duncan's address is not recorded in the 1857 New Orleans tax rolls.

5. Cf. Lafayette Tax Rolls, 1849–1850; New Orleans Tax Rolls, 1857.

6. Richard C. Wade, *Slavery in the Cities: The South, 1820–1860* (New York, 1964), 243–44.

7. Robert C. Reinders, *End of an Era: New Orleans, 1850–1860* (New Orleans 1964), 28.

8. New Orleans Tax Rolls, 1857; United States Census, 1860.

9. Based on the Robinson house plans, preserved in the Freret and Wolf records, Southeastern Architectural Archives, Tulane University, and on the Historic American Buildings Survey plan of the Brevard house; research and analysis by Davis Lee Jahncke, Jr., AIA.

10. New Orleans Tax Rolls, 1857, 2427 Camp Street. John S. Wallis, a dealer in western produce, lived at 2403 Camp Street, built 1852; Notarial Archives, Philip Prendergast, 1851, vol. 1, no. 87.

11. Notarial Archives, P. C. Cuvellier, 1852, vol. 2, no. 94.

12. Wade, 132–41.

13. Kendall, "New Orleans' 'Peculiar Institution'," 869; also Robert C. Reinders, "The Free Negro in the New Orleans Economy, 1850–1860," *Louisiana History* 6 (Summer 1965): 276.

14. James Creecy, *Scenes in the South, and Other Miscellaneous Pieces* (Washington, 1860), 25.

15. Earl F. Niehaus, *The Irish in New Orleans, 1800–1860* (Baton Rouge, 1965), 49; Olmsted, 590.

16. Wharton diary, December 11, 1853.

17. Registry of slave ship, 1831, New Orleans Public Library. Lafayette City Census, 1840, New Orleans Public Library.

18. Olmsted, 558.

19. Niehaus, 50.

20. U.S. Census, 1860.

21. Daniel E. Sutherland, *Americans and Their Servants: Domestic Service in the United States from 1800 to 1920* (Baton Rouge, 1981), 50; see also Hasia R. Diwer, *Erin's Daughters in America: Irish Immigrant Women in the Nineteenth Century* (Baltimore, 1983).

22. In the decade 1850–1860 females constituted 60 percent of the New Orleans slave population overall, a ratio that was much higher among domestics; Martin, 34.

23. Sutherland, 137–39. See also Faye E. Dudden, *Serving Women; Household Service in Nineteenth-Century America* (Middletown, 1983).

24. Based on Robinson house plan in Freret and Wolf records, Payne house plan by Koch and Wilson, architects, and Brevard house plan prepared by the Historic American Buildings Survey; Davis Lee Jahncke, Jr., AIA.

25. *Era*, October 27, 1863. The residence of George Sweet at 1236 Jackson Avenue was replaced in 1874 by the present dwelling on the site.

26. Ibid.

27. The first house at 2627 Coliseum Street was built for Thomas Allen Clarke in 1849–50 and sold to Benjamin Mackall Horrell in 1854. Notarial Archives, Lucien

Hermann, 1849, vol. 20, no. 230. After two other owners, Ellen Buckner, wife of James B. Eustis, purchased the property in 1876; a year later, 1877, the present residence was built on the site.

28. A copy of this photograph is preserved in the Historic New Orleans Collection. On the popularity of livery in the postwar era, see Sutherland, 129.

29. Vaux, *Villas and Cottages* (New York, 1857), 46.

30. Charles A. Raymond, "The Religious Life of the Negro Slave," *Harper's New Monthly Magazine* 27 (September 1863): 481–82.

31. Amelia Murray, *Letters from the United States, Cuba, and Canada* (New York, 1856), 278.

32. Notarial Archives, Philip Prendergast, 1851, vol. 1, no. 87; Alphonse Bamett, 1851, vol. 6, no. 573; Theodore O. Stark, 1853, vol. 7, 57.

33. Notarial Archives, George Rareshide, 1858, vol. 11, no. 2129. The house at 1226–28 First Street was built in 1852–54 for John Dolhonde; Notarial Archives, Achille Chiapella, 1854, vol. 35, no. 309.

34. Ellen N. Lawson and Marlene Merrill, "The Antebellum 'Talented Thousandth': Black College Students at Oberlin Before the Civil War," *Journal of Negro Education* 52 (Summer 1983): 144.

35. Henry Leovy, compiler, *Laws and General Ordinances of the City of New Orleans* (New Orleans, 1857), 257.

36. James Stuart, *Three Years in North America*, 2 vols. (Edinburgh, 1833), 2:206.

37. Harold Sinclair, *The Port of New Orleans* (New York, 1942), 191, as quoted in Martin, 11–12.

38. Wade, 59.

39. Sutherland, 49 ff.

40. Ibid, 46.

41. On the comparable situation in other southern cities see Leon F. Litwack, *Been in the Storm So Long: The Aftermath of Slavery* (New York, 1979); and Orra Langhorne, "Domestic Service in the South," *Journal of Social Science* 39 (November 1901): 170–72.

CHAPTER NINE

1. Kendall, *History of New Orleans*, 1:240–41.

2. Notarial Archives, T. I. Beck, 1860, vol. 7, no. 125; Notarial Archives, T. I. Beck, 1860, vol. 7, no. 117. Courtesy of Thomas Favrot.

3. Charles Gardner, *Gardner's New Orleans Directory for 1867* (New Orleans, 1867), 337; Notarial Archives, Robert J. Ker, 1866, vol. 27, no. 145.

4. Wharton diary, October 9, 1857.

5. Notarial Archives, Joseph Lisbony, 1859, vol. 21, no. 39.

6. Kendall, 1:232.

7. On planters who sided with the Union see James L. Roark, *Masters Without Slaves: Southern Planters in the Civil War and Reconstruction* (New York, 1977), 8–9; on southern Unionism in general see Carl N. Degler, *The Other South: Southern Dissenters in the Nineteenth Century* (New York, 1974), ch. 3–5.

8. *Daily Picayune*, March 3, 1861.

9. Robert T. Clark, Jr., "The New Orleans German Colony in the Civil War," *Louisiana Historical Quarterly* 20 (October 1937): 996, 998, 1011.

10. In 1860 John A. Peel purchased the property which now has an address of 2912 Prytania Street. Notarial Archives, William Shannon, 1860, vol. 11, no. 71. The raised cottage on the site today probably dates from the late 1860s.

11. See Charles Reagan Wilson, *Baptized in Blood: The Religion of the Lost Cause, 1865–1920* (Athens, Gal, 1980), 55.

12. On Palmer see Thomas C. Johnson, *The Life and Letters of Benjamin Morgan Palmer* (Richmond, 1906), 19, 87–91, 170.

13. Benjamin Palmer, "Thanksgiving Sermon," *Daily Delta* December 1, 1860, 3, as quoted in Robert Meyer, Jr., *Names Over New Orleans Public Schools* (New Orleans, 1975), 160.

14. *Daily Picayune*, May 6, 1890, 4.

15. Notarial Archives, William Poole, 1862, vol. 9a, no. 2293.

16. Samuel Wilson, Jr., ed., *Henry Howard, Architect: An Exhibition of Photographs of His Work by Clarence John Laughlin* (New Orleans, 1952), 2.

17. "New Orleans," *De Bow's Review* 1 (January 1866): 48–50; see also Gerald M. Capers, *Occupied City: New Orleans Under the Federals, 1862–1865* (Lexington, 1965), 145–71.

18. Notarial Archives, J. W. Breedlove, 1861, vol. 8, no. 46; J. W. Breedlove, 1862, vol. 8, no. 87; William Shannon, 1864, vol. 14, no. 51; William Shannon, 1866, vol. 17, no. 105; William Shannon, 1866, vol. 18, no. 600; E. G. Gottschalk, 1865, vol. 13, no. 28; Adolphe Mazureau, 1865, vol. 55, no. 16; Theodore Guyol, 1860, vol. 46, no. 144; A. E. Bienvenu, 1862, vol. 21, no. 106; Joseph Cuvellier, 1864, vol. 71, no. 172. Conveyance Office Book 86, folio 608, January 11, 1864.

19. Louisiana Sash Factory, Time Book and Payroll, Southeastern Architectural Archive.

20. Thomas Ewing Dabney, "The Butler Regime in Louisiana," *Louisiana Historical Quarterly* 27 (April 1944): 493; Kendall, *History of New Orleans*, 1:231, 237.

21. *Times Democrat*, November 5, 1892.

22. Dugan diaries, December 29, 1868.

23. John P. Coleman, "One of First in City with Baths," *States* April 12, 1925; Charles

Gardner, Gardner's New Orleans Directory for 1869 (New Orleans, 1869), 277. Perkins's whereabouts 1862–1869 have not been traced; his later service as consul for Sweden and Norway, and generous obituaries in the German press of New Orleans, suggest he passed the period in northern Europe.

24. 1415 Third Street. Notarial Archives, Theodore Guyol, 1862, vol. 51, no. 184.

25. Paul L. Godchaux, Jr., "The Godchaux Family of New Orleans" (New Orleans: privately printed, 1971), n.p.

26. Dabney, 505.

27. Unsigned and undated MS, courtesy Thomas Bernard, New Orleans. 1328 Harmony Street; built in 1861–62 for John Henry Campman, who had purchased the property in 1861 for $3,000. Conveyance Office Book 86, folio 195.

28. John D. Winters, *The Civil War in Louisiana* (Baton Rouge, 1963), 136. Sixty-one thousand New Orleanians took the oath, and four thousand refused.

29. Ibid, 140.

30. *Daily Picayune*, August 5, 1906, 7.

31. Notarial Archives, William Christy, 1854, vol. 64, p. 629; Amedee Ducatel, 1856, vol. 69, no. 248.

32. Notarial Archives, Hilary B. Cenas, 1854, vol.61, 601.

33. James A. Padgett, ed., "Some Letters of George Stanton Denison," *Louisiana Historical Quarterly* 23 (October 1940): 1200.

34. Conveyance Office Book 89, folio 132.

35. United States Congress, House of Representatives, *Property Seized in Louisiana*, Executive Document 102, 40th Cong., 2nd sess., 1867.

36. Captain I.W. McClure to General E. R. S. Canby, June 6, 1865. Record Group 56-S571, U.S. National Archives. Courtesy of Thomas Favrot.

37. Cotton and Abandoned Property 14380–14389, 16, 903, General Records of the Treasury Department, U.S. National Archives, Washington, D. C. Courtesy of Thomas Favrot.

38. Ibid, 16609.

39. Miriam G. Reeves, *The Governors of Louisiana* (Gretna, 1972), pp. 70–71.

40. "Surprise and Serenade to Gov. Hahn," [New Orleans] *Times*, March 30, 1864, 1.

41. Fred Harvey Harrington, *Fighting Politician: Major General N. P. Banks* (Philadelphia, 1948), Preface.

42. Mrs. Banks to General Banks, May 14, 1864. N. P. Banks file, U.S. National Archives, Washington, D.C. Courtesy of Thomas Favrot.

43. Ibid, April 20, 1864.

44. Joe Gray Taylor, *Louisiana Reconstructed, 1863–1877* (Baton Rouge, 1974) 6–8.

45. Louisiana Sash Factory, Time Book and Payroll.

46. The house at 1538 Fourth Street was built in 1864–65 for Mr. and Mrs. Samuel H. Brown. Notarial Archives, Hugh Madden, 1864, vol. 6, no. 768.

47. Minutes of the congregation. Samuel Wilson, Jr., Papers.

48. Notarial Archives, Hugh Madden, 1864, vol. 7, no. 844.

49. Notarial Archives, J. W. Breedlove, 1866, vol. 9, no. 241; also Notarial Archives, Hugh Madden, 1862, vol. 2, no. 235.

50. Winters, 137–39.

51. 1237 Jackson Avenue, now demolished. Godchaux, n.p.

52. George W. Sully built a house at 1433 Philip Street in 1845–47. The raised cottage that stands on the site today is either a remodelling of Sully's house or a new

house built by Florence A. Luling, who purchased the property in 1855 for $13,000 and sold it six years later for $20,000. Notarial Archives, William Shannon, 1861, vol. 12, no. 88.

53. *The Era*, December 5, 1863.

54. E. Merton Coulter, *The Confederate States of America, 1861–1865* (Baton Rouge, 1950), 409.

CHAPTER TEN

1. Quoted in Wilson, *Baptized in Blood*, 66.

2. Michael Wayne, *The Reshaping of Plantation Society: The Natchez District, 1860–1880* (Baton Rouge, 1983), 67.

3. Kenneth M. Stampp, *The Era of Reconstruction, 1865–1877* (New York, 1982), 4.

4. 2521–23 Prytania Street. Notarial Archives, Theodore Guyol, 1868, vol. 52, no. 96.

5. Edith Long, *The Story of 2618 Coliseum* (New Orleans, 1967), 27–33.

6. Notarial Archives, P. C. Cuvellier, 1873, vol. 31, no. 186.

7. C.D.C. 17209.

8. Roark, ch. 5.

9. *States*, March 12, 1900, 3.

10. *Daily Picayune*, October 11, 1865; Times, October 9, 1865.

11. Parish of Orleans, Civil District Court, petition of Robert H. Short, January 13, 1882. Courtesy Thomas Favrot.

12. Charles Nordhoff, *The Cotton States in the Spring and Summer of 1875* (New York, 1976), 62–63.

13. Edward King, *The Great South* (Hartford, Conn., 1875), 33.

14. Taylor, 29.

15. Kendall, *History of New Orleans*, 1:359–60.

16. On the Freedmen's Bureau in New Orleans see John W. Blassingame, *Black New Orleans, 1860–1880* (Chicago and London, 1973), 109–11.

17. C. Van Woodward, *American Counterpoint: Slavery and Racism in the North-South Dialogue* (Boston, 1971), 275.

18. *Daily Picayune*, March 2, 1873, as quoted in Taylor, 358.

19. "After the War Series," *De Bow's Review* 1 (February 1866): 219, as quoted in Taylor, 343.

20. Edward King, 61.

21. Taylor, 357.

22. Ibid, 337.

23. 3303 Coliseum Street was built in 1868–69 for Captain Thomas Pickles, who sold it in 1871 to Edward A. Palfry. See Alice Pickslay Pipes Jahncke, "The Residence of Mr. and Mrs. Davis Lee Jahncke, Jr.: 3303 Coliseum Street," (MS, December 1981), 4–12.

24. 1205 Seventh Street. Notarial Archives, Andrew Hero, Jr., 1867, vol. 3, no. 668.

25. 1427 St. Mary Street, built 1866–67 for Armant St. Amant. Notarial Archives, C. Stringer, 1865, vol. 4, no. 85.

26. Taylor, 346–47.

27. Wayne, 161–62.

28. Robert M. Davis, *The Southern Planter, The Factor and The Banker* (New Orleans, 1871), 4–5, as quoted in Wayne, 161.

29. 1331 First Street (Morris). 1620 Eighth Street (Soulè), built in 1845 for Joseph C. Clarke, a Jefferson Parish judge; designed by James Gallier, Sr. The house originally faced St. Charles Avenue but it was moved to the middle of the block on Eighth Street in 1869 by Colonel George Soulè so he could build a new house for himself on the avenue site. John Geiser III,

"Judge Clarke's House: 1620 Eighth Street," (MS, June 1971), 3–20.

30. Frederick Rodewald, a banker, built the residence at 1749 Coliseum Street in 1849 and sold it in 1871 to John Henry. In 1904 the house was sold to New Orleans author Grace King, who resided there until her death in 1932. Wilson and Lemann, *The Lower Garden District*, 86.

31. Miss Susan Hackett purchased the property at 2336 St. Charles Avenue in 1854 and built a cottage soon afterward. Notarial Archives, Hilary B. Cenas, 1854, vol. 61, no. 601. In 1873 she sold the house to Albert Walter Merriam, proprietor of the Crescent Billiard Hall, for $16,000.

32. Notarial Archives, Theodore Guyol, 1868, vol. 52, no. 96.

33. New Orleans Tax Rolls, 1864, 1867.

34. Taylor, 343.

35. Notarial Archives, Joseph Cohn, 1866, vol. 18, no. 122.

36. Notarial Archives, E. G. Gottschalk, 1866, vol. 17, no. 552.

37. James E. Reade purchased the property at 3313 Prytania Street from the heirs of James P. Freret in 1871 and built the present house soon after. Notarial Archives, P. C. Cuvellier, 1871, vol. 27, no. 184.

38. Tobacco merchant Watson Van Benthuysen built his residence at 3029 St. Charles Avenue in 1868–69. This was originally built as a five-bay house; extensively remodeled, probably in the late 1880s. Notarial Archives, George W. Christy, 1868, vol. 3, no. 301.

39. Architect Benjamin Harrod designed the residence of Col. Edward Ivy at 2113–15 Prytania Street in 1871. Robert Huyghe and Ambrose Burton built it for $9,800. Notarial Archives, John G. Eustis, 1871, vol. 2, no. 31.

40. The house at 3211 Prytania Street was built in 1866 for Clara Edith Palmer, wife of Louis C. D'Homergue; Notarial

Archives, J. W. Breedlove, 1866, vol. 9, no. 241. In December 1866 the property was sold to Edward C. Palmer for $15,455; in 1920, Miss Francis Toby Campbell began a boarding house here after she purchased the house; *States-Item*, March 15, 1977. The residence at 1224 Louisiana Avenue was built in 1868–69 for butcher Louis Gabb; Notarial Archives, E. Commagere, 1869, vol. 2, no. 300. The raised cottage at 1424 Louisiana Avenue was built in 1868–70 for Eugene Schmitt; Notarial Archives, Onesiphore Drouet, 1867, vol. 28, no. 329.

41. Frederick Wing built the house at 1329 Seventh Street in 1870–71; Notarial Archives, E. G. Gottschalk, 1870, vol. 26, no. 187. Architect William Fitzner designed the house at 1208 Eighth Street, built by H. Boensel, Jr., for William G. Murtagh at a cost of $6,500; *Daily Picayune*, September 1, 1883.

42. The Shepherd Brown residence 2833 St. Charles Avenue was built in 1872 on land purchased for $10,000 by Brown's wife, Louisa Norton Brown; now demolished. Conveyance Office Book 92, folio 584.

43. The house at 2045 Coliseum Street was built before 1872 for Thomas Jefferson Planner; Wilson and Lemann, *The Lower Garden District*, 123. 1421 Josephine Street was built for Austin W. Rountree after 1868; Wilson and Lemann, 93.

44. The sole copy of this drawing is in Samuel Wilson, Jr., Papers.

45. Henry Hudson Holly, *Holly's Country Seats* (New York, 1863).

46. "Notes on Democratic Architecture," *The Atlantic Monthly* 1 (January 1858): 261, quoted in Caldwell, 40; Hersey, quoted in Caldwell, 41.

47. Elijah Peale and Frederick Augustus William Davis built the common-wall double-frame town house at 1528–30 Fourth Street as a speculative venture in 1849–52. Samuel Wilson, Jr., Papers.

48. Notarial Archives, J. W. Breelilove, 1866, vol. 9, 202.

49. *Daily Picayune*, 6 April 1867, 6.

50. William H. McLellan of the McLellan Ship Supply Company built his 1006 Washington Avenue residence in 1868–69; Historic District Landmarks Commission nomination. The house at 2302 St. Charles Avenue was probably built for Virginia Peebles, widow of William Syer, shortly after 1871; Notarial Archives, John G. Eustis, 1871, vol. 2, no. 25; now demolished.

51. The residence of William Henderson, owner of a sugar refinery, was built at 2126 Prytania Street in 1886–88; Notarial Archives, M. T. Ducros, 1886, vol. 19, no. 373; demolished in 1970. 3005 St. Charles Avenue (Flower); Notarial Archives, P. C. Cuvellier, 1872, vol. 29, no. 36.

52. Daniel C. Byerly built his house at 1437 Eighth Street shortly after 1871; Notarial Archives, P. C. Cuvellier, 1871, vol. 28, no. 252. The house at 3120 Coliseum Street was built in 1867–68 for Mr. and Mrs. Silas Daily; Notarial Archives, George W. Christy, 1867, vol. 2, no. 229. A mansard roof by Alexander Hill was added to the house at 903 St. Charles Avenue; in John P. Coleman, "Once Show Place of St. Charles," States, January 28, 1923; now demolished.

53. Notarial Archives, P. C. Cuvellier, 1853, vol. 3, no. 38.

CHAPTER ELEVEN

1. Garnie W. McGinty, *Louisiana Redeemed: The Overthrow of Carpetbag Rule, 1876–1880* (New Orleans, 1941).

2. Taylor, 358–61; also Ella Lonn, *Reconstruction in Louisiana after 1868* (New York, 1918), 339–46.

3. Taylor, 361.

4. New Orleans Tax Rolls, 1872, 1875.

5. Mitchell, 958.

6. Joy J. Jackson, *New Orleans in the Gilded Age: Politics and Urban Progress, 1880–1896* (Baton Rouge, 1969), 212.

7. J. D. B. De Bow, "Manufacturers, the South's True Remedy," *De Bow's Review* 3 (February 1867): 176, as quoted in Paul Gaston, *The New South Creed: A Study in Southern Mythmaking* (New York, 1970), 25.

8. Frederic Cople Jaher, "Antebellum Charleston: Anatomy of an Economic Failure," in *Class, Conflict, and Consensus*, edited by Orville Burton and Robert C. McMath, Jr. (Westport, CT, 1982), 211–13.

9. *Ceremonies Connected with the unveiling of the Statue of General Robert E. Lee* (New Orleans, 1884), 38, copy in Custis-Lee Mansion, Arlington, as quoted in Thomas L. Connelly, *The Marble Man: Robert E. Lee and His Image in American Society* (New York, 1977), 93.

10. *States-Item*, March 10, 1977.

11. *Times Democrat*, November 5, 1892, 3.

12. *Daily States*, June 16, 1882, 5.

13. *Daily States*, June 13, 1896, 1.

14. *Daily Picayune*, March 31, 1869, 4.

15. Thomas Sully designed Robert Roberts's residence at 2821 St. Charles Avenue circa 1889; now demolished. Residence for Robert Roberts, Thomas Sully Collection, Southeastern Architectural Archive, Tulane University. A very similar house still stands at 3120 Coliseum Street.

16. The house at 2926 St. Charles Avenue was built for Thomas McDermott after 1880. Notarial Archives, James Fahey, 1880, vol. 20, no. 268.

17. The two double houses at 1230–32 and 1238–40 Harmony Street were probably built as rental units on property owned by Phillipine Mathilde Zimmermann (later Chalin), who was an orphaned child at the time of construction in 1872–74. Hilary S. Irvin, "1240 Harmony Street," Preservation Resource Center, New Orleans. 1329 St. Andrew Street was

built in 1883 for Edward Conery, Jr., whose father had given him the property in 1879; Notarial Archives, A. S. Beck, 1879, vol. 4, no. 65. 2604 Coliseum Street was built as the residence of James McCracken, proprietor of a Royal Street furniture store, in 1878. It was designed by Charles L. Hillger, architect, and constructed by builder Ferdinand Reusch for $7,950; Mortgage Book, vol. 167, folio 711.

18. The residence of Cornelius Bicknell Payne at 1604 Fourth Street was built in 1858 and sold in 1861 to Thomas L. Clarke for $18,000; Notarial Archives, Walter H. Peters, 1861, vol. 8, no. 83.

19. The house at 1517 Eighth Street was built in the late 1880s for wine and spirits merchant George Jurgens; Notarial Archives, John Bendernagel, 1880, vol. 7, no. 169.

20. W. J. Cash, *The Mind of the South* (New York, 1969), 146.

21. David Taylor Kearns, "The Social Mobility of New Orleans Laborers, 1870–1900" (Ph.D. dissertation, Tulane University, 1977), 162.

22. Cf. Warner, 64.

23. Louis C. Hennick and E. Harper Chariton, *The Streetcars of New Orleans* (Gretna, LA, 1975), front endsheet.

24. 2917 Magazine Street; *States*, February 12, 1933.

25. Jackson, 136, 200–201.

26. Kearns, 109–14.

27. "Local Intelligence-Homes for the People," *Republic*, April 10, 1867, 3; quoted in Caldwell, 145.

28. Jerry Toller, "The Haitian Shotgun Survives in New Orleans," *Arts Quarterly* 1 (July 1979):8–9; Caldwell, 158–66.

29. The house at 937 St. Andrew Street was built for Miss Mary Neilson in 1848; Notarial Archives, William Christy, 1848, vol. 59, p. 407. John McMillan built the

house at 1121–27 Eighth Street in 1861 and sold it later that year; Notarial Archives, James Graham, 1861, vol. 21, no. 4816.

30. Notarial Archives, Andrew Hero, Jr., 1872, vol. 14, no. 3077; W. J. Castell, 1870, vol. 26, no. 4852; W. J. Castell, 1870, vol. 34, no. 6310, as cited in Caldwell, 143.

31. Bernard Lemman, "New Orleans Prefab, 1867," *Journal of the Society of Architectural Historians* 22 (March 1963): 38–39.

32. Caldwell, 154–55. The house at 1208–10 Josephine Street was built after Hermann Henry Brinkmann purchased the property in 1877; Notarial Archives, W. J. Castell, 1877, vol. 54, no. 9777. 1230–32, 1238–40 Harmony Street.

33. Roberts & Co., *Illustrated Catalogue of Mouldings, Architectural & Ornamental Wood Work* (New Orleans, 1891).

34. Historic New Orleans Collection, 1950.5.59 i, ii.

35. Architect William Fitzner designed the double camelbacks at 1223–29 and 1233–41 Harmony Street for John Ohmstede in 1872. Builder Louis Wilkens constructed them at a cost of $18,700. Notarial Archives, Andrew Hero, Jr., 1872, vol. 14, no. 3077.

36. 2305, 2309, 2313, 2317, 2321, 2325, 2329 Coliseum Street and 1410 Philip Street. Notarial Archives, C. Pollock, 1824, vol. 16, p. 259; W. J. Castell, 1868, vol. 18, no. 3401; Theodore Guyol, 1875, vol. 59, no. 96. See also McGee and Brantley, 243–44.

37. 2731 Chestnut Street was built in 1890 for Elizabeth Ruth, widow of grocery store owner John Nutter. Notarial Archives, Marcel T. Ducrois, 1890, vol. 29, no. 76.

38. "There was one place they went a lot, they used to call it the Irish Channel." Sidney Bechet, *Treat it Gentle* (New York, 1960), 56. The houses at 2135 Jackson Avenue (Oury); 1659 St. Thomas Street (Kelly); 3221 Baronne Street (Williams); 1425 Leontine Street (Dusen); 3912 Laurel Street (Dutrey); Seventh Street near St. Charles Avenue (Dodds).

39. Jackson, 145–46.

40. Cash, 186.

41. Don Harrison Doyle, "Urbanization and Southern Culture: Economic Elites in Four New South Cities (Atlanta, Nashville, Charleston, Mobile) c. 1865–1910," in *Toward a New South?*, edited by Orville Burton and Robert C. McMath, Jr. (Westport, CT, 1982), 22–31.

42. Twain, 249.

43. Doyle, 24–25.

44. Jackson, 89.

45. See S. Frederick Starr, "St. Charles Avenue, New Orleans," and Jan Cigliano, "Introduction," in *Grand American Avenue, 1850–1920*, edited by Cigliano and Sarah Bradford Landau (San Francisco and Washington, D.C., 1994).

46. 1206 Second Street. Built in 1866 for Charles H. Adams by James Freret, architect, for $7,950. *Daily Picayune*, September 1, 1886.

47. The residence of Mrs. Isidor Scooller at 3203 Prytania Street was built in 1893. The house at 2115 Palmer Avenue is described by Thomas Friedheim, "Fornaris-Rinker House Landmarked," *Preservation In Print* 9 (December 1982).

48. John Ferguson has made available his unpublished research on Sully, which the author gratefully acknowledges.

49. 4010 St. Charles Avenue, and 1305 and 1531 Carrollton Avenue.

50. Interview by John Ferguson with Sully's daughter, Jeanne Sully West.

51. *Biographical and Historical Memoirs of Louisiana*, 1892 edition, 1:473–74; also *Times Democrat*, January 9, 1898; *Daily Picayune*, January 7, 1898, January 9, 1898. The Hernsheim residence, 3811 St. Charles Avenue.

52. Alcée Fortier, ed., *Louisiana*, 3 vols. (New Orleans, 1914), 3: 322–24; also *Daily Picayune*, December 1, 1909. Newman's house stood at 3607 St. Charles Avenue; now demolished.

53. Fortier, 3:507; also *Daily Item*, August 8, 1894. 3512 St. Charles Avenue; now demolished.

54. *Times Democrat*, June 25, 1893; also *Biographical and Historical Memoirs of Louisiana*, 2:439. The Joseph A. Walker residence at 2503 St. Charles Avenue was built in 1885–86; Notarial Archives, W. O. Hart, 1885, vol. 5, no. 1237; Residence for Joseph Walker, Thomas Sully Collection.

55. Fortier, 3: 643–46; also *National Cyclopedia of American Biography*, 22: 336. The John A. Morris residence at 2525 St.

Charles Avenue was built in 1890; Notarial Archives, N. H. Trist, 1888, vol. 19, no. 2871; Residence for J. A. Morris, Thomas Sully Collection.

56. *Times-Picayune*, March 29, 1918, 5. The house at 2362 Camp Street was built in 1889 for Mr. and Mrs. Albert S. Ranlett on property bought by Miss Cora Mathilda Semmes in that year; Notarial Archives, Charles T. Soniat, 1889, vol. 26, nos. 59, 60.

57. *Daily Picayune*, March 19, 1908, 12. John S. Rainey purchased the property at 2631 Prytania Street in 1890, and built the house in 1890; Notarial Archives, W. D. Denegre, 1890, vol. 1, no. 32.

58. *Times Picayune*, January 14, 1936, 1. The Samuel Adams Trufant residence at 1239 Philip Street was built in 1891; designed by Thomas Sully.

59. Francis Johnson and Francis R. Johnson, his son, partners in the firm of F. Johnson & Son, Undertakers, commissioned B. J. Schneider, builder, to construct the residence at 2727 St. Charles Avenue in 1891. Notarial Archives, John Bendernagel, 1891, vol. 33, no. 47; Residence for F. Johnson, Thomas Sully Collection.

60. Residence for Dr. J. D. Bloom, Thomas Sully Collection.

61. *Daily States*, January 30, 1890; *Weekly States*, February 19, 1886.

BIBLIOGRAPHY

GENERAL WORKS

Amos, Harriet E. *Cotton City: Urban Development in Antebellum Mobile.* University of Alabama Press, University, Alabama, 1985.

Amos, Harriet E. "'Birds of Passage' in a Cotton Port: Northerners and Foreigners Among the Urban Leaders of Mobile." In *Class, Conflict, and Consensus.* Edited by Orville V. Burton and Robert C. McMath, Jr. Westport, CT, Greenwood Press, 1982, 232–26.

"The Anglo-American Suburb." *AD (Architectural Design)* 51 (Oct–Nov 1981):19.

Archer, John. "Country and City in the American Romantic Suburb." *Journal of the Society of Architectural Historians* 42 (May 1983): 139–56.

Archer, John. "Ideology and Aspiration, Individualism, the Middle Class, and the Genesis of the Anglo-American Suburb." *Journal of Urban History* 14:2 (Feb 1988): 214–53.

Beecher, Catherine E., and Harriet Beecher Stowe. *The American Woman's Home.* New York, 1869.

Binford, Henry C. *The First Suburbs: Residential Communities on the Boston Periphery, 1815–1860.* Chicago, University of Chicago Press, 1985.

Christian, Marcus Bruce. *Negro Ironworkers in Louisiana, 1718–1900.* Gretna, LA, Pelican Publishing Company, 1972.

Cigliano, Jan and Sarah Bradford Landau, editors. *Grand American Avenue, 1850–1920.* San Francisco and Washington, D.C., Pomegranate Artbooks and American Architectural Foundation, 1994.

Connelly, Thomas L. *The Marble Man: Robert E. Lee and His Image in American Society.* New York, Knopf, 1977.

Cooledge, Harold N. *Samuel Sloan, Architect of Philadelphia 1818–1884.* Philadelphia, University of Pennsylvania Press, 1986.

Creecy, James. *Scenes in the South, and Other Miscellaneous Pieces.* Washington, 1860.

Davis, Robert M. *The Southern Planter, The Factor and The Banker.* New Orleans, 1871.

De Bow, J. D. B. "Manufacturers, the South's True Remedy," *De Bow's Review* 3 (Feb 1867).

Degler, Carl N. *The Other South: Southern Dissenters in the Nineteenth Century.* New York, Harper & Row, 1974.

Downing, Andrew Jackson. *The Architecture of Country Houses.* New York, D. Appleton & Co., 1850.

Downing, Andrew Jackson. *Cottage Residences.* New York, 1844.

Dudden, Faye E. *Serving Women: Household Service in Nineteenth-Century America.* Middletown, Wesleyan University Press, 1983.

Dwight, Theodore. *Things as They Are.* New York, 1834.

Ebner, Michael. *Creating Chicago's North Shore: A Suburban History.* Chicago, University of Chicago Press, 1988.

Fishman, Robert. *Bourgeois Utopias: The Rise and Fall of Suburbia.* New York, Basic Books, 1987.

Fitzgerald, Oscar P. *Three Centuries of American Furniture.* Englewood Cliffs, N.J., Prentice-Hall, 1982.

Gaston, Paul. *The New South Creed; A Study in Southern Mythmaking.* New York, Knopf, 1970.

Gillette, Howard Jr., and Zane L. Miller, editors. *American Urbanism: A Historiographical Review.* New York, Greenwood Press, 1987.

Gowans, Alan. *Images of American Living,* New York, Harper & Row, 1976.

Greiff, Constance M. *John Notman, Architect: 1810–1865.* Philadelphia, Athenaeum of Philadelphia, 1979.

Holly, Henry Hudson. *Holly's Country Seats.* New York, D. Appleton, 1863.

Holly, Henry Hudson. *Modern Dwellings in Town and Country.* New York, Harper & Brothers, 1878.

Jackson, Kenneth T. *Crabgrass Frontier: The Suburbanizing of the United States.* New York and Oxford, Oxford University Press, 1985.

Jenkins, Frank. *Architect and Patron.* London. Oxford University Press, 1961.

Jordy, William H. and Monkhouse, Christopher P. *Buildings on Paper: Rhode Island Architectural Drawings 1825–1945.* Providence, Bell Gallery, List Art Center, Brown University, 1982.

King, Edward. *The Great South.* Hartford, Conn., American Publishing Company, 1875.

Langhome, Orra. "Domestic Service in the South. " *Journal of Social Science* 39 (Nov 1901).

Lawson, Ellen N. and Marlene Merrill. "The Antebellum 'Talented Thousandth': Black College Students at Oberlin Before the Civil War." *Journal of Negro Education* 52 (Summer 1983).

Litwack, Leon F. *Been in the Storm So Long: The Aftermath of Slavery.* New York, Knopf, 1979.

Lockwood, Charles. "The Italianate Dwelling House in New York City. " *Journal of the Society of Architectural Historians* 31 (May 1972): 145–51.

Maass, John. *The Gingerbread Age.* New York, Bramhall House, 1957.

Murtagh, William J. "The Philadelphia Row House. " *Journal of the Society of Architectural Historians* 16 (Dec 1957): 8–13.

Nordhoff, Charles. *The Cotton States in the Spring and Summer of 1875.* New York, 1876.

Norgress, Rachael Edna. "History of the Cypress Lumber Industry in Louisiana." *Louisiana Historical Quarterly* 30 (July 1947): 981–98.

O'Connor, Carol A. "Sorting Out the Suburbs: Patterns of Land Use, Class, and Culture." *American Quarterly,* 37:3 (1985): 382–94.

Olmsted, Frederick L. *A Journey in the Seaboard Slave States, with Remarks on Their Economy.* New York, 1856.

Pearce, John N., Lorraine W. Pearce, and Robert C. Smith, "The Meeks Family of Cabinetmakers." *Antiques* 85 (April 1964): 417.

Pitthandlin, David. *The American House: Architecture and Society 1815–1915.* Boston and Toronto, Little, Brown and Company, 1979.

Roark, James L. *Masters Without Slaves; Southern Planters in the Civil War and Reconstruction.* New York, Norton, 1977.

Rosenberg, Hans. *Die Weltwirtschaftshrisis von 1857–1859.* Berlin and Stuttgart, W. Kohlhammer, 1934.

Schuyler, David. *The New Urban Landscape: The Redefinition of City Form in Nineteenth Century America.* Baltimore, Johns Hopkins University Press, 1986.

Schuyler, Montgomery. "The Small City House in New York." *Architectural Record* 8 (April–June 1899): 857 ff.

Scott, Frank J. *The Art of Beautifying the House Grounds.* New York, 1870.

Sloan, Samuel. *The Model Architect.* 2 vols. Philadelphia, 1851.

Stern, Robert A. M. "La Ville Bourgeoise." *AD (Architectural Design)* 51 (Oct–Nov 1981): 4.

Stone, Alfred H. "The Cotton Factorage System of the Southern States. " *American Historical Review* 20 (1915): 516.

Sutherland, Daniel E. *Americans and Their Servants: Domestic Service in the United States from 1800 to 1920.* Baton Rouge, Louisiana State University Press, 1981.

Taylor, George Rogers. *The Transportation Revolution, 1815–1860.* New York, Rinehart, 1951.

Trollope, Mrs. Frances. *Domestic Manners of the Americans.* London, 1832.

Tunnard, Christopher, and Reed, Henry Hope. *American Skyline: The Growth and Form of Our Cities and Towns.* Boston, Houghton Mifflin, 1955.

Wade, Richard C. *Slavery in the Cities: The South, 1820–1860.* New York, Oxford University Press, 1964.

Waring, George E. "Out of Sight, Out of Mind: Methods of Sewage Disposal. " *Century Magazine* 47 (1894): 439 ff.

Wayne, Michael. *The Reshaping of Plantation Society: The Natchez District, 1850–1880.* Baton Rouge, Louisiana State University Press, 1983.

Warner, Sam Bass, Jr. *Streetcar Suburbs: The Process of Growth in Boston, 1870–1900.* Cambridge. Harvard University Press, 1983.

Wheeler, Gervace. *Homes for the People, in the Suburb and Country.* New York, 1855.

Vaux, Calvert. *Villas and Cottages.* New York, 1857.

PUBLISHED GENERAL SOURCES ON NEW ORLEANS

Abbey, Kathryn T. "The Land Ventures of General Lafayette in the Territory of Orleans and the State of Louisiana." *Louisiana Historical Quarterly* 16 (July 1933): 359 ff.

Adams, Lynn. "Research Reveals One of Oldest Shotguns. " *The Historic New Orleans Collection Newsletter* III no. 2 (Spring 1985): 10.

Arndt, Karl J. R., ed. "A Bavarian's Journey to New Orleans and Nacogdoches in 1853–1854." *Louisiana Historical Quarterly* 23 (April 1940).

Arthur, Stanley C. *A History of the United States Custom House.* New Orleans, 1940.

Bechet, Sydney. *Treat it Gentle.* New York, Hill and Wang, 1960.

Blassingame, John W. *Black New Orleans, 1860–1880.* Chicago and London, University of Chicago Press, 1973.

Browne, Daniel, "Burnside's Grave." *Times Democrat* (August 24, 1890): 3.

Burns, Francis P. "Lafayette Visits New Orleans." *Louisiana Historical Quarterly* 29 (April 1946): 296 ff.

Burns, Francis P. "The Graviers and Faubourg Ste. Marie. " *Louisiana Historical Quarterly* 22 (April 1939): 395–97.

Capers, Gerald M. *Occupied City: New Orleans Under the Federals, 1862–1865.* Lexington, Kentucky, University of Kentucky Press, 1965.

Cash, W. J. *The Mind of the South.* New York, Vintage Books, 1969.

Ceremonies Connected with the Unveiling of the Statue of General Robert E. Lee. New Orleans, 1884.

Chenault, William W., and Robert C. Reinders. "The Northern-born Community of New Orleans in the 1850s." *Journal of American History* 51 (September 1964): 232–47.

City Council of New Orleans. *Report of the Sanitary Commission of New Orleans on the Epidemic of Yellow Fever of 1853.* New Orleans, 1854.

Clapp, Rev. Theodore. *Autobiographical Sketches and Recollections, During a Thirty-Five Years' Residence in New Orleans.* Boston, 1857.

Clark, Robert T., Jr. "The New Orleans German Colony in the Civil War." *Louisiana Historical Quarterly* (October 1937).

Cohen's New Orleans Directory. New Orleans, 1854.

Cohen's New Orleans City Directory for 1855. New Orleans, 1855.

Dabney, Thomas Ewing. "The Butler Regime in Louisiana." *Louisiana Historical Quarterly* (April 1944).

Davis, Edwin, Adams. *The Story of Louisiana.* 4 vols. New Orleans, J. F. Hyer, 1960.

De Bow, James. "Natives and Inhabitants of the Leading Cities." *De Bow's Review* 19 (September 1855): 262.

Didimus, H. *New Orleans As I Found It.* New York, 1845.

Ferguson, John. "Decay, Vandals Seal Plantation's Fate." *Times Picayune/States-ltem* (February 6, 1982): 16.

Fortier, Alcée, ed. *Louisiana.* New Orleans, Century Historical Association, 1914.

Fossier, A. E. "A Funeral Ceremony of Napoleon in New Orleans, December 19, 1821." *Louisiana Historical Quarterly* 13 (April 1930): 246–52.

Friedheim, Thomas. "Fornaris-Rinker House Landmarked." *Preservation In Print* 9 (December 1982): 3.

Friends of the Cabildo. *New Orleans Architecture.* 6 vols. Gretna, LA, Pelican Publishing Co., 1971–1980.

Gallier, James. *The American Builder's General Price Book and Estimator.* New York, 1833.

Gardner, Charles. *Gardner's New Orleans Directory for 1867.* New Orleans, 1867.

Hall, A. Oakey. *The Manhattaner in New Orleans.* New York, 1851.

Hardy, D. Clive. *The World's Industrial and Cotton Centennial Exposition.* New Orleans, The Historic New Orleans Collection, 1978.

Hennick, Louis C., Louis C. Charlton, and E. Harper. *The Streetcars of New Orleans.* Gretna, LA, Pelican Publishing Co., 1975.

Hill, Henry Bertram, and Larry Gara. "A French Traveler's View of Antebellum New Orleans." *Louisiana History* 1 (Autumn 1960): 337.

Jackson, Joy J. *New Orleans in the Gilded Age; Politics and Urban Progress, 1880–1896.* Baton Rouge, Louisiana State University Press, 1969.

Jewell, Edwin L., editor and compiler. *Jewell's Crescent City Illustrated .* New Orleans, 1873.

Johnson, Thomas C. *The Life and Letters of Benjamin Morgan Palmer.* Richmond, Presbyterian Committee of Publication, 1906.

Kendall, John S. "New Orleans' 'Peculiar Institution.'" *Louisiana Historical Quarterly* 23 (July 1940).

King, Grace. *Grace King of New Orleans; A Selection of her Writings.* Edited by Robert Bush. Baton Rouge, Louisiana State University Press, 1973.

Latrobe, Benjamin Henry Boneval. *Impressions Respecting New Orleans.* Edited by Samuel Wilson, Jr. New York, Columbia University Press, 1951.

Lemman, Bernard. "New Orleans Prefab, 1867." *Journal of the Society of Architectural Historians* 22 (March 1963): 38–39.

Leovy, Henry, compiler. *Laws and General Ordinances of The City of New Orleans.* New Orleans, 1857.

Lonn, Ella. *Reconstruction in Louisiana after 1868.* New York, G. P. Putnam's Sons, 1918.

McGinty, Garnie W. *Louisiana Redeemed: The Overthrow of Carpetbag Rule, 1876–1880.* New Orleans, 1941.

Meyer, Robert, Jr. *Names Over New Orleans Public Schools.* New Orleans, Namesake Press, 1975.

Mitchell, Harry A. "The Development of New Orleans as a Wholesale Trading Center. " *Louisiana Historical Quarterly* 27 (October 1944): 944–57.

Murray, Amelia. *Letters from the United States, Cuba, and Canada.* New York, 1856.

"New Orleans. " *De Bow's Review* 1 (January 1866): 48–50.

Nolte, Vincent. *Fifty Years in Both Hemispheres; Or, Reminiscences of the Life of a Former Merchant.* New York, 1854.

Palmer, Benjamin Morgan. "Thanksgiving Sermon. " *Daily Delta* (December 1, 1860): 3.

Reinders, Robert C. "The Free Negro in the New Orleans Economy, 1850–1860." *Louisiana History* 6 (Summer 1965).

Ripley, Eliza. *Social Life in Old New Orleans.* New York and London, D. Appleton and Company, 1912.

Roberts & Co. Illustrated Catalogue of Mouldings. New Orleans, 1891.

Robinson, William L. *The Diary of a Samaritan.* New York, 1860.

Ronstrom, Maude O'Bryan. "Seignouret and Mallard, Cabinetmakers." *Antiques* 46 (August 1944).

Scully, Arthur, Jr. *James Dakin, Architect.* Baton Rouge, Louisiana State University Press, 1973.

Sinclair, Harold. *The Port of New Orleans.* New York, Doubleday, 1942.

Soniat, Meloncy C. "The Faubourgs Forming the Upper Section of the City of New Orleans." *Louisiana Historical Quarterly* 20 (January 1937): 192–99.

Soulé, Leon Cyprian. *The Know Nothing Party in New Orleans; A Reappraisal.* Baton Rouge, Louisiana Historical Association, 1962.

Stuart, James. *Three Years in North America.* 2 vols. Edinburgh, 1833.

Swanson, Betsy. *Historic Jefferson Parish.* Gretna, LA, Pelican Publishing Co., 1975.

Taylor, Joe Gray. *Louisiana Reconstructed, 1863–1877.* Baton Rouge, Louisiana State University Press, 1974.

Toby, Thomas. *A Vindication of the Conduct of the Agency of Texas in New Orleans.* New Orleans, 1836.

Toledano, Roulhac. *The National Trust Guide to New Orleans.* New York, Preservation Press/John Wiley & Sons, 1996.

Tregle, Joseph George, Jr. "Louisiana and the Tariff 1817–1846." *Louisiana Historical Quarterly* 25 (January 1942): 33–121.

Toller, Jerry. "The Haitian Shotgun Survives in New Orleans." *Arts Quarterly* 1 (July 1979): 8–9.

Wilmer, J. P. B. *Annual Address of the Bishop of Louisiana, to the Council of the Diocese; MDCCCLXXIV.* New Orleans, 1874.

Wilson, Samuel, Jr. "Ignace Francois Broutin." *In Frenchmen and French Ways in the Mississippi Valley,* edited by John Francis McDermott. Urbana, IL, University of Illinois Press, 1969.

Wilson, Samuel, Jr., and Leonard V. Huber. *The Cabildo on Jackson Square.* New Orleans, Friends of the Cabildo, 1970.

Wilson, Samuel, Jr., ed. *Henry Howard, Architect: An Exhibition of Photographs of His Work by Clarence John Laughlin.* New Orleans, 1952.

Winters, John D. *The Civil War in Louisiana.* Baton Rouge, Louisiana State University Press, 1963.

Wood, Minter. "Life in New Orleans in the Spanish Period. " *Louisiana Historical Quarterly* 22 (July 1939): 642–709.

PUBLISHED SOURCES ON THE GARDEN DISTRICT

Briede, Kathryn C. "A History of the City of Lafayette. " *Louisiana Historical Quarterly* 20 (October 1937): 904–908.

Carey, Rita Katherine. "Samuel Jarvis Peters." *Louisiana Historical Quarterly* 30 (April 1947): 441 ff.

Coleman, John P. "The Buckner-Eustis Residence. " *States* (April 8, 1923).

Coleman, John P. "First Home of English Lawyer." *States* (May 13, 1924).

Coleman, John P. "One of First in City with Baths." *States* (April 12, 1925).

Coleman, John P. "A Palatial Prytania House." *States* (November 4, 1923).

Coleman, John P. "The Hunt Henderson Residence." *States* (December 23, 1923).

"Death of a Great Architect." *Times-Democrat* (November 26, 1884): 3.

Dixon, Brandt V. B. *A Brief History of the Sophie Newcomb Memorial College 1887–1919.* New Orleans, Hauser Printing Company, 1928.

Eshleman, Martha. "Toby Westfeldt House, 2340 Prytania Street." MS, January 1967.

Evans, Harry Howard. "James Robb, Banker and Pioneer Railroad Builder of Antebellum Louisiana. " *Louisiana Historical Quarterly* 23 (January 1940): 170–258.

Gardner, Charles. *Gardner & Wharton's New Orleans Directory for the Year 1858.* New Orleans, 1858.

Godchaux, Paul L., Jr. "The Godchaux Family of New Orleans." New Orleans, privately printed, 1971.

Hamer, Collin B., Jr. "Records of the City of Lafayette (1833–1852) in the City Archives Department of the New Orleans Public Library." *Louisiana History* 13 (Fall 1972): 413–31.

Harrington, Fred Harvey. *Fighting Politician: Major General N. P. Banks.* Philadelphia, University of Pennsylvania Press, 1948.

Jordan, George E. "Robb and Clay: Politicians and Scholars." *New Orleans Art Review* 3 (January–February 1984): 6–7.

Kellogg, Miner K. *Justice to Hiram Powers, Addressed to the Citizens of New Orleans.* Cincinnati, 1848.

Kendall, John Smith. *History of New Orleans.* 3 vols. Chicago and New York, 1927.

Long, Edith. *The Story of 2618 Coliseum.* New Orleans, 1967.

Masson, Ann. *Cast Iron and the Crescent City.* New Orleans, Gallier House, 1975.

Menn, Joseph Karl. *The Large Slaveholders of Louisiana–1860.* New Orleans, Pelican Publishing Co., 1964.

Niehaus, Earl F. *The Irish in New Orleans, 1800–1860.* Baton Rouge, Louisiana State University Press, 1965.

Norman's New Orleans and Environs. New Orleans, 1845.

Padgett, James A., ed. "Some Letters of George Stanton Denison." *Louisiana Historical Quarterly* 23 (October 1940): 1200.

Poesch, Jessie. *Newcomb Pottery: An Enterprise for Southern Women, 1895–1940.* Exton, Pennsylvania, Schiffer Publishing, 1984.

Renshaw, James A. "The Lost City of Lafayette." *Louisiana Historical Quarterly* 2 (January 1919): 47–55.

Reynolds, Lewis E. *The Mysteries of Masonry.* Philadelphia, 1870.

Reynolds, Lewis E. *A Treatise on Handrailing, Comprising Three Original Systems of Applying the Trammel.* New Orleans, 1849.

Robinson, Elisha. *Atlas of the City of New Orleans, Louisiana.* New York, 1883.

Samuel, Martha Ann Brett, and Samuel, Ray. *The Great Days of the Garden District.* New Orleans, Parents' League of the Louise S. McGehee School, 1961.

Schmit, Patricia Brady. "Robb Papers Discovered." *The Historic New Orleans Collection Newsletter* IV no. 1 (Winter, 1986): 3–4.

Schmit, Patricia Brady, and Lynn D. Adams. "New Evidence: Robb's Twin Houses." *The Historic New Orleans Collection Newsletter* IV no. 1 (Winter, 1986): 7.

"Surprise and Serenade to Gov. Hahn." *Times* (March 30,1864): 1.

Twain, Mark. *Life on the Mississippi.* New York, Bantam Books, 1976.

United States Congress, House of Representatives. *Property Seized in Louisiana.* Executive Document 102, 40th Cong., 2d sess., 1867.

Wilson, Samuel Jr. "Episcopal Diocese Preserving One of Last Gallier-Designed Homes." *States* 12 (June 1953): 6.

NEWSPAPERS

Cincinnati Commercial.
Daily Crescent.
Daily Delta.
Daily Picayune.
Daily States.
Daily Southern Star.
Democrat.
Deutsche Zeitung.
The Era.
Lafayette City Advertiser.
Louisiana Courier.
New Orleans Democrat.
New Orleans Republican.
New Orleans States.
Republic.
States.
States-Item.
Times Democrat.

UNPUBLISHED DISSERTATIONS AND SCHOLARLY MANUSCRIPTS

Bos, Harriet, P. "Barthelemy Lafon." M.A. thesis, Tulane University, 1977.

Caldwell, Joan G., "Italianate Domestic Architecture in New Orleans, 1850–1880." Ph.D. dissertation, Tulane University, 1975.

Cigliano, Jan. "The Architectural Profession in America, 1830–1930; The Social History of a Profession." MS, Washington, D.C., 1985.

Dunbar, Prescott N. "History of the New Orleans Museum of Art." MS, New Orleans, n.d.

Farrell, Nancy Clow. "Hiram Powers: His Life and His Art." M.A. thesis, Michigan State University, 1959.

Jahncke, Alice Pickslay Pipes. "The Residence of Mr. and Mrs. Davis Lee Jahncke, Jr.: 3303 Coliseum Street." MS, 1981.

Kayman, Eleanor K. "Leisure-Time Activities in New Orleans, 1855–1863." M.A. thesis, Tulane University, 1966.

Kearns, David Taylor. "The Social Mobility of New Orleans Laborers, 1870–1900." Ph.D. dissertation, Tulane University, 1977.

Martin, Jerrye Louise. "New Orleans Slavery, 1840–1860: Testing the Wade Theory." M.A. thesis, Tulane University, 1972.

McGee, Victor, and Brantley, Robert S. "Greek Revival to Greek Tragedy, Henry Howard, Architect (1818–1884)." MS, New Orleans, 1983.

Pinner, Sylvia J. "A History of the Irish Channel, 1840–1860." M.A. thesis, Tulane University, 1954.

Somers, Dale A. "The Rise of Sports in New Orleans, 1850–1900." Ph.D. dissertation, Tulane University, 1966.

ARCHIVAL SOURCES

Arrivals and Port Register, 1834, City of Lafayette, Tulane University Archives.

Banks, [N.P.], file, United States National Archives, Washington, D.C. Courtesy of Thomas Favrot.

Benson, John, Company ledger, Hermann-Grima/Gallier Historic Houses, New Orleans.

Cotton and Abandoned Property 14380–14389, 16, 903, General Records of the Treasury Department, United States National Archives, Washington, D.C. Courtesy of Thomas Favrot.

Civil District Court Records, New Orleans.

Coleman, John P., published and unpublished writings, The Historic New Orleans Collection.

Conveyance Office Records, City of New Orleans.

Cook and Moorhouse ledger, Southeastern Architectural Archive, Tulane University.

Dugan, Louise, diaries (1868–1879), MS, Howard-Tilton Memorial Library, Tulane University.

Freret and Wolf Records, Southeastern Architectural Archive, Tulane University.

Gates of Heaven Synogogue congregation, minutes. Samuel Wilson, Jr., papers, Southeastern Architectural Archive, Tulane University.

Gallier Papers, Labrot Collection, Southeastern Architectural Archive, Tulane University.

Historic District Landmarks Commission.

Historic American Buildings Survey, National Park Service, United States Department of the Interior.

Jefferson Parish Notarial Records.

Lafayette City Census, 1840, 1850, New Orleans Public Library.

Louisiana Sash Factory, Time Book and Payroll, Southeastern Architectural Archive, Tulane University.

New Orleans Parish Mortgage Books, New Orleans Public Library.

New Orleans Tax Rolls, 1857, New Orleans Public Library.

Orleans Parish Notarial Archives, Plan Books, New Orleans Public Library.

Orleans Parish court records, New Orleans.

Hiram Powers Papers, Cincinnati Historical Society.

Registry of slave ship, 1831, New Orleans Public Library.

Robb Papers, The Historic New Orleans Collection.

1328 Harmony Street, unsigned and undated MS, property of Thomas Bernard, New Orleans.

United States Census, 1840, Louisiana.

United State Census, 1860, New Orleans.

United States Census, 1860, Slave Inhabitants of Louisiana, II.

United States Second District Court, New Orleans, Deed Books.

United States Tax Records, New Orleans.

Wharton, Thomas Kelah, diary, MS, New York Public Library.

Wilson, Samuel, Jr., papers, Southeastern Architectural Archive, Tulane University.

INDEX

Italicized page numbers indicate a photograph